Law, Responsibility and Vulnerability

This book addresses how law and public policy cause or exacerbate vulnerability in individuals and groups.

Bringing together scholars, judges and practitioners, it identifies how individuals and groups can become vulnerabilised through the operation of law, and examines how the State can acknowledge and remedy that impact. The book offers not only a theoretical, ethical and normative conception of vulnerability in law, but also an evaluation of the diverse practices of responding to vulnerability in law through accountability mechanisms and public campaigns. The analysis of vulnerability contained in this volume is enhanced by the common use of Ireland as a case study. Despite the robust rights protections available at national, regional and international level, Ireland remains a state where at-risk people have experienced vulnerability across a range of thematic areas, such as criminal law, migration and asylum, historical abuse, LGBTI rights and austerity. Drawing on comparative analyses and a consideration of the role of international law in domestic settings, this book offers a comparison of diverse national and transnational attempts to ensure State accountability and responsiveness to legally created vulnerabilities. The book demonstrates lessons learned from theory and practice regarding how vulnerability can be experienced by individuals and groups, structured by law and addressed through legal and political action.

This book will be of considerable interest to socio-legal and "law and society" scholars, as well as others working in international human rights, jurisprudence, philosophy, legal theory, political theory, feminist theory, and ethics.

James Gallen and **Tanya Ní Mhuirthile** are based at the School of Law and Government, Dublin City University.

Gender in Law, Culture, and Society

Series Editor

Martha Albertson Fineman

Emory University School of Law, USA

Gender in Law, Culture, and Society will address key issues and theoretical debates related to gender, culture, and the law. Its titles will advance understanding of the ways in which a society's cultural and legal approaches to gender intersect, clash, and are reconciled or remain in tension. The series will further examine connections between gender and economic and political systems, as well as various other cultural and societal influences on gender construction and presentation, including social and legal consequences that men and women uniquely or differently encounter. Intended for a scholarly readership as well as for courses, its titles will be a mix of single-authored volumes and collections of original essays that will be both pragmatic and theoretical. It will draw from the perspectives of critical and feminist legal theory, as well as other schools of jurisprudence. Interdisciplinary, and international in scope, the series will offer a range of voices speaking to significant questions arising from the study of law in relation to gender, including the very nature of law itself.

Other titles in the series

Exploring Masculinities: Feminist Legal Theory Reflections
Edited by Martha Albertson Fineman and Michael Thomson
ISBN 978-1-472-41511-0 (hbk)
ISBN 978-1-472-41512-7 (pbk)

Feminism, Law, and Religion
Edited by Marie Failinger, Elizabeth Schiltz and Susan J. Stabile
ISBN 978-1-409-44419-0 (hbk)
ISBNc978-1-409-44421-3 (pbk)

Critical Queer Studies: Law, Film, and Fiction in Contemporary American Culture
Casey Charles
ISBN 978-1-409-44406-0 (hbk)
ISBN 978-1-138-27176-0 (pbk)

For more information about this series, please visit: www.routledge.com

Law, Responsibility and Vulnerability

State Accountability and Responsiveness

Edited by James Gallen and Tanya Ní Mhuirthile

Routledge
Taylor & Francis Group
a GlassHouse Book

First published 2022
by Routledge
2 Park Square, Milton Park, Abingdon, Oxon OX14 4RN

and by Routledge
605 Third Avenue, New York, NY 10158
a GlassHouse book

Routledge is an imprint of the Taylor & Francis Group, an informa business

British Library Cataloguing-in-Publication Data
A catalogue record for this book is available from the British Library

Library of Congress Cataloging-in-Publication Data
A catalog record for this book has been requested

ISBN: 978-0-367-08581-0 (hbk)
ISBN: 978-1-032-07533-4 (pbk)
ISBN: 978-0-429-02314-9 (ebk)

DOI: 10.4324/9780429023149

Typeset in Bembo
by Apex CoVantage, LLC

Contents

Notes on contributors

Koldo Casla is Lecturer in Law and a member of the Human Rights Centre in the University of Essex.

Stephen Coutts is Lecturer in Law in School of Law in University College Cork.

Gladys Ganiel is Reader in the School of Social Sciences, Education and Social Work and a member of The Senator George J. Mitchell Institute for Global Peace, Security and Justice in Queen's University Belfast.

James Gallen is Associate Professor in Law in the School of Law and Government at Dublin City University.

Liz Heffernan is Associate Professor in the School of Law at Trinity College Dublin.

Máire Leane is Senior Lecturer in Social Policy, Co-Chair of the Board of Women's Studies and Chair of the University Autism Friendly Project at University College Cork.

Darren McStravick is Senior Lecturer in Law in School of Law, Social and Behavioural Sciences in Kingston University London.

Luke Moffett is Senior Lecturer in the School of Law and member of The Senator George J. Mitchell Institute for Global Peace, Security and Justice in Queen's University Belfast.

Tanya Ní Mhuirthile is Assistant Professor in Law in the School of Law and Government at Dublin City University.

Fiachra Ó Súilleabháin is Lecturer in Social Work in the School of Applied Social Studies in University College Cork.

Antonia Porter is Lecturer in Law at Kent Law School, University of Kent.

Ann Power Forde is an Irish judge who has served as a Judge of the Court of Appeal since November 2019. She previously served as a Presiding Judge of the Kosovo Specialist Chambers and Specialist Prosecutor's Office from 2017 to 2019 and a Judge of the European Court of Human Rights from 2008 to 2020.

Fergus Ryan is Associate Professor (Senior Lecturer) in Law at the Department of Law, Maynooth University.

Claire-Michelle Smyth is Principal Lecturer in Law at Brighton Business School.

Acknowledgments

The editors would like to thank all of our contributors to this volume and all who contributed to the 2016 conference at Dublin City University on vulnerability and the law. We are very appreciative of the support from the School of Law and Government at Dublin City University.

Introduction

State accountability and responsiveness

James Gallen and Tanya Ní Mhuirthile
Dublin City University

Introducing vulnerability theory

In recent years, vulnerability theory and discourse has emerged to describe how human beings are susceptible to change in our physical and social well-being. Martha Fineman's theory of vulnerability captures how individuals experience multiple forms of risk or harm, through an examination of the State's role in shaping, enabling or curtailing social institutions.[1] For Fineman, there are four key aspects of vulnerability. It is universal, constant, complex and particular.[2] Vulnerability is universal as it is something inherent to all humanity. By contrast, the liberal subject, typified by the reasonable man, is not truly, as it claims, a universal subject. There are times in everyone's life when one cannot be autonomous, self-sufficient and independent.[3] Therefore the vulnerability describes the universal, inevitable enduring aspect of the human conditions. As Cooper states, a shared, universal understanding of vulnerability enables the argument 'that we need a strong state to help us prevent injuries and recover from those that occur anyways'.[4]

The second key aspect of vulnerability is constancy. Fineman argues that, rather than being independent, the liberal subject 'is enmeshed in a web of relationships'.[5] This interdependency is routinely ignored, or assumed to be adequately managed, usually in the private sphere of the family.[6] As vulnerability arises from our embodiment, there is always the possibility of harm whether

1 Martha Albertson Fineman, 'Gender and the New Legal Realism' 2005 *University of Wisconsin Law Review* 405 (2005); Nina Kohn, 'Vulnerability Theory and the Role of Government' (2014) 26(1) *Yale Journal of Law and Feminism* 1–27; Martha Albertson Fineman, 'The Vulnerable Subject: Anchoring Equality in the Human Condition' (2008–9) 20 *Yale Journal of Law and Feminism* 1–23, 20–21.

2 Martha Albertson Fineman, 'The Vulnerable Subject and the Responsive State' (2010) 60 *Emory Law Journal* 251, 268.

3 Martha Albertson Fineman, 'Feminism, Masculinities, and Multiple Identities' (2013) 13 *Nevada Law Journal* 619, 620.

4 Frank Rudy Cooper, 'Always Already Suspect: Revising Vulnerability Theory' (2015) 93 *North Carolina Law Review* 1399, 1358.

5 Martha Albertson Fineman, 'The Vulnerable Subject' (n 1), 11.

6 Ibid.

DOI: 10.4324/9780429023149-1

by disease, natural disaster, economic or institutional factors.[7] This constant possibility of harm means that vulnerability, unlike dependency, cannot be hidden.[8] A vulnerability perspective highlights our interdependency. Furthermore, Fineman notes that the liberal subject is assumed to be an adult of sound mind. Therefore, it only reflects a portion of human experience and cannot account for childhood or moments of illness. The vulnerability theory, rooted in its acceptance of the total human experience, acknowledges that life is bookended by 'dependency and lack of capacity', thus vulnerability is constant.[9]

The third key aspect of vulnerability theory is its complexity. There is a multiplicity of ways in which vulnerability can manifest. As noted above, there is the constant possibility of physical harm, which may impact upon those around us thus harming our relationships, whether they be with other people or institutions.[10] Such harm may be social or economic and may be inherited or passed intergenerationally.[11] Consequently, membership of social groups can contribute to vulnerability.

The final key aspect of vulnerability is that it is particular. Vulnerability is rooted in our embodiment and thus it is 'experienced uniquely by each of us and this experience is greatly influenced by the quality and quantity of resources we possess or can command'.[12] In order to become legally recognisable, Fineman argues that vulnerability must be particularised.[13] She notes two ways within which the vulnerable legal subject can be construed. The first way focuses on differences in human embodiment, such as physical, mental, race and gender. Recognition of these differences has resulted in differential power relationships and hierarchies historically, which has caused the creation of 'vulnerable categories' that both obscure universal vulnerability and stigmatise those who fall within the category.[14] Fineman argues that the appropriate response is to reduce the possibility of discrimination by striving for substantive equality, as formal equality 'does not challenge existing allocation of resources and power'.[15] The second mode of particularising the vulnerable legal subject is through a focus on social location. Our options and opportunities are outlined by our relationships with people and institutions.[16] These are important, as they provide us with the resources necessary to address our vulnerability. Therefore the vulnerable subject shifts the focus from individual identity towards

7 Ibid, 9.

8 Ibid, 3, 11.

9 Ibid, 12.

10 Martha Albertson Fineman 'The Vulnerable Subject and the Responsive State' (2010) 60 *Emory Law Journal* 251, 268.

11 Ibid.

12 Martha Albertson Fineman, The Vulnerable Subject' (n 1) 10.

13 Martha Albertson Fineman, 'Feminism, Masculinities, and Multiple Identities' (n 3) 637.

14 Ibid.

15 Martha Albertson Fineman, '"Elderly" as Vulnerable: Rethinking the Nature of Individual and Societal Responsibility' (2012) 20 *Elder Law Journal* 101, 132.

16 Martha Albertson Fineman, 'Feminism, Masculinities, and Multiple Identities' (n 3) 619, 638.

'interrogating the institutional practices that produce the identities and inequalities in the first place'.[17]

Vulnerability theory and the vulnerable

While for Fineman inherent vulnerability is posited as universal, others have emphasised that vulnerability may also be understood as situational and may be caused or exacerbated by the personal, social, political, economic or environmental situations of individuals.[18] A particular form of situational vulnerabilities are pathogenic vulnerabilities, including morally dysfunctional or abusive interpersonal and social relationships and sociopolitical oppression or injustice.[19] Pathogenic vulnerabilities may particularly arise in situations of embodied dependency, where an individual, such as a child, requires the support and care of another.[20] Fineman insists that the experience of embodied dependency is also universal and inevitable: all of us have been dependent as infants and many will in our later years become dependent on others for resources, care and support.[21] By emphasising that all people are vulnerable and experience dependency over the course of their lives, vulnerability theory seeks to de-stigmatise the term 'vulnerable'.[22] Fineman has consistently critiqued the attribution of vulnerability to specific individuals or groups, suggesting that 'some people are viewed as more or less vulnerable, or as differently or uniquely vulnerable. This perspective ignores the universality and constancy of vulnerability as I use the term and is merely another way of identifying bias, discrimination and social disadvantage rather than focusing on structural arrangements that affect everyone.'[23]

Vulnerability theory also assesses whether the structure and distribution of societal resources result in the privileging of some and the disadvantage of others,[24] suggesting an affirmative obligation for the State to either justify disparate circumstances of conferred privilege or remedy them.[25] Nina Kohn

17 Martha Albertson Fineman, 'The Vulnerable Subject' (n 1) 16.

18 Robert Goodin, *Protecting the Vulnerable: A Reanalysis of Our Social Responsibilities* (Chicago: University of Chicago Press 1986) 112.

19 Catriona Mackenzie, Wendy Rogers and Susan Dodds, 'Introduction: What is Vulnerability, and Why Does it Matter for Moral Theory?' in C. Mackenzie, W. Rogers and S. Dodds (eds) *Vulnerability: New Essays in Ethics and Feminist Philosophy* (Oxford University Press 2014), 1–32, 9–10.

20 Susan Dodds, 'Dependence Care and Vulnerability' in C. Mackenzie, W. Rogers and S. Dodds (eds) *Vulnerability: New Essays in Ethics and Feminist Philosophy* (Oxford University Press 2014), 181–203, 182–3.

21 Martha Albertson Fineman, 'Cracking the Foundational Myths: Independence, Autonomy, and Self-Sufficiency' (2000) 8 *American University Journal of Gender Social Policy and Law* 13–29, 18.

22 Nina Kohn, 'Vulnerability Theory and the Role of Government' (n 1), 9.

23 Martha Albertson Fineman, 'Vulnerability and Inevitable Inequality' (2017) 4 *Oslo Law Review* 133–149, 142.

24 Martha Albertson Fineman, 'The Vulnerable Subject' (n 1) 20.

25 Ibid, 22.

has argued that the universality of vulnerability encourages comprehensive approaches to addressing situations of vulnerability and dependency, rather than piecemeal population-by-population interventions.[26]

By contrast, Vanessa Munro has expressed concern that the concept of vulnerability has and can be used to construct 'highly conditional and precarious, conceptions of who counts as "vulnerable"'.[27] Munro emphasises the risks that attend to an ambiguous and open textured concept.[28] Its use risks othering the recipients of a label of particular vulnerability (or dependency), 'marking them out as peculiar exceptions to the less precarious and more resilient norm, and often in ways that stigmatise and oppress, or further entrench their vulnerability'.[29] Peroni and Timmer offer a more nuanced account of vulnerability, suggesting that when judicial and legislative authorities invoke a particularised approach to vulnerability, they should employ specific justifications about why a group is especially vulnerable and why an individual should be treated as a member of that group.[30] Any new application of vulnerability theory, such as that proposed in this book, must continue to be mindful of these risks and criticisms.

Vulnerability theory and human rights

Fineman is clear in her explanation that vulnerability theory is not an alternative method of articulating the principles underlying human rights law. 'The abstract and inevitably contested legal principles often referred to in human rights literature, such as equality, liberty and dignity' are not the standards by which vulnerability are measured.[31] Yet vulnerability theory and human rights law resonate with each other. Both highlight the fragility of human experience. Both begin from the premises that these are inherent attributes of all human beings. We are all vulnerable; we all have inalienable human rights. Yet these inherent aspects of the human experience go unnoticed until we encounter challenges. It is only when we are censored, and told not to speak, that we actively engage with the importance of freedom of speech. This catch-22 is at the heart of human rights law. Wall argues that embedded in the text of the

26 Nina Kohn, 'Vulnerability Theory and the Role of Government' (n 1) 10.
27 Vanessa Munro, 'Shifting Sands? Consent, Context and Vulnerability in Contemporary Sexual Offences Policy in England and Wales' (2017) *Social & Legal Studies* 417–440.
28 Ibid, 429; John L. Hill, 'Exploitation' (1993) 79 Cornell Law Review 631–699, 632; Martha Albertson Fineman, 'The Vulnerable Subject: Anchoring Equality in the Human Condition' (n 2), 9.
29 Vanessa Munro, 'Shifting Sands?' (n 27) 429.
30 Lourdes Peroni and Alexandra Timmer, 'Vulnerable Groups: The Promise of an Emerging Concept in European Human Rights Convention Law' (2013) 11(4) *International Journal of Constitutional Law* 1056–1085.
31 Martha Albertson Fineman, 'Vulnerability and Inevitable Inequality' (n 23) 133, 143.

Preamble to the Universal Declaration of Human Rights is this acknowledgment that 'we find human rights through their violation'.[32]

In a similar vein it can be argued that it is only when something happens to draw our attention to our vulnerability that we become conscious of it. As Fineman explains, social structures, including both the State and law, are set up to facilitate the liberal, able-bodied subject who is of sound mind.[33] As such, she contends that when it comes to achieving social justice equality discourse is limited.[34] The search for a comparator inevitably highlights difference, and the response of the State to difference is piecemeal, focused on a specific individual at a specific moment in time.[35] In so doing, Fineman argues that formal equality ignores context and inevitable, material inequalities that may exist between people. In leaving 'existing institutional arrangements that privilege some and disadvantage others' undisturbed, formal equality legitimises those structures.[36] The strength of the vulnerability thesis is that it challenges this legitimisation by interrogating the 'hidden assumptions and biases' that underpin law's structures and practices.[37]

Both vulnerability theory and human rights law demonstrate the instances where the State fails to respect our shared humanity. Both call on the State to account for this failure and demand that it responds in a manner which builds resilience necessary to withstand such incursions in the future. Both have at their centre the person as a member of the human family, an interconnected embodied person who has had experiences which have exacerbated rather than ameliorated their vulnerability. Heikkilä et al. argue that both universal and particular obligations of responsive states are needed ensure substantive equality for all.[38] As with vulnerability theory, the inherent core of human right law is its universality. It is this very universality that requires rights to be interpreted in context and with regard to the particular individual vulnerabilities and resilience of each person. Thus they conclude that in operationalising the obligations arising from such rights, the human rights project and the vulnerability theory complement and reinforce each other in terms of specifying the rationale and the detailed benchmarks for State action.[39]

32 Illan Rua Wall, 'On Pain and the Sense of Human Rights' (2008) 29 *Australian Feminist Law Journal* 53, 54. The second sentence of the Preamble to the UDHR states that 'disregard and contempt for human rights have resulted in barbarous acts which have outraged the conscience of mankind'.

33 Martha Albertson Fineman 'The Vulnerable Subject' (n 1) 1.

34 Martha Albertson Fineman, 'Vulnerability and Inevitable Inequality' (n 23) 133, 134.

35 Ibid, 135.

36 Martha Albertson Fineman 'The Vulnerable Subject and the Responsive State' (n 2) 266.

37 Ibid, 266 fn 53.

38 Mikaela Heikkilä, Hisayo Katsui and Maija Mustaniemi-Laakso, 'Disability and Vulnerability: A Human Rights Reading of the Responsive State' (2020) 24(8) *International Journal of Human Rights* 1180.

39 Ibid, 1200.

Examining the interplay of the universal and the particular

Scholarship on vulnerability to date has addressed several substantive issues, such as the legal organisation of work, public responsibility in the context of privatisation, and the role of law regarding the elderly.[40] This volume concerns several areas of national and international law and policy which are ostensibly concerned with 'vulnerable' groups and individuals. However, contrary to Fineman's approach, such areas typically reflect a narrow conception of vulnerability which maintains the concept as exceptional and isolated, and not a universal human condition. In other words, the areas could be considered as classified according to moments of manifest disadvantage rather than vulnerability as Fineman would define it.

This volume evaluates the extent to which existing law and policy concerning the thematic areas of regional international law, the criminal law, historical institutional abuse, socio-economic and LGBTIQ rights meaningfully describe and engage with inherent conceptions of vulnerability and compare the theoretical and empirical descriptions of universal human vulnerability with the construction of vulnerability offered by thematic areas of law and policy. The book assesses the extent to which it is possible or desirable to destigmatise the term 'vulnerable', aligning with Nina Kohn's suggestion that a universal conception of vulnerability has a destigmatising potential.[41]

In particular, the book considers how the conceptual framework of universal vulnerability, particular situational vulnerabilities and dependencies interact with modern, fragmented legal regulation at international, regional and national levels. It considers the application of universal conceptions of vulnerability in a transnational perspective, drawing from comparative experiences and understandings of vulnerability across legal cultures to better inform and understand how law frames and conceptualises vulnerability, both inherent and situational, in individuals and groups in society.

The book is also concerned to consider the nature of, and strategic engagement with, a 'responsive State'. In Fineman's work, the State should play a critical role in redressing harms generated by vulnerability and dependencies, by creating mechanisms whereby individuals can 'accumulate the resilience or resources that they need to confront the social, material and practical implications of their vulnerability'.[42] Resilience is 'what provides an individual with

40 Martha Albertson Fineman and Jonathan W. Fineman (eds), *Vulnerability and the Legal Organisation of Work* (London: Routledge 2017); M. Fineman, T. Mattsson and U. Andersson (eds), *Privatisation, Vulnerability and Social Responsibility* (London: Routledge 2016); Martha Albertson Fineman, 'Elderly as Vulnerable: Rethinking the Nature of Individual and Societal Responsibility' (2012) 20(2) *Elder Law Journal* 71–112.

41 Nina Kohn, 'Vulnerability Theory and the Role of Government' (n 1) 9.

42 Martha Albertson Fineman 'Equality, Autonomy and the Vulnerable Subject in Law and Politics', in M. Fineman and A. Gear (eds) *Vulnerability: Reflections on a New Ethical Foundation for Law and Politics* (Aldershot, UK: Ashgate 2013) 13–28, 19.

the means and ability to recover from harm, setbacks and the misfortunes that affect our lives'.[43] Resilience is not inherent. Rather, it is experientially acquired through interactions with social structures and institutions, whether public or private.[44] It is the nature and quality of these interactions that can either enhance or reduce resilience such that a person's inherent vulnerability can be construed as a situational vulnerability that may be alleviated or exacerbated by the response of the State. In responding to vulnerability and dependencies, there are at least five different types of resources or assets that societal organisations and institutions can provide: physical, human, social, ecological or environmental, and existential. A lack of resilience is often a function of unequal access to certain societal structures or the result of unequal allocations of privilege and power within those structures.[45] Similarly, Goodin concluded that vulnerability analysis was enhanced by its ability to 'clearly finger' those who are, or should be, particularly responsible for seeing to it that a person's interests are protected.[46]

Vulnerability theory may inform these concerns by focusing on the State's responsibility to use law to structure the interactions and liabilities of social institutions such that they maximise the resilience of those who engage in these interactions. To date, the role of vulnerability as a mechanism of redressing concrete injustices has been inadequately charted.[47] The approach of this book is to emphasise the relationship of universal vulnerability across seemingly diverse areas of acute marginalisation. Strategies for advocating for greater State responsiveness to acute vulnerability and dependency can be compared and shared across the areas of criminal law, historical abuse and LGBTIQ rights. Although not always substantively overlapping as a matter of law and policy, the structure of the engagement of the State, advocacy organisations and those subject to the area of legal regulation reveals shared broader structures and patterns that frame, affirm or dismiss the existence of human vulnerability that are acknowledged, articulated and challenged in this book.

In Chapter 1, Power Forde argues that the manner in which the ECHR has interpreted vulnerability, eschewing definitions and responding instead on a case-by-case basis, respects the inherent vulnerability of all. Operating in this manner, she contends that the Court both enables a response to the particular situations of applicants before the Court while also remaining open to the universal reality of vulnerability. In acknowledging the systemic failures to safeguard against states exacerbating vulnerability, the Court uses human rights norms to identify strategies to build resilience. Drawing on Peroni and

43 Martha Albertson Fineman, 'Vulnerability and Inevitable Inequality' (n 23) 133–149, 146.

44 Martha Albertson Fineman, 'Vulnerability, Resilience, and LGBT Youth' (2014) 23(2) *Temple Political & Civil Rights Law Review* 307.

45 Martha Albertson Fineman, 'Vulnerability and Inevitable Inequality' (n 23) 133–149, 146–147.

46 Robert Goodin, *Protecting the Vulnerable* (n 18) 117.

47 A. Cole, 'All of Us Are Vulnerable, But Some Are More Vulnerable Than Others: The Politics Ambiguity of Vulnerability Studies, an Ambivalent Critique' (2016) 17(2) *Critical Horizons* 260–277.

Timmer's work, she acknowledges that there is a risk that grouping people according to their vulnerabilities will result in the stigmatising that Fineman cautions against. Thus Power Forde argues that it is essential that the focus remains on the circumstances and contexts that create, sustain and exacerbate vulnerability.

Coutts echoes the argument that the deployment of human rights norms can create a space where courts can engage with issues of vulnerability in a more open and effective manner in his analysis of migration and asylum cases before the Court of Justice of the European Union in Chapter 2. However, he notes that systemic concerns about the unity and integrity of European Union law can operate to stymie an approach that prioritises universal vulnerability.

Chapters 3 to 5 consider vulnerability theory in the context of the criminal justice system.

The full potential of vulnerability theory and its demonstrable universality is evident in restorative justice programmes, according to McStravick. He contends that such programmes create meso-communities of care, concern and accountability, ably supported by criminal justice agencies and a responsive State both financially and by way of case referrals, which enable an alternative outlook on the notion of victimhood and vulnerability. Through this shared experience, all parties to the programme come to an awareness that they are all subject to vulnerabilities, human limitations and frailties.

Porter argues that the particularised way in which our vulnerability is experienced is intimately dependent upon our variant resilience. Therefore, the State must be responsive to the varying resilience of people by being attentive to those conditions which exacerbate vulnerability and erode resilience. The first step in such attentiveness is that the State acknowledges its own contribution to the erosion of resilience. In responding to vulnerability, the State must do so sensitively and empathetically. Porter highlights a limitation in vulnerability in the context of domestic abuse as it does not provide a solution in circumstances where a victim of domestic abuse wished to withdraw from a prosecution. Yet, she acknowledges that vulnerability theory requires us to take a big-picture perspective and is not intended to operate as a checklist to solve specific instances of vulnerability. Rather its focus is on reconceptualising our responsibilities to each other and the responsibilities of the State to its citizens. In this way it exposes the systemic structures and practices that erode resilience.

For Heffernan, vulnerability theory offers a potentially insightful way of exploring human engagement with the criminal trial process. With its emphasis on actual human experience, it encourages us to rethink the role of courts in shaping social identities. She notes that giving witness testimony in a criminal trial is an exceptional occurrence for most people, which finds them thrust into an alien environment for which many people may not have the necessary resilience. Thus the courts have developed practices, known as special measures, to support 'vulnerable' witnesses and protect them from stress and trauma. In this context 'vulnerable' was narrowly construed, but the absence of a clear definition has opened the possibility for a broadening of access to the special measures to a wider range of witnesses. She concludes that vulnerability theory may assist in this process by prompting reflection on the lived experience of giving witness testimony. A vulnerability approach brings the obligations of the State to nurture resilience into sharp focus which resonates with the perspective of the trial as a place where witnesses and victims are active participants who have the opportunity to have their experiences heard.

The responsiveness of the State to historic violence and abuse is considered in Chapters 6 to 8.

Moffett examines the interplay of vulnerability and resilience in the context of transitional justice. He argues that transitional justice mechanisms can and do boost the resilience of victims once they are properly resourced and take into account the varying needs of the population. However, he notes that by treating the situation in Northern Ireland as if it were an ordinary justice issue rather than by managing it as a post-conflict situation which involved extraordinary sectarian driven violence, the response of the State falls flat and exacerbates rather than narrows the gap between vulnerability and resilience for victims, carers and affected communities. In order to be meaningful, transitional justice mechanisms must be timely and the State must be more responsive in order to avoid compounding vulnerabilities experienced as a result of conflict.

In her chapter, Ganiel pushes the application of vulnerability theory beyond the State, arguing it can be a useful point of engagement for churches and other institutions implicated in abuse. She persuasively argues for this application on the basis that the Church is one of the main providers of existential resources necessary for human flourishing and resilience. In a situation where the State has delegated responsibility for vulnerable people to the Church, the interplay between Church and State in response to historic abuse is interesting. Ganiel notes how the apologies from the State have been welcomed, while those from the Church have not. In part she offers that this could be due to inability of survivors to build resilience resulting from confinement to a church-run institution such as a Magdalene laundry, mother and baby home or industrial school. Ganiel argues that there is much that the Church could learn from Truth and Reconciliation Commissions (TRCs) in Canada that would promote greater resilience. The act of listening as part of a TRC can go a long way to meet the need of survivors to be heard and acknowledged. It is in this that resilience can be nurtured.

Developing this theme, Gallen identifies in vulnerability theory an opportunity to guide the development of tort law on vicarious liability in a more coherent fashion. He points to the obligations of the State in Fineman's conception of vulnerability to structure interactions such that people can build the necessary resilience to respond to their vulnerability. He details how the response of the Canadian courts to claims of vicarious liability for historic abuse emphasises both the dependency of the victim and the control the employer had over the abusive employees such that the role of the institution in creating and exacerbating vulnerability is exposed. The expansionary trend evident in the UK cases Gallen examines reflects this commitment to protect the vulnerable from institutionally created harm. He notes the early rejection of vicarious liability for historical abuse in Ireland but that more recent cases have seen a reflection of the more expansive approach. Gallen concedes that the expansion of the role of vulnerability in vicarious liability is predicated on a particularised conception of vulnerability. Yet he argues that vulnerability theory usefully clarifies the relationships between concepts such as vulnerability, dependency and control that are central to institutional liability. As a result, he concludes that vulnerability theory facilitates a multi-player analysis of responsibility or wrongdoing at individual, institutional or structural levels.

Whether vulnerability theory can create a space to enable increased realisation of socioeconomic rights is the focus of Chapters 9 and 10.

Smyth employs Fineman's vulnerability thesis to argue that a responsive state must engage in unequal treatment in order to build the resilience of those experiencing disadvantageous treatment due to particular vulnerability, whether that is inherent or locational. Adopting a policy of 'vulnerability proofing' budgetary decision-making would better result in stronger protection for economic, social and cultural rights than the present practice of 'human rights proofing'.

Casla recognises that, while we are all vulnerable, socio-economic disadvantage is not shared equally across society. He contends that vindication of socio-economic rights is the material condition of freedom within a given community or society. Thus he argues that adopting a vulnerability approach can bring human rights closer to home by refocusing them from a global individualistic perspective towards a local communitarian one.

In many respects recent legal changes such as the introduction of marriage equality and gender recognition may be considered to have fixed any discriminatory vulnerability experienced by LGBT+ people. Chapters 11 to 13 interrogate whether the response of the State has adequately built the resilience in this context.

In teasing through how Fineman's vulnerability theory applies in the context of the LGBT+ community, Ryan accepts her contention that, notwithstanding the universality of vulnerability, specific identity categories do have a place within this theoretical framework, as vulnerability is also particular, varied and unique. Nonetheless he argues that heteronormativity continues to predominate in social practices and transgressing the boundaries of acceptable gender performance comes at a social cost. Where laws were designed to support and uphold the heteronormative hegemonic perspective on the world and could not recognise the reality of the lived experiences of those who did not conform to that worldview, LGBT+ people could find themselves in a precarious position. Despite increasing acknowledgment of diversity and the introduction of legal reforms such as marriage equality, Ryan argues that vulnerability in the LGBTQ community persists. He charts through a series of examples where the State fails to respond to the vulnerability of LGBTQ people and enables a building of their resilience. Thus, he cautions that it is necessary to keep a 'keenly political, critical lens' on particularly vulnerable LGBTQ people.

Leane and Ó Súilleabháin build on this theme and argue that in its entrenched binary understanding of gender the State fails to recognise transgender youth. It therefore entrenches the particularised vulnerability which this community experiences. The persistent failure to recognise them strips trans youth of the ability to become resilient to challenges they may face. For Leane and Ó Súilleabháin, the strength of the vulnerability lens is that it enables a critical reappraisal of particular vulnerability and, in so doing, it facilitates a redefinition of the parameters of justice.

Such a reappraisal is what Ní Mhuirthile argues can prompt law to consider adopting a different doctrinal path to the one immediately obvious when responding to particular vulnerabilities. Employing a vulnerability lens enables an understanding that traditional negligence or medical malpractice precedent are insufficient to achieve justice for intersex people. The vulnerability lens can refocus law towards alternative approaches, equally doctrinally sound, such as considering medical and/or surgical interventions to be experimentation which results in an outcome enabling people with intersex variations to choose for themselves whether and when to engage with medical management of their bodies. Thus, adopting the vulnerability approach builds their resilience and returns to people with intersex variations control over their bodies and futures which traditional legal responses have facilitated removing.

In this book we have deliberately chosen to focus on groups that are typically framed as vulnerable, but in a particular, specialised and isolated fashion. For example, migrants and asylum seekers, as framed in legal materials and literature, do not share an understanding of solidarity in vulnerability, nor a shared challenge in seeking better engagement in fostering a responsive state. The selection of seemingly disparate substantive areas of law and regulation, and of those areas not already within the vulnerability discourse, offers the means to explore the extent to which these areas share common challenges and obstacles. How do these areas experience the tension between universal conceptions of vulnerability and particular forms of vulnerability that are situational or pathogenic in nature?

The State creates institutions and relationships using law and policy. This book seeks to unpack whether in the construction of these institutions and relationships the State is solely focused on the liberal subject Fineman argues is a fiction, or whether it can be responsive to the universal vulnerability inherent in us all. In other words, is it possible for the State to build the resilience of those subject to its laws? The book argues that, despite the seeming persistence of particularised approaches to vulnerability in courts and literature, adopting a holistic response, grounded in vulnerability theory, can prompt imaginative solutions in law that foster resilience and thereby address and respond to disadvantage.

1 'Vulnerability' as a factor in the assessment of claims before the European Court of Human Rights

Ann Power Forde[1]

I have been asked to address you on the issue of 'vulnerability' under the European Convention of Human Rights (ECHR), a subject that was of particular interest to me during my time as a Judge of the Strasbourg Court. The liberal notion that humans are born free and remain autonomous throughout their lives has shaped how international human rights law has developed. It posits that states exist because individuals, who are free by nature, join together and consent to the creation of an entity – the State – to act on their behalf. Their rights and freedom are protected against encroachment by other individuals and by the State. States must justify any interference with the individual's human rights.

A new movement in legal philosophy – the 'vulnerability movement' – is now questioning this foundational principle. Inspired by the work of Martha Fineman, the 'vulnerability movement' argues that the human being is born physically and socially dependent on its environment and remains dependent on that environment for the rest of its life. Vulnerability replaces autonomy as the essential characteristic of the human person. The movement posits that unless we have regard to vulnerability in our notions on law, a constituent component of the person is neglected. It claims that the 'autonomy myth' has produced institutional arrangements that fail to take account of the dependency inherent in the human condition resulting in major social inequalities. Fineman calls for a refocusing of law and policy away from autonomy and towards vulnerability.

The paradox of vulnerability

Vulnerability is, as Peroni and Timmer point out, a paradoxical concept.[2] It is universal in that we are all vulnerable and it is particular in that we each

1 Ann Power Forde is a former Judge of the European Court on Human Rights. The views expressed herein are expressed in her personal capacity and not as a representative of the Court.

2 Lourdes Peroni and Alexandra Timmer, 'Vulnerable Groups: The Promise of an Emerging Concept in European Human Rights Convention Law' (2013) 11(4) International Journal of Constitutional Law 1056–1085.

DOI: 10.4324/9780429023149-2

experience it differently. It is burdensome in that we are constantly susceptible to harm – but it has its benefits in that it inspires intimacy and makes us 'reach out to others, to form relationships, and build institutions'.[3] Although vulnerability has been mentioned in several hundred rulings of the Strasbourg Court, the Court has not defined vulnerability or vulnerable individuals or groups. It identifies on a case-by-case basis whether the applicant or a person involved in the case is in a condition of vulnerability. As a result, there is a diversity of persons that the Court has recognised as vulnerable subjects.

In 2001, the Court first mentioned the concept of 'vulnerable groups'.[4] In this early formulation, the Court identified two factors that pointed towards vulnerability: (i) the applicant's membership of a minority group (Roma); and (ii) the lack of consideration of its minority lifestyle in the State's decision-making processes. This early articulation of vulnerability had already put in place the elements that would later shape the Court's subsequent formulations of 'vulnerable groups': membership of a minority group whose vulnerability is partly constructed by broader societal, political and institutional circumstances.

Categories of vulnerable persons

Yussef Al Tamimi has analysed over 500 judgments of the Court since *Dudgeon*[5] and has identified those groups whose claims receive 'vulnerability' attention from the Court.

Detainees

With mentions of vulnerability in over 236 cases, detainees are identified as by far the most frequently mentioned vulnerable category in the Court's judgments. In early cases, detainees who had been the subject of ill-treatment or who were experiencing mental illness or who did not speak the language of the judicial officer were deemed vulnerable.[6] Quickly, however, the Court came to the view that all persons who are held in detention are in a 'vulnerable position'. In *Salman v. Turkey*, the Grand Chamber noted: '[p]ersons in custody are in a vulnerable position and the authorities are under a duty to protect them'.[7]

3 Martha Albertson Fineman, '"Elderly" as Vulnerable: Rethinking the Nature of Individual and Societal Responsibility' (2012) 20(1) Elder Law Journal 96.

4 *Chapman v. the United Kingdom* Application no. 27238/95, Judgment (Merits and Just Satisfaction) 18 January 2001.

5 *Dudgeon v. United Kingdom*, Application no. 7525/76, 22 October 1981.

6 *TW v. Malta* Application no. 25644/94, Judgment (Grand Chamber) 29 April 1999; *Stanev v. Bulgaria* Application no. 36760/06 Judgment (Merits and Just Satisfaction) (Grand Chamber) 17 January 2012; *Murray v. the United Kingdom* Application no. 14310/88 Judgment (Merits and Just Satisfaction) (Grand Chamber) 28 October 1994.

7 *Salman v. Turkey* Application no. 21986/93 Judgment (Merits and Just Satisfaction) (Grand Chamber) 27 June 2000, at para. 99.

Because of this vulnerable status of prisoners, substantive and positive obligations on states have been developed to ensure that the prisoner's right to life is respected under Article 2, to protect prisoners from self-harming acts and from harm from others.[8] In addition, those who are deprived of their liberty and under the full control of the authorities are deemed to be most vulnerable to, and at risk of, abuse of State power, including torture and ill-treatment under Article 3. Recognition of the inherent vulnerability of detainees led to the European Committee for the Prevention of Torture (CPT) being explicitly mandated to visit persons deprived of their liberty so as to ensure their protection from torture and from inhuman or degrading treatment or punishment.[9] The types of treatment identified and condemned by the Court include Palestinian hanging (*Aksoy v. Turkey*);[10] severe forms of beating (*Selmouni v. France*, *Dikme v. Turkey*);[11] denial of medical treatment (*Ilhan v. Turkey*);[12] electric shocks (*Akkoç v. Turkey*);[13] rape (*Aydin v. Turkey*);[14] beatings on the soles of the feet (*Salman v. Turkey*,[15] *Greek* case[16]); sleep and food deprivation. The worst offenders in the case law are Turkey, Romania, Russia, Bulgaria and Ukraine.

To offset the vulnerable status of detainees, CPT standards require that every Council of Europe (COE) Member State must provide fundamental safeguards to protect detainees against ill-treatment. These include: the right of the detainee to have the fact of his detention notified to a third party of his choice (family member, friend, consulate); the right of access to a lawyer; the right to request a medical examination by a doctor of his choice; and an obligation on states to maintain custody records from the first moment of detention.[17] Where a death or injury occurs in custody, there is a heightened burden on the government to provide a satisfactory explanation through detailed and accurate

8 *Keenan v. United Kingdom* Application no. 27229/95 Judgment (Merits and Just Satisfaction) 3 April 2001; *Ketreb v. France* Application no. 38447/09, 19 July 2012; *Edwards v. United Kingdom* Application nos. 39647/98 40461/98 Judgment (Merits and Just Satisfaction) (Grand Chamber) 27 October 2004.

9 Article 1 of the European Convention for the Prevention of Torture and Inhuman or Degrading Treatment or Punishment ETS No. 126.

10 *Aksoy v. Turkey*, Application no. 21987/93 Judgment (Merits and Just Satisfaction) 18 December 1996.

11 *Selmouni v. France* Application no. 25803/94 Judgment (Merits and Just Satisfaction) (Grand Chamber) 28 July 1999; *Dikme v. Turkey*, Application no. 20869/92, Judgment (Merits and Just Satisfaction) 11 July 2000.

12 *İlhan v. Turkey* Application no. 22277/93, Judgment (Merits and Just Satisfaction) 27 June 2000.

13 *Akkoç v. Turkey*, Application nos. 22947/93 and 22948/93 Judgment (Merits and Just Satisfaction) 10 October 2000.

14 *Aydın v. Turkey*, Application no. 23178/94 Judgment (Merits and Just Satisfaction) (Grand Chamber) 25 September 1997.

15 *Salman v. Turkey* Application no. 21986/93 Judgment (Merits and Just Satisfaction) (Grand Chamber) 27 June 2000.

16 *Denmark et al. v. Greece,* Application no. 3321/67, Commission Report of 5 November 1969, Yearbook 12.

17 2nd General Report of the European Committee for the Prevention of Torture (1992), available at https://rm.coe.int/1680696a3f, para. 36 (last visited 14 December 2020).

records concerning the person's detention, and they should be able to account convincingly for any injuries.[18] The Court considers that detainees with a mental disorder are 'particularly vulnerable'. The cases of *Stanev v. Bulgaria*[19] and *Murray v. Netherlands*[20] are particularly worthy of note.

Children

Children constitute the second highest grouping on the list of 'vulnerable groups' in ECtHR judgments, where they are entitled to state protection in criminal proceedings,[21] and in the context of migration, where I have raised concerns about the level of protection.[22] In *Mayeka and Mitunga v. Belgium*,[23] the first applicant arrived in Canada in 2000 from the Democratic Republic of the Congo (DRC) and was granted refugee status in 2001. She asked her brother, a Dutch national, to go and collect her daughter, the second applicant, from her grandmother in the DRC and to mind her until she could be reunited. He arrived in Brussels in August 2002 without immigration papers for the child and claimed that she was his daughter. He was refused entry and returned to the Netherlands. The second applicant was put into detention in an adult detention centre. In October 2002, the Belgian courts ordered her release from detention and her return to the DRC. The Court found several violations of the Convention. It considered that the second applicant's 'extremely vulnerable situation' should take precedence over considerations relating to her status as an illegal immigrant.[24]

Victims

There are over thirty cases involving victims where vulnerability plays a role in the Court's judgments, including in cases involving domestic violence, sexual offences, trafficking and other offences. The Court's approach to victim vulnerability is very individualised and it rarely makes categorical statements about

18 *Salman v. Turkey* Application no. 21986/93 Judgment (Merits and Just Satisfaction) (Grand Chamber) 27 June 2000.

19 *Stanev v. Bulgaria* Application no. 36760/06 Judgment (Merits and Just Satisfaction) (Grand Chamber) 7 January 2012.

20 *Murray v. The Netherlands* Application no. 10511/10 Judgment (Merits and Just Satisfaction) (Grand Chamber) 26 April 2016.

21 *T v. United Kingdom* Application no. 24724/94 Judgment (Merits and Just Satisfaction) (Grand Chamber) 16 December 1999.

22 See dissents of Judge Power Forde in *MYH and Others v. Sweden* Application no. 50859/10 Judgment (Merits and Just Satisfaction) 27 June 2013; *KAB v. Sweden* Application no. 886/11 Judgment (Merits and Just Satisfaction) 5 September 2013; *F.G. v. Sweden* Application no. 43611/11 Judgment (Merits and Just Satisfaction) (Grand Chamber) 23 March 2016.

23 *Mayeka and Mitunga v. Belgium*, Application no. 13178/03, Judgment (Merits and Just Satisfaction) 12 October 2006.

24 Ibid, at para. 55.

victims, with the exception, perhaps, of victims of torture and ill-treatment. The Court refers, frequently, to international treaties in victim cases. It has, for example, referred to the United Nations General Assembly Declaration on the Elimination of Violence against Women and to reports of the Commission on Human Rights of the UN Economic and Social Council. In recent cases, the Court has used such treaties to declare that victims of domestic violence are vulnerable persons.

In *Opuz v. Turkey*, for example, the Court affirmed the obligation of the State to provide protection to vulnerable victims of domestic violence.[25] The applicant and her mother had been victims of numerous assaults and threatening behaviour on the part of the applicant's husband. Ultimately, the applicant's mother was shot and killed by the applicant's husband. The applicant complained, inter alia, under Articles 2 and 3 of the Convention. The Court considered whether the authorities displayed due diligence to prevent violence against the applicant and her mother by pursuing criminal or other appropriate preventive measures against the applicant's husband, despite the withdrawal of complaints by the victims.[26] It observed that, generally speaking, certain factors are taken into account when deciding whether or not to prosecute. These include:

- the seriousness of the offence
- whether the victim's injuries are physical or psychological
- whether the accused used a weapon
- whether there had been subsequent threats or attacks
- whether the attack was planned
- the effect on children living in the household
- the continuing threat to the health and safety of the victim or anyone else who became involved
- the history of the relationship
- the accused's criminal history and, in particular, whether any violence was involved in the past.

The Court observed that the application of those provisions and the cumulative failure of the domestic authorities to pursue criminal proceedings against the applicant's husband deprived the applicant's mother of the protection of her life.[27] It noted that, in the light of the State's positive obligation to take preventative operational measures to protect an individual whose life is at risk, it might have been expected that the authorities, when faced with a suspect known to have a criminal record of perpetrating violent attacks, would take special measures consonant with the gravity of the situation with a view

25 *Opuz v. Turkey* Application no. 33401/02, Judgment (Merits and Just Satisfaction) 9 June 2009.

26 Ibid, at para. 131.

27 Ibid, at para. 145.

to protecting the applicant's mother. While the authorities remained mostly passive for almost two weeks, the applicant's husband had shot and killed the applicant's mother. In those circumstances, the Court concluded that the national authorities did not display due diligence and, therefore, failed in their positive obligation to protect the right to life of the applicant's mother within the meaning of Article 2 of the Convention. It found a violation of Article 3 based on the applicant's complaint that she had been subjected to violence, injury and death threats several times and that the authorities had been negligent in responding to her situation. The Court considered the applicant fell within the group of 'vulnerable individuals' entitled to State protection.

The Court has also addressed the experience of vulnerability of trafficked victims. In *Siliadin v. France*, the applicant was a minor girl trafficked to France from Togo for the purpose of forced labour.[28] She was obliged to work in harsh conditions, effectively, as an unpaid servant. The Court found a lack of adequate protection provided within the domestic law of France in circumstances where the applicant was fully dependent and required to perform forced unpaid labour.[29] The Court held that there is a positive obligation that requires the penalisation and effective prosecution of any act aimed at maintaining a minor in such a situation.

Immigrants

Some commentators have criticised the Court's case law for being discernibly pro-state when it comes to immigration cases. For example, Dembour contends that the Court's 'normal reasoning is to put border controls before human rights'.[30] Frequently, in immigration cases, the Court reiterates that under Article 8 (the right to respect for private and family life), a state is entitled under internationals law to control both the entry of aliens into its territory and their residence there and to deport those found to be illegally present. The Convention does not guarantee the right of an alien to enter or to reside in a particular country.[31] There is no general obligation on the part of a Contracting State to respect the choice by married couples of the country of their matrimonial residence and to accept the non-national spouses for settlement in that country.[32] Regard must be had to a fair balance to be struck between the competing interests of the individual and of the community. In both contexts the State enjoys a certain margin of appreciation. The extent of a

28 *Siliadin v. France* Application no. 73316/01 Judgment (Merits and Just Satisfaction) 26 July 2005.

29 Ibid, at paras. 102–149.

30 Marie-Benedicte Dembour, *When Humans Become Migrants* (Oxford University Press 2–15).

31 *I.A.A. and Others v. the United Kingdom* Application no. 25960/13 Judgment (Admissibility) 8 March 2016.

32 *Uner v. The Netherlands* Application no. 46410/99, Judgment (Merits and Just Satisfaction) (Grand Chamber) 18 October 2006.

state's obligations to admit relatives of residents will vary according to a variety of factors, including:

- the extent of family rupture
- the extent of the ties in the Contracting State
- any insurmountable obstacles to family life elsewhere
- any factors of immigration control or considerations of public order weighing in favour of exclusion
- whether family life was created when its continuance was known to be precarious.

Where so known, then the removal of the non-national member will be incompatible with Article 8 only in the most exceptional circumstances. The interests of the child will be afforded significant, though not determinate, weight.

Until *M.S.S. v. Belgium and Greece*, the Court had declined to recognise migrants and asylum seekers who find themselves in foreign lands often unaccompanied and desperately impoverished as 'vulnerable'.[33] That case may be considered groundbreaking when considering vulnerability as a factor in the Court's assessment of the application. The applicant was an Afghan asylum seeker who fled Kabul in 2008, entered the European Union through Greece and travelled on to Belgium, where he applied for asylum. By virtue of the Dublin II Regulation of the EU (Regulation 343/2003), Greece was the responsible Member sSate for the examination of his asylum application. The applicant applied for a stay of execution in Belgium due to the deficiencies in the asylum procedure in Greece. His application was rejected and the Belgian authorities transferred him back to Greece in June 2009. There, he faced detention in desperate conditions. After his release, he lived on the streets and had, only occasionally, received aid from local residents and church groups. Allegedly, steps had been taken to find him accommodation, but according to his submissions no housing was ever offered to him. One of the important questions raised in the case was whether the detention and living conditions of M.S.S. in Greece amounted to inhuman and degrading treatment under Article 3 of the Convention. The Court observed:

> In the present case the Court must take into account that the applicant, being an asylum seeker, was particularly vulnerable because of everything he had been through during his migration and the traumatic experiences he was likely to have endured previously.[34]

At first sight, this wording points to the specific experiences of the applicant. Thus, one might conclude that those individual experiences are critical to

33 *M.S.S. v. Belgium and Greece*, Application no. 30696/09, Judgment (Merits and Just Satisfaction) (Grand Chamber) 21 January 2011.

34 Ibid, at para. 232.

the Court's vulnerability decision. In the next paragraph, however, the Court referred to the particular vulnerability of asylum seekers in a more general manner, as though it were a constituent attribute of the entire class. It stated that: '[T]he applicant's distress was accentuated by the vulnerability inherent in his situation as an asylum seeker.'[35] The Court also stated: '[t]he Court attaches considerable importance to the applicant's status as an asylum seeker and, as such, a member of a particularly underprivileged and vulnerable population group in need of special protection.'[36]

The majority of the Grand Chamber found that M.S.S. was particularly vulnerable because he was 'wholly dependent on State support [….] unable to cater for his most basic needs.'[37] The dependency argument is familiar – taken, as it is, from other Article 3 cases concerning prisoners and detainees. Moreover, the majority recognised that the applicant's situation was representative of a bigger picture due to a series of institutional shortcomings inherent in the Greek asylum system. These shortcomings included the lack of sufficient reception centres to accommodate asylum seekers, administrative obstacles impeding their access to the job market and the lengthy procedures involved in examining their asylum requests. By unveiling all these deficiencies in the Greek asylum system, the Court was pointing, essentially, to the institutional causes of vulnerability among asylum seekers in Greece.

M.S.S. seems to indicate that the Court has deemed asylum seekers to be vulnerable on a number of interrelated grounds, including:

(i) the reality for asylum seekers in Greece – one that is characterised by material and psychological deprivation
(ii) asylum seekers' absolute dependence on the State
(iii) the inherent vulnerability of asylum seekers arising from everything they have been through during the process of migration and the trauma that often accompanies this
(iv) the systemic deficiencies of the Greek asylum system.

It is not quite clear whether *all* asylum seekers are to be considered vulnerable or just those who were in Greece under the conditions prevailing at the time. However, it is clear that the Court's analysis in *M.S.S.* challenges simplistic characterisations of group vulnerability, opening the way for more nuanced and complex formulations. That said, the general approach tends to be that, despite the numerous difficulties attaching to their status – unfamiliarity with a new culture and language, interpretation difficulties and sometimes a history of trauma – migrants are, for the most part, treated as being as adept and as robust as any other applicants. The dissenting judge in *M.S.S.* argued that, unlike other

35 Ibid, at para. 233.
36 Ibid, at para. 251.
37 Ibid, at paras 253–254.

'particularly vulnerable groups' in the Court's case law, asylum seekers 'are not a group historically subject to prejudice with lasting consequences, resulting in their social exclusion'. In his view, the concept of vulnerable groups has a 'specific meaning in the jurisprudence of the Court' and asylum seekers simply do not fit the concept.[38] His concern points to the potential problem of the open-endedness of the vulnerable-group concept.

Members of the Roma community

Members of the Roma community have also been recognised as 'vulnerable' in over twenty rulings of the Strasbourg Court. In *Chapman v. the United Kingdom*, the applicant, a British gypsy, alleged a violation of Article 8 as she was refused planning permission to station her caravans on land she had purchased.[39] She also complained that actions taken against her to enforce planning measures violated Articles 8 and 14 of the Convention and that those measures interfered with her peaceful enjoyment of her land, contrary to Article 1 of the First Protocol of the Convention. The Court considered that the vulnerable position of gypsies as a minority meant that some special consideration should be given to their needs and their different lifestyle in reaching decisions in particular cases. In its judgment there is a certain overlap between the concepts of vulnerable groups and minorities. On the facts of the case, however, the Court was not persuaded that no alternative had been available to the applicant apart from occupying land in a 'Green Belt' area without planning permission. Humanitarian considerations could not be used to exempt her from the implementation of national planning laws.

In terms of advancing the issue of vulnerability, perhaps the most significant judgment delivered during my time on the Court was that of the *Centre for Legal Resources [CLR] on behalf of Valentin Câmpeanu v. Romania*.[40] With that case, new ground was broken in terms of the Court's approach to vulnerable individuals. Born in Romania, the applicant was a Roma child abandoned at birth by his mother. Throughout his life, he had suffered severe intellectual disability, he was HIV-positive and had been burdened by several other medical conditions. He had no relatives, legal guardians or representatives. He had lived in various public orphanages and children's centres. He had received no proper health treatment or educational support and when found he was in a distressed condition. He died at the age of 18 in the Poiana Mare Neuropsychiatric Hospital. The CLR had taken the case to the Strasbourg Court on behalf of Mr Câmpeanu.

38 Partially Concurring and Partially Dissenting Opinion of Judge Sajó.

39 *Chapman v. the United* Kingdom Application no. 27238/95, Judgment (Merits and Just Satisfaction) 18 January 2001.

40 *Centre for Legal Resources on behalf of Valentin Câmpeanu v. Romania* 47848/08 Judgment (Merits and Just Satisfaction) (Grand Chamber) 17 July 2014.

The CLR complained that, due to the combined actions and omissions on the part of State agencies, the applicant had been unlawfully deprived of his life, in contravention of the State's legal obligation to provide him with care and treatment. They also complained that the authorities had failed to put in place an effective mechanism to safeguard the rights of people with disabilities who were placed in long-stay institutions. For example, there were no effective processes for initiating investigations into suspicious deaths. Consequently, the official investigation in Romania into allegations of ill-treatment had not been in compliance with the State's procedural obligation under Article 3. The CLR also complained that Mr Câmpeanu had been subjected to inhuman and degrading treatment, arguing that the threshold for inhuman and degrading treatment was met by the serious flaws in his care and treatment, his living conditions, and the general attitude of the authorities over the last months of his life.

The Government objected, claiming that the CLR did not have *locus standi* to lodge an application on behalf of the applicant. They contended that the case was, therefore, inadmissible and incompatible with the provisions of Article 34 of the Convention. The Court recognised that this case concerned a highly vulnerable person with no next of kin.[41] It noted 'that when he reached the age of majority no competent person or guardian had been appointed by the State to take care of his interests, whether legal or otherwise, despite the statutory requirement to do so'.[42] The Court thus held that:

> in the exceptional circumstances of this case and bearing in mind the serious nature of the allegations, it should be open to the CLR to act as a representative of Mr Câmpeanu, notwithstanding the fact that it had no power of attorney to act on his behalf and that he died before the application was lodged under the Convention. To find otherwise would amount to preventing such serious allegations of a violation of the Convention from being examined at an international level, with the risk that the respondent State might escape accountability under the Convention as a result of its own failure to appoint a legal representative to act on his behalf as it was required to do under national law.[43]

Ultimately, the Court found a violation of Article 13 in conjunction with Article 2 of the Convention, on account of the State's failure to implement an appropriate legal framework that would have enabled complaints concerning the applicant to have been examined by an independent authority.[44] The Court recommended that the respondent State put in place necessary general measures

41 Ibid. at para. 111.
42 Ibid. at para. 111.
43 Ibid, at para. 112.
44 Ibid, at para. 160.

to ensure that mentally disabled persons are afforded independent representation, so as to enable them to have Convention complaints relating to their health and treatment examined, either before a court or another independent body.[45]

In his concurring opinion, Judge Pinto de Albuquerque argued that, instead of relying on the 'exceptional circumstances' of the case, it may have been preferable to rise above the specificities, and address the question of principle raised by the case, namely, 'what are the contours of the concept of representation of extremely vulnerable persons before the Court?'[46] He continued:

> The Court should have established a concept of de facto representation, for cases involving extremely vulnerable victims who have no relatives, legal guardians or representatives. These two cumulative conditions, namely the extreme vulnerability of the alleged victim and the absence of any relatives, legal guardians or representatives, should have been laid down clearly by the Court. Extreme vulnerability of a person is a broad concept that should include, for the above purposes, people of tender age, or elderly, gravely sick or disabled people, people belonging to minorities, or groups subject to discrimination based on race, ethnicity, sex, sexual orientation or any other ground. The absence of relatives, legal guardians or representatives is an additional condition that must be assessed according to the facts known to the authorities at the material time.
>
> What is relevant is the fact that the victim has no known next-of-kin and no representative or guardian appointed by the competent authority to take care of his or her interests. These two conditions would have provided legal certainty to the Contracting Parties to the Convention and guidance to any interested institutions and persons who might be willing in future to lodge applications on behalf of other extremely vulnerable victims of human rights violations. By not providing clear and general criteria, and by linking its finding to the 'extraordinary circumstances' of the case, the Court's judgment not only weakens the authority of its reasoning and restricts the scope of its findings and their interpretative value, but also provides less guidance, or no guidance at all, to States Parties and interested institutions and persons who might be willing to intervene in favour of helpless, vulnerable victims of human rights violations. Instead of extending the benefit of its work to as many individuals as possible, the Court has restricted the reach of its work to the bare confines of the present case.[47]

Characteristics of a vulnerable group in the ECtHR

Peroni and Timmer provide analysis of the Court's approach to 'vulnerability' in its case law and I am indebted to those authors for several of the

45 Ibid, at para. 161.
46 Concurring Opinion of Judge Pinto de Albuquerque.
47 Ibid. at para. 11.

following observations.[48] In the years following *Chapman*, the Court has not only reaffirmed the vulnerability of Roma in different contexts but it has also extended the list of 'vulnerable groups' to persons with mental disabilities, people living with HIV, and to asylum seekers.[49] However, what, precisely, ties these groups together is not clear. The Court has not, as of yet, developed a coherent set of indicators to determine what renders a group vulnerable.[50] In its jurisprudence, references to European or international human rights reports and resolutions serve to confirm rather than to establish group vulnerability.[51] Nonetheless, Peroni and Timmer claim that the concept of group vulnerability, as used by the Court, has three distinct characteristics:

> The Court's account of group vulnerability *is first of all relational* [...] The Court locates vulnerability not in the individual alone but rather in her wider social circumstances ...
>
> The Court's vulnerable subject is not the inherently vulnerable human being. Rather, *the Court's vulnerable subject is a particular group member* ... By 'particular,' we mean that the Court's vulnerable subject is a group member whose vulnerability is shaped by specific group-based experiences ...
>
> A third characteristic of the Court's formulation of group vulnerability in the post-Chapman case law is its *focus on harm*. Indeed, all the indicators that the Court has employed to determine group vulnerability show that harm features centrally in the Court's account of group vulnerability ... Thus, one clear set of indicators that emerges from the Court's case law is (historical) prejudice and stigmatization. These indicators point to the harm of misrecognition, which ... takes place when 'institutionalized patterns of cultural value constitute some actors as inferior, excluded, wholly other, or simply invisible – in other words, as less than full partners in social interaction' [52] ... These indicators have played out in the Court's group-vulnerability analysis, most notably in the context of discrimination [emphasis added].[53]

48 Lourdes Peroni and Alexandra Timmer, 'Vulnerable Groups: The Promise of an Emerging Concept in European Human Rights Convention Law' (2013) 11(4) International Journal of Constitutional Law 1056–1085.

49 Ibid, 1064.

50 Ibid.

51 Ibid.

52 Nancy Fraser, 'Rethinking Recognition' (2000) 3 New Left Review, 107, 113, as cited in Lourdes Peroni and Alexandra Timmer, 'Vulnerable Groups: The Promise of an Emerging Concept in European Human Rights Convention Law' (2013) 11(4) International Journal of Constitutional Law (n 2), 1056–1085, 1064–1065.

53 Lourdes Peroni and Alexandra Timmer, 'Vulnerable Groups: The Promise of an Emerging Concept in European Human Rights Convention Law' (2013) 11(4) International Journal of Constitutional Law (n 2), 1056–1085, 1064–1065.

Gaps in ECtHR vulnerability jurisprudence

Using prejudice, stigmatisation, social disadvantage and exclusion as factors in the assessment of group vulnerability, it could be argued that there are certain gaps in the Court's approach to vulnerable groups. For example, the Court has, at times, been silent on group vulnerability in its case law concerning Roma applicants, notably, in cases where the harm inflicted upon them occurs in the broader context of prejudice and discrimination within which vulnerability to violence originates. While it acknowledges that segregation in classrooms or forced sterilisation of Roma requires analysis of this group's vulnerability, it sometimes declines to have regard to their vulnerability in the context of violence and fatal killings. It has, at times, found violations of Article 2 or 3 in respect of members of the Roma community but it has declined to examine such complaints in conjunction with Article 14 – discrimination on the basis of ethnicity – unless the killing had been accompanied by expressly racist language.[54] This overlooks the fact that racial prejudice towards vulnerable minorities is far more subtle than the use of express verbal abuse and, because of its subtlety, more sinister and more difficult to tackle. I raised this matter in a partly dissenting opinion in *Carabulea v. Romania*[55] and observed that where there are recurring factors giving cause for concern about systemic discrimination against an ethnic minority within a State, then the onus should shift to the State to show, by reference to objective data, that the assaults and deaths were not racially motivated. Since *Carabulea*, some progress has been made, but the rate of such progress is slow.[56]

Muslim women wearing the full veil – a minority within a religious minority in Europe – may be classified as a vulnerable group within the sense established by the Court's jurisprudence. There is some evidence that they can be subjected to prejudice and stereotyping in European countries.[57] One negative stereotype is that such Muslim women are not free and are oppressed. Undertones of this stereotype can be detected in earlier cases such as *Dahlab v. Switzerland*.[58] Though progress has been made in challenging stereotyping religious groups (see *Eweida and other v. United Kingdom*),[59] nevertheless it seems to me that work remains to be done to ensure that safeguards are in place to protect Muslim women from indirect discrimination in the workplace arising from the

54 *V.C. v. Slovakia*, Application no. 18968/07, Judgment (Merits and Just Satisfaction) 8 November 2011, at para. 146.

55 *Carabulea v. Romania*, Application no. 45661/99 Judgment (Merits and Just Satisfaction) 13 July 2010.

56 *Balazs v. Hungary*, Application no. 15529/12 Judgment (Merits and Just Satisfaction) (Second Section) 20 October 2015.

57 Thomas Hammarberg, *Human Rights in Europe: No Grounds for Complacency* (Council of Europe Publishing 2–11), 36–39, 47–48.

58 *Dahlab v. Switzerland* Application no. 42393/98, Judgment (Merits and Just Satisfaction) 15 February 2001.

59 *Eweida and Others v. the United Kingdom*, Application nos. 48420/10, 36516/10, 51671/10, 59842/10, 15 January 2013.

manifestation, in practice, of their religious beliefs through the wearing of the hijab or face veil.

The homeless do not feature, prominently, as a vulnerable group in the Court's jurisprudence. In *Hutten-Czapska v. Poland,* the Court ruled that tenants are 'often' vulnerable individuals. Nevertheless, it found that the government had struck a fair balance between the interests of the landowner and the tenants.[60] In *McCann v. United Kingdom*, the Court rejected the respondent State's argument that a case concerning vulnerable Roma people[61] was not applicable to the case at hand. The Court rejected this argument:

> The Court is unable to accept the Government's argument that the reasoning in Connors was to be confined only to cases involving the eviction of Roma or cases where the applicant sought to challenge the law itself rather than its application in his particular case. The loss of one's home is a most extreme form of interference with the right to respect for the home. Any person at risk of an interference of this magnitude should in principle be able to have the proportionality of the measure determined by an independent tribunal in the light of the relevant principles under Article 8 of the Convention, notwithstanding that, under domestic law, his right of occupation has come to an end.[62]

This judgment may be indicative of the Court's willingness to extend and apply its reasoning on vulnerable groups or individuals to other subjects. Vulnerability reasoning could, potentially, lay the basis for more extensive protection.

Risks inherent in a focus on vulnerability

Finally, it is worth noting that a focus on vulnerability is not without difficulties. Peroni and Timmer identify certain risks that should be avoided when dealing with group vulnerability. There is, first, the risk of reinforcing vulnerability and ignoring other aspects of group identity. In *Kiyutin v. Russia*, for example, the stigmatisation of people living with HIV was central to the Court's finding that they constituted a vulnerable group.[63] Paradoxically, the authors claim, the Court itself risks stigmatising vulnerable groups by applying the very term 'vulnerable', which, for many people, carries solely negative connotations, such as harm or injury. The Court, in their view, should be wary of stigmatisation, especially as it is possible that vulnerability can take

60 *Hutten-Czapska v. Poland* Application no. 35014/97 Judgment (Merits and Just Satisfaction) (Grand Chamber) 19 June 2006, para. 225.

61 *Connors v. the United Kingdom* Application nos. 39665/98 40086/98 Judgment (Merits and Just Satisfaction) 15 July 2002.

62 *McCann v. United Kingdom* Application no. 19009/04, Judgment (Merits and Just Satisfaction) 13 May 2008, para. 50.

63 *Kiyutin v. Russia*, App. No. 2700/10, Judgment (Merits and Just Satisfaction) 10 March 2011.

on a 'master status'. This occurs when 'the defining attribute eclipses all other aspects of stigmatized persons, their talents and abilities'.[64] When vulnerability overshadows all other aspects of an applicant's identity in the Court's reasoning, it has taken on a master status.

Peroni and Timmer have also admonished the Court for engaging in 'misplaced paternalism' when it comes to its group-vulnerability reasoning.[65] In *D.H. v. Czech Republic*, in response to the government's objection that the Roma children would not have been placed in special schools had their parents not consented to it, the majority of the Grand Chamber held that '[i]n the circumstances of the present case, the Court is not satisfied that the parents of the Roma children, who were members of a disadvantaged community and often poorly educated, were capable of weighing up all the aspects of the situation and the consequences of giving their consent'.[66] By denying the Roma parents' capacity to make an informed decision about placing their children in special schools, the Court, for Peroni and Timmer, may tend to reinforce their powerlessness.

To prevent group-vulnerability reasoning from reducing applicants to pure victims and from stigmatising their vulnerability, the Court should, in their view, always make sure that it does not apply vulnerability as simply a 'label' (a label turns easily into a stigma), but rather as a 'layered' concept. They argue that the focus should be on the various *circumstances* that render certain groups vulnerable and not on which groups are vulnerable. They also argue that the Court should insist on and strengthen its contextual inquiry to determine whether a group may be deemed vulnerable or not. This approach will help avoid a reified conception of group vulnerability, as the focus is expanded towards the social and historical forces that originate, maintain or reinforce the vulnerability of a group.[67]

Finally, a note of caution is sounded on the need to be aware of the temptation of turning group vulnerability into an easy and straightforward narrative: people are rendered vulnerable due to a complex set of causes, including: economic disempowerment, social attitudes and physical limitations. It must, simultaneously, be recalled that people always possess sources of resilience in the face of their vulnerabilities.[68] Humanity, after all, is both free and vulnerable.

64 Lourdes Peroni and Alexandra Timmer, 'Vulnerable Groups: The Promise of an Emerging Concept in European Human Rights Convention Law' (2013) 11(4) International Journal of Constitutional Law (n 2), 1056–1085, 1072.

65 Ibid.

66 *D.H. and others v. the Czech Republic* Application no. 57325/00 Judgment (Merits and Just Satisfaction) (Grand Chamber) 13 November 2007, at para. 203.

67 Lourdes Peroni and Alexandra Timmer, 'Vulnerable Groups: The Promise of an Emerging Concept in European Human Rights Convention Law' (2013) 11(4) International Journal of Constitutional Law 1056–1085 (n 2), 1073.

68 Ibid, 1074.

2 The impact of the Charter of Fundamental Rights

The case of the Returns Directive

Stephen Coutts
University College Cork

Introduction

The European Union has not historically been considered a human rights organisation. As is well known, it has primarily been concerned with economic integration and its fundamental rights jurisprudence was developed in response to challenges from national constitutional courts, especially the German Constitutional Court and the Italian constitutional court.[1] Similarly, the Court of Justice has been accused of not 'taking rights seriously', being overly concerned with ensuring the effectiveness of Union law and the constitutional imperative of integration.[2] This picture has changed somewhat in recent years and the advent of the Treaty of Lisbon offers an opportunity to reassess the human rights credentials of the European Union and Court of Justice. As pointed out by de Búrca, the Treaty of Lisbon introduced important human rights innovations.[3] In Article 6 TEU it now outlines the sources of human rights in the European Union, of which there are three: the general principles, the Charter of Fundamental Rights (CFR) and, finally, an obligation on the European Union to accede to the European Convention on Human Rights.[4] The adoption of the Charter is especially important. It codifies and extends existing fundamental rights, providing a modern set of rights. It also provides the Court of Justice with the language and a textual basis for a more active and rights-conscious interpretative strategy.

1 See Gráinne de Búrca, 'The Evolution of EU Human Rights Law' in Paul Craig and Gráinne de Búrca (eds.) *The Evolution of EU Law* (2nd edn, Oxford University Press 2011) at 477 ff.

2 Jason Coppel and Aidan O'Neill, 'The European Court of Justice: Taking Rights Seriously?' (1992) 29 Common Market Law Review 669. Although see the riposte in J.H.H. Weiler and Nicolas Lockhart, '"Taking Rights Seriously" Seriously: The European Court and its Fundamental Rights Jurisprudence – Part I' (1995) 32 Common Market Law Review 51 and J.H.H. Weiler and Nicolas Lockhart, '"Taking Rights Seriously" Seriously: The European Court and its Fundamental Rights Jurisprudence – Part II' (1995) 32 Common Market Law Review 579.

3 Gráinne de Búrca, 'After the EU Charter of Fundamental Rights: The Court of Justice as a Human Rights Actor?' (2013) 20 Maastricht Journal of European and Comparative Law 168.

4 These three sources have been characterised as the Union's fundamental rights unwritten principles, an internal bill of rights and an external bill of rights.

DOI: 10.4324/9780429023149-3

Important as the adoption of the Charter is, however, its significance cannot be appreciated in isolation from other constitutional changes introduced in the Treaty of Lisbon, of which two are especially relevant. First is the extension of the Union's competences to areas which are particularly sensitive to human rights concerns or, in fact, can be considered specific manifestations of human rights.[5] Asylum law and criminal law are important cases in point. The Union therefore has an important *legislative* role in developing certain fundamental rights such as the right to asylum itself and rights of individuals in the field of criminal law.[6] This expansion in the legislative competence of the Union also has implications for the scope of Union law and therefore the scope of the Charter. Finally, the jurisdiction of the Court in these key fields has been normalised after the Treaty of Lisbon from a previously restrictive practice after the Treaty of Amsterdam. The combined result of these changes – increased textual basis for fundamental rights in the Charter, increased competence and expanded jurisdiction of the Court – lay the foundations for a much more human-rights-orientated approach by the Court of Justice, which now has the potential to act as a genuine human rights court.[7] At the same time, the Court remains the apex court of a system designed above all to secure legal integration. The old imperatives of unity, effectiveness and primacy of Union law remain and, while they can at times be complementary, they can also sometimes exist in tension.

This chapter assess the claim that the introduction of the Charter has led to the Court of Justice acting more as a human rights court by assessing a number of judgments of the Returns Directive[8] before and after the Treaty of Lisbon. It will be noted that the interpretative strategy of the Court of Justice shifted profoundly with the introduction of the Treaty of Lisbon and the elevating of the Charter of Fundamental Rights to primary law status. The Court of Justice now uses fundamental rights to protect individuals. This has led not only to a fundamental rights-compliant interpretation of the Returns Directive, but an extension of its scope and of the protection it offers beyond the text of the

5 For an overview of the changes introduced in the Treaty of Lisbon, see Steve Peers, 'Justice and Home Affairs Law since the Treaty of Lisbon: A Fairy-Tale Ending?' in Diego Acosta Arcarazo and Cian Murphy (eds.) *EU Security and Justice Law* (Hart 2014). See also Steve Peers, *EU Justice and Home Affairs Law*, vol. 1, *EU Immigration and Asylum Law* (Oxford University Press 2016), ch 2.

6 Mitsilegas in particular stresses this fact in the field of criminal law. See Valsamis Mitsilegas, *EU Criminal Law after Lisbon* (Hart 2016), chapter 6. See also Andrew Williams, 'Human Rights in the EU' in Anthony Arnull and Damian Chalmers (eds.) *The Oxford Handbook of European Union Law* (Oxford University Press 2015), who notes the importance of non-judicial actors in the promotion of human rights in EU law and policy.

7 De Búrca, 'After the EU Charter of Fundamental Rights: The Court of Justice as a Human Rights Actor?' (n 3).

8 Directive 2008/115/EC on common standards and procedures in member states for returning illegally staying third-country nationals [2008] OJ L 348/98. For an assessment of the text, see Anneliesse Baldaccini, 'The Return and Removal of Irregular Migrants under EU Law: An Analysis of the Returns Directive' (2009) 11 European Journal of Migration and Law 1.

Directive. The language of fundamental rights has also provided the Court with the normative resources to deploy an approach which addresses issues of vulnerability in a more open and effective manner. This is demonstrated most clearly in the judgment of *Achiba*. At the same time, systemic concerns relating to the unity and effectiveness of Union law remain, as is evidenced by constitutional judgments relating to the operation of mutual recognition systems. The old dynamics of protecting the integrity of Union law therefore displace concerns relating to individual protection and displace issues of vulnerability. The inhuman, and some might say insensitive, aspect of Union law can at times prevail.

The Returns Directive before and after Lisbon: the role of the Charter

Pre-Lisbon: the Returns Directive and classic interpretative strategies

The Returns Directive[9] was adopted in order to harmonise the conditions under which an individual should be issued with a decision to leave the European Union and under which an individual may be detained for that purpose.[10] It is therefore an exclusionary and arguably repressive measure. Nonetheless, the Directive does contain a number of rights respecting provisions, particularly concerning procedural rights and around the use of detention. The overall objective of the Directive is that '[c]lear, transparent and fair rules need to be fixed to provide for an effective return policy as a necessary element of a well-managed migration policy.'[11]

Teleological, or result-orientated, interpretation is a hallmark of the Court of Justice's jurisprudence.[12] This is generally seen as the approach of a Court more concerned with developing and promoting the effectiveness of its own legal order vis-à-vis, for example, member state legal rules and in indirectly securing its autonomy. Often, as in the case of *Melloni*,[13] in which higher national standards of fundamental rights were set aside to ensure the effective application of Union law, this can be seen to conflict with the interests of the individual. However, in *El Dridi*,[14] in which the applicant resisted the imposi-

9 Returns Directive (n 8).

10 It is therefore more accurately described as an immigration rather than asylum measure. However, it is the case that a failed international protection applicant who remains in the European Union (and fails to secure another regular status) is likely to fall within the scope of the Directive. For an overview, see Baldaccini, 'The Return and Removal of Irregular Migrants under EU Law: An Analysis of the Returns Directive'.

11 Returns Directive (n 8) preamble, point (4).

12 See Gerard Conway, *The Limits of Legal Reasoning and the European Court of Justice* (Cambridge University Press 2012), chs 1–2.

13 Case C-399/11 *Stefano Melloni v Ministerio Fiscal* EU:C:2013:107.

14 Case C-61/11 PPU *Hassen El Dridi* EU:C:2011:268, [2011] ECR I-3015.

tion of a prison sentence imposed following his failure to voluntarily depart following the issuance of a removal order, teleological reasoning operated in an individual-friendly manner.[15] The Court of Justice found that detention under the Returns Directive is only justified for the purposes of ensuring removal of the individual. Imprisoning the individual would clearly have the effect of delaying the enforcement of the return decision and thereby risk 'jeopardising the attainment of the objective pursued by [the] directive, namely, the establishment of an effective policy of removal and repatriation of illegally staying third-country nationals'.[16] A custodial sanction imposed on an individual for failure to comply with a returns decision had therefore to be set aside. The result is quite remarkable; the effectiveness of Union law – and in particular the Returns Directive – in removing as expeditiously as possible third-country nationals justifies the setting aside of national criminal law. It is important to note, however, that this is not achieved on the basis of fundamental rights per se but rather on the classic grounds of effectiveness of Union law. Note also the absence of the individual and his or her specific concerns regarding removal from the judgment, which operates at systemic level. The classic interpretative strategies of the Court of Justice leave little room for considerations of the needs of individuals, who, while occupying a prominent place in the Union's legal order, are frequently instrumentalised in the process.[17]

In *Abdida*[18] the Returns Directive was again at stake; however, now fundamental rights and the Charter take centre stage. This in turn provides the normative resources to take the vulnerable situation of Mr Abdida seriously and as a central motivating aspect of the Court's judgment. In *Abdida* a Nigerian man whose initial asylum application was rejected was facing a removal after leave to remain on humanitarian grounds - initially granted on the basis of a visual impairment suffered as a consequence of an assault- had been withdrawn. While he challenged the removal order he lost all access to social assistance with the exception of emergency medical care.[19] On the basis of the asylum acquis[20] the national court raised questions regarding the absence of an

15 Case C-61/11 PPU *Hassen El Dridi* (Opinion of AG Mazák) EU:C:2011:205, [2011] ECR I-3015, paras 2–4.

16 *El Dridi* (14) para 59.

17 See an interpretation of van Gen den Loos, see Damian Chalmers and Luis Barroso, 'What *Van Gend en Loos* stands for' (2014) 12 International Journal of Constitutional Law 105. Specifically in relation to EU citizenship, see Michelle Everson, 'The Legacy of the Market Citizen' in Jo Shaw and Gillian More (eds.), *New Legal Dynamics of European Union* (Clarendon Press 1995).

18 Case C-562/13 *Centre public d'action sociale d'Ottignies-Louvain-La-Neuve v Moussa Abdida* EU:C:2014:2453.

19 Case 562/13 *Centre public d'action sociale d'Ottignies-Louvain-La-Neuve v Moussa Abdida* (Opinion of AG Bot) EU:C:2014:2167, paras 55–58.

20 In particular the Directive 2004/83/EC on minimum standards for the qualification and status of third country nationals or stateless persons as refugees or as persons who otherwise need international protection and the content of the protection granted [2004] OJ L 304/12, since replaced by Directive 2011/95/EU on standards for the qualification of third-country nationals or stateless

automatic suspensive effect on appeals from removal orders and the extent to which any applicant in such a case is entitled to have his or her basic subsistence needs met.

In its judgment the Court of Justice, found that the matter fell within Union law. As a third-country national illegally resident in a member state, Mr Abdida, was subject to the Returns Directive,[21] which 'seeks to guarantee, in accordance with the fundamental rights of the persons concerned, the effective protection of their interests, in particular repatriation under humane and dignified conditions'.[22] Human dignity and the risk of inhuman and degrading treatment then provide the means for the Court to extend protection to Mr Abdida, appropriately reflecting, in a manner not available to effectiveness-type reasoning, his vulnerable position. Not applying an automatic suspensive effect to removal orders in situations such as that of Mr Abdida risked removing an individual to a situation where he would risk facing inhuman and degrading treatment, possibly breaching his right to non-refoulement found in Article 19(2) CFR read in conjunction with the right to good administration found in Article 47 CFR.[23] At the same time Mr Abdida, as someone subject to a removal order under appeal, was entitled to emergency medical care under Article 14(1)(b) of the Directive, a right that would be rendered 'meaningless' if basic subsistence was not also provided.[24]

Important is the manner in which the Court arrives at this conclusion and the respective roles played by secondary legislation (in this case, the Returns Directive) and the Charter. The matter is brought within the scope of Union law by the Returns Directive, thus confirming de Búrca's point that how the expansion of the Union's legislative activities to areas where fundamental rights implications are more apparent is likely to expand the role of the Union in general and the Court of Justice in particular in the field of human rights.[25] But the Court of Justice goes beyond what is envisaged either in the Charter or in the Returns Directive to develop this right into a right to remain for humanitarian reasons. Both findings of the Court in *Abdida* – that appeal from a removal order shall have automatic suspensive effect and that the means of subsistence

---

persons as beneficiaries of international protection, for a uniform status for refugees or for persons eligible for subsidiary protection, and for the content of the protection granted [2011] OJ L 337/9, Directive 2003/9/EC laying down minimum standards for the reception of asylum seekers [2003] OJ L31/18 since replaced by Directive 2013/33/EU laying down standards for the reception of applicants for international protection (recast) [2013] OJ L 180/96 and Directive 2005/85/EC on minimum standards on procedures in member states for granting and withdrawing refugee status [2005] OJ L 326/13 (n 9) since replaced by Directive 2013/32/EU on common procedures for granting and withdrawing international protection (recast) [2013] OJ L 180/60.

21 *Abdida*, para 39.

22 *Abdida* (Opinion of AG Bot) (n 19) para 105.

23 *Abdida* (n 18) para 45.

24 Ibid, para 60.

25 De Búrca, 'After the EU Charter of Fundamental Rights: The Court of Justice as a Human Rights Actor?' (n 3) at 169.

should be provided for applicants in such situations – go against the legislative intent, as described by AG Bot,[26] and yet flow from the jurisprudence of the ECtHR, which, as is indicated in Article 52(3) CFR, should guide the Court of Justice when interpreting the Charter. Thus, while secondary legislation brings the matter within the scope of Union law, once this occurs, the Charter, though importing the jurisprudence of the ECtHR, expands significantly on the protection offered by the Directive and leads to an interpretation going beyond the legislative intent.

Systemic concerns meet fundamental rights: the case of mutual trust

However, if in *Abdida* we see the Court of Justice acting as a fundamental rights court, supplementing the rights provided for in legislation and interpreting that legislation in a manner consistent with the fundamental rights regime established by the Treaty of Lisbon, we have not seen an unambiguous shift in the attitude of the Court of Justice towards a rights-based approach. The Court of Justice is an institution which has over the years developed an idiosyncratic law of integration[27] and sees itself as presiding over a legal system which has as its *raison d'être* the integration of the member states of the Union. The language of effectiveness, primacy and unity of Union law remain central to the jurisprudence of the Court of Justice and at times resurface in direct tension with fundamental rights. The Court is now juxtaposing its traditional role as a court of integration with a new role as a human rights court. This tension can be seen in cases relating to the mutual recognition of national decisions in the Area of Freedom, Security and Justice, including where individuals are transferred from one member state to another within the so-called Dublin system.

The judgment in *NS,* in which the Court found that an individual may resist transfer to another member state if there was a risk of inhuman and degrading treatment, is a perfect illustration of the tensions between fundamental rights and the law of integration. The Court of Justice does concede to the need for some fundamental rights protection within the CEAS; however, it does so against a background concern to secure the effectiveness of the Dublin system as a whole. A number of points in the judgment reflect this overall systemic concern, to the detriment of the individual asylum applicant's interests and a consideration of his or her individual situation.[28] First, the analysis is foregrounded by a discussion of the need to ensure the effectiveness

26 *Abdida* (Opinion of AG Bot) (n 19) para 80.

27 See the defining work of Pierre Pescatore, *Le Droit de l'intégration* (A.W. Sijthoff 1972). For a modern restatement, see Julio Baquero Cruz, *What's Left of the Law of Integration? Decay and Resistance in European Union Law* (Oxford University Press 2018).

28 For the contrary, individualised approach, see *Tarakhel v Switzerland* App No 29217/12 (Grand Chamber) 4 November 2014.

of the Dublin system and the need to have a system for clearly identifying the responsible state and effective transfers speedily.[29] Indeed, in a somewhat enigmatic phrase, the Court of Justice finds that '[a]t issue…is the raison d'être of the European Union and the creation of an area of freedom, security and justice…based on mutual confidence and a presumption of compliance by other member states, with European Union law and, in particular, fundamental rights'.[30]

Second, while this presumption may be set aside in some circumstances, they are very limited. The Court outlines a clear and strict test: 'if there are substantial grounds for believing that there are systemic flaws in the asylum procedure and reception conditions for asylum applicants in the member state responsible, resulting in inhuman or degrading treatment, within the meaning of Article 4 of the Charter…the transfer would be incompatible with that provision'.[31] Note that there must be *substantial* grounds for believing there are *systemic flaws* in the member state such that a risk of inhuman and degrading treatment (and not other rights violations) will be experienced. The reference to systemic flaws is important, as it precludes an individual assessment of the asylum seeker's situation,[32] a finding which later would bring the *NS* judgment in tension, if not conflict, with the parallel line of ECtHR jurisprudence.[33] A more recent response from the Court of Justice has conceded in *CK* that individual concerns may be taken into account.[34] However, as pointed out by Imamović and Muir, the Court does stress the exceptional nature of this case and that in most cases the *NS* test will continue to apply.[35]

This tension is again evident in *Opinion 2/13*[36] concerning the accession of the European Union to the European Convention of Human Rights as, it will be recalled, it is obliged to do under Article 6(2) TEU. A previous attempt at

29 See Joined Cases C-411/10 and C-493/10 *NS v Secretary of State for the Home Department and ME and Others v Refugee Applications Commissioner and Minister for Justice, Equality and Law Reform* EU:C:2011:865, [2011] ECR I-13905, paras 79–85.

30 Ibid, para 83.

31 Ibid, para 86.

32 An individual assessment can of course work against the individual concerned, as has occurred in the analogous cases dealing with transfer within the European Arrest Warrant system, where both systemic flaws *and* an individual risk need to be taken into account, meaning an individual many be surrendered to a state where there are systemic flaws but no individual risk. See Case C-216/18 PPU *Minister for Justice and Equality v LM* EU:C:2018:586.

33 In particular the judgment in *Tarakhel*. For an analysis of the two lines of caselaw, see Guilia Vicini, 'The Dublin Regulation between Strasbourg and Luxembourg: Reshaping *Non-Refoulement* in the Name of Trust' (2015) 8 European Journal of Legal Studies 50.

34 Case C-578/16 *CK and Others v Republika Slovenija* EU:C:2017:127.

35 Šeila Imamović and Elise Muir, 'The Dublin III System: More Derogations to the Duty to Transfer Individual Asylum Seekers?' (2017) 2 European Papers 719, at 726.

36 *Opinion 2/13 Accession to the European Convention on Human Rights* EU:C:2014:2454. For an analysis, see Daniel Halberstam, '*"It's the Autonomy, Stupid!"* A Modest Defence of *Opinion 2/13* on EU Accession to the ECHR, and the Way Forward' (2015) 16 Guernsey Law Journal 105.

accession failed due to lack of competence in *Opinion 2/94*.[37] That competence was duly provided in the Treaty of Lisbon, but the Treaty of Lisbon also included a protocol in which any accession to the ECtHR should not compromise the essential features of Union law among other conditions.[38] One of those essential features identified by the Court of Justice in its Opinion rejecting the draft accession agreement as incompatible with the Treaties, and in particular with Protocol 8 EU, was the mutual confidence presumed by Union law between member states in their collective compliance with fundamental rights when they were acting within the scope of Union law. The importance given to the system of integration is evident in the constitutional language used by the Court noting that:

> essential characteristics of EU law have given rise to a structured network of principles, rules and mutually interdependent legal relations linking the EU and its Member States and its Member States with each other, which are now engaged…in a process of creating an ever-closer union among the peoples of Europe.
>
> This legal structure is based on the fundamental premiss that each Member State shares with all the other Member States, and recognises that they share with it, a set of common values on which the EU is founded, as stated in Article 2 TEU. That premiss implies and justifies the existence of mutual trust between the Member States that those values will be recognised and, therefore, that the law of the EU that implements them will be respected.[39]

The result is that any accession of the EU to the ECtHR must contain some mechanism that ensures that member states are not obliged to check if another member state has complied with fundamental rights. To allow otherwise would be 'liable to upset the underlying balance of the EU and undermine the autonomy of EU law'.[40] External review of fundamental rights compliance of the component parts of the Union's composite constitution[41] must not compromise the well-functioning of that legal system and the resulting legal integration. The result is that the interests of individuals and any consideration of their potentially vulnerable situation must be subordinated to the broader interests in the functioning of mutual recognition systems in EU law, including the Dublin system. It limits the extent to which Union law can be responsive to individual vulnerable situations.

37 *Opinion 2/94 Accession by the Community to the European Convention for the Protection of Human Rights and Fundamental Freedoms* EU:C:1996:229 [2006] ECR I-2827.

38 See Protocol 8 EU.

39 *Opinion 2/13* (n 36) paras 167–168.

40 Ibid, para 194.

41 See Leonard Besselink, *A Composite European Constitution* (Europa Law Publishing 2007).

Conclusion

This chapter has argued that, despite the fact that there was no radical structural change to the human rights competence of the Union after the Treaty of Lisbon, in the sense that the Union did not gain a general human rights competence and did not become a human rights organisation per se, changes in the Treaty of Lisbon – including the adoption of the Charter as primary law, the expansion of the Union's substantive competences to areas more typically associated with fundamental rights and the widening of the jurisdiction of the Court of Justice – has created a genuine human rights competence for the Court in specific areas. This has been demonstrated by an assessment of the jurisprudence of the Returns Directive before and after the adoption of the Treaty of Lisbon. We can see in cases before the Treaty of Lisbon that the Court, while seeking to achieve an outcome respectful of the individual's interests, refrained from deploying the language of fundamental rights, falling back on classic Union law interpretive tools such as the principle of effectiveness in *El Dridi*.[42] *Abdida*[43] provides a clear contrast with the Court of Justice using the Charter in combination with legislative provisions to provide a new right of leave to remain on the basis of humanitarian grounds by extending the right to *non-refoulement* found in the Returns Directive[44] and the Charter,[45] to situations of medical need and extreme deprivation.

We can therefore witness a clear shift and the introduction of a new discourse into the reasoning of the Court of Justice after the Treaty of Lisbon. However, it is important to note that this new set of norms and judicial reasoning does not displace the older forms of reasoning of the Court, such as teleological, systemic methods and the principle of effectiveness. These different families of reasoning are not necessarily in conflict, even when the needs of individuals are at stake. In *Abdida*,[46] both discourses are at stake and both are deployed to protect the interests of the individual: fundamental rights to find and extend the right to non-refoulement to cover the situation of the applicant and a classic effectiveness argument to extend rights to subsistence from the right to emergency care found in the Returns Directive itself. Interpretive tools are malleable, perhaps none more so than teleological and effectiveness-based ones, and can be deployed to secure a variety of ends.

However, when questions of constitutional integrity and systemic concerns arise, as in *NS* and *Opinion 2/13*, fundamental rights concerns are subordinated.

42 *El Dridi* (n 14).
43 *Abdida* (n 18).
44 Returns Directive (n 8), art 5.
45 CFR, art 18.
46 *Abdida* (n 18).

The result is a weakness in the ability of Union law to recognise the position of individuals and adjust to their vulnerable position. Thus, while de Búrca's prediction that combination of changes in the Treaty of Lisbon has expanded the role of human rights in the Union's legal order, and the Court of Justice as a human rights court, an assessment of its jurisprudence in the area of asylum and illegal migrants demonstrates that it is not *only* a human rights court and this new role does not displace its more fundamental vocation as a court of integration.

3 Prosecuting domestic abuse

Vulnerability theory as heuristic

Antonia Porter
University of Kent

Introduction

'Law and order' and improving the conviction rate has become the dominant paradigm for dealing with domestic abuse in England and Wales.[1] Criminal prosecutions are key to the UK government's strategy to end violence against women and girls[2] and 'Guidelines for Prosecutors', introduced between 2005 and 2008, announced that the Crown Prosecution Service (CPS)[3] regards domestic abuse offences as 'particularly serious'.[4] Yet, while prosecutors are told the 'public interest' will invariably require pursuance of such offences through the criminal courts,[5] victims[6] of domestic abuse often express their reluctance to support a State prosecution. The Crown Prosecutor must therefore resolve the conflict between achieving convictions on the one hand and victim retraction on the other. The danger for victims is that, as prosecutors now frequently proceed with cases against a victim's stated wishes,[7] intimate partner coercion might simply be replaced with State coercion.[8] This chapter considers how vulnerability theory might assist the prosecutor in exercising

1 See Antonia Porter, 'Prosecuting Domestic Abuse in England and Wales: Crown Prosecution Service "Working Practice" and New Public Managerialism' (2019) 28(4) Social and Legal Studies 493; Mimi Kim, 'Challenging the Pursuit of Criminalisation in an Era of Mass Incarceration: The Limitations of Social Work Responses to Domestic Violence in the USA' (2012) 43(7) British Journal of Social Work 1276.

2 The first government Violence Against Women and Girls strategy was: HM Government, 'Together We Can End Violence Against Women and Girls: A Strategy' (Home Office 2009).

3 Crown Prosecution Service, 'Domestic Abuse Guidelines for Prosecutors' www.cps.gov.uk/legal-guidance/domestic-abuse-guidelines-prosecutors accessed 6 June 2019.

4 Ibid.

5 Ibid.

6 The use of the word 'victim' here reflects its use in the criminal justice system vis-à-vis the 'complainant'. In no way do I intend to totalise women's experiences or overlook empowered agency of women who have experienced domestic abuse.

7 Antonia Porter, 'Prosecuting Domestic Abuse in England and Wales: Crown Prosecution Service "Working Practice" and New Public Managerialism' (n 1).

8 Donna Coker, 'Crime Control and Feminist Law Reform in Domestic Violence Law' (2001) 4(2) British Columbia Law Review 80.

DOI: 10.4324/9780429023149-4

their discretion, to proceed with a case or not, when a victim of domestic abuse expresses her wish for case discontinuance. The chapter contemplates how vulnerability theory might offer a disruption to existing prosecutorial normative appraisals of domestic abuse cases so as to avoid, or at least reduce, detrimental (safety or autonomy compromising) outcomes for victims of domestic abuse.

The chapter starts by setting out how prevailing feminist and neoliberal discourses have identified a 'vulnerable' category of persons – abused women – and how these drivers have contributed to a reliance on the 'penal equation'.[9] Next, it interrogates how Fineman's vulnerability theory has the effect of 'turn[ing] the previous conversation on its head'.[10] Vulnerability, for Fineman, is ontological, and the theory demands that the State recognises this. In turn, the State and its actors have a responsibility to be responsive in ways that promote the resilience of all citizens. However, the question of *how exactly* the State fulfils this obligation is missing from vulnerability theory, and real-world predicaments, such as the one contemplated in this chapter, highlight the shortcoming.

Given the lacuna – between what vulnerability theory offers in its current form and its potential to contribute to existing practices, structures and procedures – it is no wonder that, when specific and tangible dilemmas present, some 'vulnerability' academics have turned to bodies of scholarship that already offer decades of thought, for example, in the fields of relational autonomy or the capabilities approach.[11] Mackenzie, for example, has resisted conceptualising vulnerability and autonomy in oppositional terms and has persuasively argued that frames such as relational autonomy and capabilities offer precisely the sort of guidance deficient in vulnerability theory.[12]

The chapter concludes, however, not by writing off vulnerability theory, but by revisiting Fineman's theory as heuristic. If, as Fineman contends, 'vulnerability' is simply to be understood as *the* universal (human) condition, starting with categorisations or taxonomies of the 'more' or 'less' vulnerable will always be misguided. Moreover, Fineman urges us not to fall into the trap of aspiring to 'empowerment' or 'autonomy' (whether relational or not) because such goals engage the same individualised identity-based neoliberal registers that her vulnerability theory expressly set out to resist. As such, the chapter recognises that the theory will not, as it stands, provide a 'silver bullet' for State

9 Alan Norrie, *Law and the Beautiful Soul* (Glass House 2005) 75. Norrie refers to the 'penal equation' as the formula which requires that 'crime, plus responsibility, equals punishment'.

10 Maxine Eichner, 'Dependency and the Liberal Polity: On Martha Fineman's "The Autonomy Myth"' (2005) 93 Californian Law Review 1285.

11 See, e.g., Catriona Mackenzie, Wendy Rogers and Susan Dodds (eds.) *Vulnerability: New Essays in Ethics and Feminist Philosophy* (Oxford University Press 2014).

12 Catriona Mackenzie, 'The Importance of Relational Autonomy and Capabilities for an Ethics of Vulnerability' in Catriona Mackenzie, Wendy Rogers and Susan Dodds (eds.) *Vulnerability: New Essays in Ethics and Feminist Philosophy* (Oxford University Press 2014) 33.

actors functioning in existing structures and arrangements. If the theory is to offer tangible ameliorations, and if it is to transcend being labelled as mere 'provocative social criticism',[13] it requires us to step back from the instant problematic (and others like it) that operate within existing frames. Fineman provokes us to rethink and theorise our fundamental social relationships, values and institutional organisation. Perhaps only when we have revisited the deep-rooted assumptions that guide and organise us might we return to the question of how the State might best support the victim of domestic abuse. Unfortunately, for the prosecutor working within existing confines of the criminal justice system, dealing with the daily demands of how to proceed in cases where the victim is unsupportive, the theory in its current form, holds limited purchase.

The domestic abuse victim and the penal equation

Victims of domestic abuse are considerably more likely to retract their support for a criminal prosecution, or fail to attend trial to give evidence, as compared to other criminal offences. One in three domestic abuse prosecutions fail in this way,[14] accounting for over 7500 cases annually.[15] This compares to one in ten prosecutions generally.[16] Domestic abuse victims withdraw from the criminal process for myriad reasons,[17] but may include the fear of retaliation by the perpetrator, a wish to preserve the relationship or family arrangements or concerns about the court procedure itself.[18]

When faced with an unsupportive complainant, the options available to prosecutors include discontinuing the case, requiring the victim to give evidence at trial by issuing a witness summons or pursuing a 'victimless' prosecution in her absence when other corroborative evidence allows. Noting that the CPS celebrates successive annual rises in conviction rates and has ambitions to 'bring more perpetrators to justice',[19] the criminal prosecutor operates with

13 Morgan Cloud, 'More than Utopia' in Martha Fineman and Anna Grear (eds.) *Vulnerability: Reflections on a New Ethical Foundation for Law and Politics* (Ashgate 2013) 77.

14 Crown Prosecution Service, 'Violence Against Women and Girls Crime Report, 2015–16' (CPS 2016).

15 Crown Prosecution Service, 'Violence Against Women and Girls Crime Report, 2010–2011' (CPS 2011).

16 Crown Prosecution Service, 'Violence Against Women and Girls Crime Report, 2015–16' (CPS 2016).

17 See, e.g., Sarah Buel, '50 Obstacles to Leaving aka Why Victims Stay' (1999) 28 Colorado Lawyer 1.

18 Andrea Nichols, 'No-Drop Prosecution in Domestic Violence Cases' (2014) 29(11) Journal of Interpersonal Violence 2114; Eve Buzawa and Carl Buzawa, *Domestic Violence: The Criminal Justice Response* (3rd edn, Sage 2003).

19 Crown Prosecution Service, 'Violence Against Women and Girls Report, 2016–17' (CPS 2017) www.cps.gov.uk/sites/default/files/documents/publications/cps-vawg-report-2017.pf accessed 6 June 2019.

the expectation that proceeding to trial (by summonsing the victim or persevering without her) will invariably be in the 'public interest'.[20]

The current prosecutorial working assumption stands in contrast to approaches of the past when criminal intervention was rare in cases of violence between intimates and was only engaged for the most serious infractions.[21] Moreover, even if the matter was charged, the effect of the victim withdrawing her support had 'an almost a singular effect – namely discontinuance'.[22] The feminist and women's movements of the 1960s–1980s vociferously demanded the State be more proactive and take privately occurring abuse seriously. More recently, committed to provoking State action, feminist campaigners have found recent neoliberal governments particularly hospitable in the area of criminal justice and crime control.[23] A succession of CPS public consultations with groups such as, inter alia, the Fawcett Society, Women's Aid, Refuge and the UK Network of Sexwork Projects has informed and shaped the prosecutorial approach to domestic abuse. It can be argued that the CPS has responded admirably to the challenge not to ignore domestic abuse. Indeed, domestic abuse conviction rates continue to rise year on year.[24]

As part of this commitment, the CPS appears to have reacted to feminist critique about the liberal legal subject. In the past, the Crown may have been accused of identifying abused women who did not support a case (who may have also expressed a wish to remain with an abusive partner) as failing to meet the standards of the logical, autonomous and self-determining liberal legal subject.[25] If unsupportive of prosecution, the victim of domestic abuse was invariably considered irrational, her capacity to be a witness compromised and her testimony likely unreliable. The inability of abused women to be recognisably 'rational' legal subjects and witnesses provided justification for prosecutors to habitually discontinue cases on evidential grounds.[26]

20 Antonia Porter, 'Prosecuting Domestic Abuse in England and Wales: Crown Prosecution Service "Working Practice" and New Public Managerialism' (n 1).

21 Rebecca Dobash and Russell Dobash, *Violence Against Wives: A Case Against the Patriarchy* (New York: Free Press 1979) 210–211.

22 Louise Ellison, 'Prosecuting Domestic Violence without Victim Participation' (2002) 65(6) Modern Law Review 834; see also Antonia Cretney and Gwynn Davis, 'Prosecuting Domestic Assault: Victims Failing Courts, or Courts Failing Victims?' (1997) 36(2) Howard Journal of Crime and Justice 146.

23 Kristin Bumiller, *In an Abusive State: How Neoliberalism Appropriated the Feminist Movement Against Sexual Violence* (Duke University Press 2009); Janet Halley et al., *Governance Feminism: An Introduction* (University of Minnesota Press 2018).

24 Crown Prosecution Service, 'Violence Against Women and Girls Report, 2017–18' (CPS 2018) www.cps.gov.uk/sites/default/files/documents/publications/cps-vawg-report-2018.pdf accessed 6 June 2019.

25 Ngaire Naffine, 'Sexing the Subject (of Law)' in Margaret Thornton (ed.), *Public and Private: Feminist Legal Debates* (Oxford University Press 1995) 20.

26 Ibid. See also Antonia Cretney and Gwynn Davis, 'Prosecuting Domestic Assault: Victims Failing Courts, or Courts Failing Victims?' (1997) 36(2) Howard Journal of Crime and Justice 146.

More recently, however, CPS policy requires prosecutors to 'flag' all domestic abuse files as having a 'vulnerable/intimidated victim'.[27] 'Vulnerable' victims merit particular 'enhanced' treatment by the Service. 'Vulnerable' victims merit particular 'enhanced' treatment by the Service and committed domestic abuse prosecutions demonstrate that the prosecutor is taking the offence seriously.[28]

Using 'vulnerability': some caveats

The CPS appear, therefore, to have reassessed the status of the unsupportive victim. No longer dismissed as an irrational actor incapable of knowing what is in her best interests (as a liberal conception of the legal subject might previously have concluded), prosecutors are now encouraged to be mindful of her vulnerability and the consequent responsibility the State has towards her. Vulnerability becomes a benchmark for assessing how far short of expected norms she has fallen and the extent to which the State is required, therefore, to intervene.

Deployed in the quotidian, as in CPS policy, 'vulnerability' is merely a descriptor. It implies someone's risk of and exposure to potential harm. Its use creates classes of those who are 'vulnerable', as distinct from the remainder, the fictitious 'invulnerable'. While the effect of using this terminology might have been to motivate prosecutors to respond, great caution should be exercised before unquestioningly embracing 'vulnerability' as a legitimising call to action.

The everyday use of the word 'vulnerable' is fluid and malleable. As the term enjoys ethical appeal across political agendas, it has been used to meet the ends of any range of mainstream political groupings under the guise of State altruism. Identifying vulnerable groups can become a means of justifying State intervention in people's lives and there is potential for its use to extend didactic neoliberal governance.[29] For example, in response to our vulnerability to terrorism, stronger surveillance policies are green-lighted. In response to vulnerable sex workers and migrants, securitisation through border controls and criminalisation is assented and, in response to the vulnerable victim of domestic violence, the perpetrator must be brought to justice and future risk to the victim must be managed by the State (through, inter alia, criminal prosecution).

Objections to using the term 'vulnerability' to effect these ends are concerned with oppressive paternalism capable of expanding State control on the one hand and the stigmatisation and exclusion of those so labelled on the other.[30] Seeking to improve the lot of a particular specified group – abuse victims – has predictably resulted in treating the social problem of domestic abuse as something that can be controlled and managed through criminalisation. This State

27 Crown Prosecution Service, 'Domestic Abuse Guidelines for Prosecutors' (n 3).

28 Antonia Porter, 'Prosecuting Domestic Abuse in England and Wales: Crown Prosecution Service Working Practice and New Public Managerialism' (n 1).

29 Vanessa Munro and Jane Scoular, 'Abusing Vulnerability? Contemporary Law and Policy Responses to Sex Work in the UK' (2012) 20(3) Feminist Legal Studies 189.

30 Kate Brown, '"Vulnerability": Handle with Care' (2011) 5(3) Ethics and Social Welfare 313, 316.

treatment of domestic abuse forms part of a stock of 'law and order' responses typical of successive neoliberal governments.[31] Fineman's vulnerability theory, by contrast, aims to mediate calls for 'individual responsibility' (and its associated punitive rhetoric). By reconceptualising the responsibility of the State to its citizens through the lens of universal vulnerability, the State's responsibility is not to provide 'just deserts' to offending individuals and resultant 'justice' for victims, but – wider than criminal justice responses – it is to furnish resources that facilitate its people's resilience.

Dependency: a paradigm shift for conceiving the legal subject

Fineman's productive and transformative way of reconceiving the legal subject based in human experience and the human condition had roots in her work regarding the 'autonomy myth'.[32] Rather than contending that 'sameness of treatment' will facilitate disadvantaged groups' equal status, Fineman began by identifying 'disadvantage' in the West's dominant conception of the universal subject as self-sufficient, capable and independent and free to carve out a successful life for oneself. This libertarian autonomy that dominates the political arena ignores that *dependency* is an inevitable consequence of being human; during life's course, we are all dependent during childhood, sickness or old age. Society therefore labours under the misapprehension of the desirability and attainability of autonomy and its attendant ideals of individualism, self-reliance and achievement.[33] In so doing, society fails to meet its collective responsibility to 'inevitable depandents' (the looked-after) and 'derivative dependants' (the caretakers). Dependency and its derivatives become stigmatised because they are seen to fall short of the efficient execution of an autonomous life. In fact, dependency should be regarded as normal and unavoidable and social contract theories of justice have been wrong to omit the inevitability of human dependency.[34]

By treating the family akin to a public body assigned the responsibility of taking care of children, the elderly and the unwell, rather than the 'natural' and discrete place to do so, Fineman rearranges preceding feminist thought about the overdrawn segregation of public and private.[35] Prior to Fineman,

31 See, e.g., David Garland, *The Culture of Control: Crime and Social Order in Contemporary Society* (Oxford University Press 2001); Emma Bell, *Criminal Justice and Neoliberalism* (Palgrave Macmillan 2011); Pat O'Malley, 'Neoliberalism, Crime and Criminal Justice' (2016) 16(10) Sydney Law School Research 1.

32 Martha Fineman, *The Autonomy Myth* (New Press 2004).

33 Pamela Anderson also suggested that there is 'an unachievable ideal of autonomy' in Pamela Anderson, 'Autonomy, Vulnerability and Gender' (2003) 4(2) Feminist Theory 149, 157.

34 Eva Kittay, *Love's Labor: Essays on Women, Equality and Dependency* (Routledge 2013).

35 Maxine Eichner, 'Dependency and the Liberal Polity: On Martha Fineman's "The Autonomy Myth"' (2005) 93 Californian Law Review 1285, 1290.

feminists advocated that the solution to gender inequality would be the sharing of childcare responsibilities between the sexes (parental parity).[36] They encouraged employers to adopt practices to assist caretaking and urged genuine, not merely symbolic and partial, attempts at sharing household chores. These ameliorations, they asserted, would go far in reducing inherent injustices in the traditional gender-structured family and society. Fineman, however, reconceives the solution not in terms of demanding gender equality in the home and at work, but rather in terms of society recognising dependency as inevitable. If the State continues to assign the burdens of caretaking to families (as against other societal institutions) Fineman argues that the State must take responsibility to publicly support and subsidise carers.

Fineman's theory of dependency, however, can be criticised for failing to acknowledge that inevitable dependency is episodic (we have periods of dependency in our lives that come and go) and that 'derivative dependency' is performed by 'choice'. Consequently, recognising that people eventually transcend these periods, and that derivative dependants have chosen to care for others, critics have often failed to include dependency in their theories about justice and liberty. The traditional division between public and private spheres remains resistant to dismantling, and traditional legal theorists continue to assert that dependency can rightly be confined to a concern of the private sphere. Social and political theories can and should, critics say, carry on without consideration of dependency.[37]

This is, however, an unhelpful perspective to those women who continue to suffer by feeling trapped in abusive relationships because of their derivative dependency (usually due to their care roles to children). They may feel forced to remain within the private family home until such time as the children are no longer dependent and their consequent economic dependency on their abusive partner does not feel so total. Are critics of, or those who ignore, Fineman's analysis of dependency really suggesting that abused mothers can be expected to wait until that period of their lives has passed before they are able to start financial independence? Second, can it be right that they are suggesting that mothers are derivatively dependent on their abusive partners through choice? Or is it possible, as Fineman argues, that through effective State subsidies for childcare (and housing) such women would be able to establish financial independence through employment? Those who fail to engage with the inevitability of dependency absolve the State of responsibility for supporting mothers/carers with violent partners to effect life ameliorations away from their partner.

36 See, e.g., Susan Okin, *Justice, Gender and the Family* (University of Chicago Press 1989) is typical; Jerry Jacobs and Kathleen Geerson, *The Time Divide: Work, Family and Gender Inequality* (Harvard University Press 2004); and Frances Olsen, 'The Family and the Market: A Study of Ideology and Legal Reform' (1983) 96(7) Harvard Law Review 1497.

37 Martha Fineman and Anna Grear, 'Introduction' in Martha Fineman and Anna Grear (eds.) *Vulnerability: Reflections on a New Ethical Foundation for Law and Politics* (Ashgate 2013) 19.

Vulnerability theory: the ontological human condition

Nonetheless, as a consequence of the critique of dependency theory, Fineman developed her 'vulnerability theory'. While incorporating dependency theory, vulnerability theory recognises 'vulnerability' as a universal and *continuous* part of the human condition. It is therefore more 'theoretically powerful'[38] in the call for a more just society and reconceptualisation of the subject. Yet, while vulnerability might be universal, Fineman acknowledges that it is simultaneously differentially experienced and will not therefore manifest in the same way for everyone. This 'embodied difference' comes about because our 'experience of vulnerability varies according to the quality and quantity of resources we possess or can command'.[39] Vulnerable populations *can* emerge due to social and historical treatment of different human embodiments and characteristics. They can also emerge because we are not born equal; we inherit wealth and unequal social and economic advantages.

Despite this, to recognise vulnerable groups – such as 'abused women' – as the starting point for improvement is pernicious.[40] Groups which successfully mobilise are able to marshal change, leaving those groups who do not rally excluded. Furthermore, those who fall within an organised active alliance may not always benefit as differences and variance within the group are not always recognised or tailored to. By being perceived as part of a vulnerable group, individuals become stigmatised and somehow 'other', while the group's shared characteristics with those outside the group become obscured. Fineman comments that such categorising is therefore either always over- or under-inclusive. More than that, focus on the underprivileged group deflects 'attention away from the institutional arrangements and systems that distribute disadvantage across people and groups'.[41]

The State should not, therefore, begin by responding to disadvantaged groups through 'sameness of treatment'. This positions discrimination as the nemesis of equality. It also suggests there is equivalence in people's abilities and possibilities. It assumes that women who have or who are experiencing domestic abuse would simply expect their partners to face justice, just as any other victim of crime. 'Sameness of treatment' is convergent with modern political ideology about autonomy and accomplishment, which, as discussed, is unrealistic. We are not isolated and emotionless individuals but embodied and interconnected and fallible humans. In short, we are all vulnerable to injury,

38 Martha Fineman, 'The Vulnerable Subject and the Responsive State' (2010) 60 Emory Law Journal 251.

39 Ibid, 251.

40 Martha Fineman, 'What it Means to be Human: Vulnerability and the Human Condition' (2013) Emory Law School Lecture www.youtube.com/watch?v=MEgeTrzOm1o accessed 5 June 2019.

41 Martha Fineman, 'The Vulnerable Subject: Anchoring Equality in the Human Condition' (2008) 20(1) Yale Journal of Law and Feminism 8, 20.

misfortune, ageing and failure. The political and legal subject built on the Western legal tradition does not sufficiently recognise this, preferring instead to segment society into those victims who are vulnerable, and the remainder – the invulnerable. By replacing the traditionally conceived legal subject with the 'vulnerable subject', our potential to be less than self-sufficient becomes recognised, not stigmatised.

The 'vulnerable subject' is embodied and is therefore positioned as a site that foregrounds the fleshiness of what it is to be human: requiring nourishment, hydration and sleep and being susceptible to harm or illness. It is also exposed to environmental threats such as famine, flood or fire. It is this inescapable reality that renders us ontologically vulnerable. Fineman refers to these biological processes on the one hand, and external threats to the body on the other, as our 'embodied vulnerability'.[42] Recognising the interrelationality of humans with each other and with society, the embodied individual is also 'embedded' within institutions and relationships.[43] Our bodily vulnerability can thus be compounded by the vagaries of institutions – for example, if one falls ill, social and economic disruption may follow.

In the same way that our vulnerability is universal yet variantly experienced, so too is its counterpoint, resilience. The central question that should be posed by the State is not one of 'Who is more or less vulnerable?' but more one of 'Who is more or less resilient and how did they get that way?'[44] Marvel suggests that the inequality of resilience, not vulnerability, is at the core of vulnerability theory. In times of crisis, such as the infliction of violence by a partner, one's accumulated resources impact one's realistic options. The extent of our agency and available options is dependent on our resilience.

Our resilience depends, according to Fineman, on at least five resource areas or 'assets': physical (material goods, assets affecting our economic quality of life); human (our capability to make the most of a situation, dependent on education, knowledge, resources and experience); social (our family, social networks and communities); ecological (our natural or physical environment); and existential (our beliefs, religion, culture, art, politics, which allow us to see the beauty in life).[45] So, while vulnerability is ontological, it is also particularly experienced depending on our variant resilience. It is to our resilience that the State must attend. This next section considers how this imperative might assist criminal prosecutors faced with a resistant domestic abuse witness.

42 Martha Fineman, speaking at 'A Workshop on Vulnerability and Social Justice' (2016) Leeds University.

43 Ibid.

44 Stu Marvel, 'The Vulnerable Subject of Rape Law: Rethinking Agency and Consent. A Response to Deborah Tuerkheimer, Rape On and Off Campus' (2016) 65 Emory Law Journal Online 2035.

45 Martha Fineman, 'Equality, Autonomy, and the Vulnerable Subject in Law and Politics' in Martha Fineman and Anna Grear (eds.) *Vulnerability: Reflections on a New Ethical Foundation for Law and Politics* (Ashgate 2013) 22–23.

What would a responsive State look like for abused women?

Rather than to the vulnerable group, the State must be responsive to the conditions that exacerbate vulnerability – not in ways which are authoritarian but, Fineman argues, in ways which 'empower' subjects.[46] The State's first priority in this conception is to confront its own contribution to individuals' diminishing resilience. As a foundation to prosecutorial decision-making, such an approach is laudable. Indeed, as far as the criminal justice system is concerned, such acknowledgment of State responsibility is reflected, I suggest, in both the 'presumption to arrest'[47] and ostensible 'presumption to prosecute,'[48] emphases now found in England and Wales. Presumptions to arrest and to prosecute are commendable steps by the State's criminal justice system in addressing its contribution towards diminishing the resilience of abused women.

As already mentioned, in the past, the State could have been accused of enabling violence against women in the home to persist through criminal justice agencies' reluctance to intervene. Criminal prosecutions however, according to the crime control model,[49] can be at once educational and also act as a deterrent thereby reducing incidents of violence. Accordingly, Madden-Dempsey has argued that pushing for aggressive prosecution of domestic violence offences that tend to sustain and perpetuate patriarchy means that, when prosecutors (representatives of the State) so act, they assist in reconstituting their communities as less patriarchal.[50] In tangible terms, aggressive prosecutions are justified, according to Madden-Dempsey, in instances where the intimate relationship bears the hallmarks of stereotypical gender expectations, where men control the woman's finances, where she is disempowered in her social life and where her access to work opportunities is restricted due to caring responsibilities.[51] Madden-Dempsey's approach attends to the patriarchal structures that she argues are conducive to domestic violence in which the male partner is coercive and controlling or, as she calls it, domestic violence in its 'strong' sense. The new presumptions towards prosecution, it could therefore be argued as far as the criminal justice system is concerned, are not *unresponsive* to domestic

46 Martha Fineman, 'The Vulnerable Subject: Anchoring Equality in the Human Condition' (n 41) 19.

47 Hoyle and Sanders identify that there have been pro-arrest policies operating in many police services since 1993. Carolyn Hoyle and Andrew Sanders, 'Police Response to Domestic Violence: From Victim Choice to Victim Empowerment' (2000) 40 British Journal of Criminology 14, 79.

48 In cases where the evidential test is met but the DA complainant withdraws her support for the prosecution, 'it will be rare for the public interest stage not to be met': CPS 'Domestic Abuse Guidelines for Prosecutors' (n 3).

49 Herbert Packer, 'Two Models of the Criminal Process' (1964) 113(1) University of Pennsylvania Law Review 1.

50 Michelle Madden-Dempsey, *Prosecuting Domestic Violence: A Philosophical Analysis* (Oxford University Press 2009) 45–99.

51 Michelle Madden-Dempsey, 'Toward a Feminist State: What does Prosecution of Domestic Violence Mean?' (2007) 70(6) Modern Law Review 908.

abuse. Indeed, the new approach goes some way to addressing the 'embedded' or 'structural' aspects of vulnerability through deterrence, education and challenging patriarchal structures and ideology.

But, while a presumption to prosecute might demonstrate State responsiveness to some of the conditions that produce domestic abuse, there remain occasions when it may not be preferable for the presumption to be followed. Madden-Dempsey herself, committed in practice to aggressive prosecution, considered that 'upon reflection' she 'found justification lacking in many instances'.[52] Is it here that vulnerability theory might encourage prosecutors to tailor their response and look at how they can respond to ameliorate the 'assets' of abused women? This would mean that prosecutors would look to address her physical, human, social, ecological and existential aspects. However, what these assets are, and what their importance is, remains thinly drawn, and a rich theorising of *how* to sustain and bolster these assets does not arise from Fineman's work, at least as it currently stands.

It seems, then, that vulnerability theory can only assist the prosecutor so far. To summarise, Fineman's critique of the libertarian formulation of the self-sufficient subject is valuable. Construction of the subject in those terms becomes a way of justifying minimal State intervention. The consequences exacerbate societal inequalities, which particularly affect domestically abused women. Fineman's demand that the State be responsive to the ways it can facilitate resilience to structural or 'embedded' vulnerability is also commendable. Starting with the presumption to arrest and the presumption to prosecute is, for the criminal justice system, laudable in that it begins to break down ideology that supports structural vulnerability. However, in the area of domestic abuse prosecution, vulnerability theory leaves questions about how exactly the State should best respond when a woman no longer supports criminal prosecution. How best can the State address mechanisms that effect structural/embedded vulnerability on one hand and embodied vulnerability on the other? What is the State's responsibility towards individual sources of vulnerability, the 'embodied' vulnerability that interacts with or is embedded within social structures?

Before considering how to proceed from here, there is a final cue from vulnerability theory that might assist the prosecutor: Fineman demands that the State responds *sensitively* to the vulnerable subject. Vulnerability theory encourages prosecutors to plug an 'empathy gap' in their praxis. Distinct from sympathy (reserved for the identity-based anti-discrimination approach, where 'they' not 'us' are targeted), empathy draws out commonalities between individuals so that women who experience domestic abuse are not wholly defined by it. Rather than suppressing empathy as an illegitimate response, vulnerability theory gives prosecutors permission to engage with female victims of domestic

52 Michelle Madden-Dempsey, *Prosecuting Domestic Violence: A Philosophical Analysis* (Oxford University Press 2009) 3.

abuse by asking the following question: 'What would *I* want and need the State to do for me?' By allowing an empathetic approach, the prosecutor cannot help but engage the question of what is in the best interests of each woman.

Fineman herself has used the term 'empowerment' as a commendable focus for governments wishing to avoid authoritarian decision-making.[53] But the rhetoric of 'empowerment', entwined as it is with our capacity to self-determination, self-care and responsibilisation, is fraught with echoes of (neo) libertarian individualism. How, then, does she conceive 'empowerment' and how does she reconcile it with her critique of 'autonomy' – our desire or need for self-determination? If the State is to be 'constructed around a well-defined responsibility [which will] implement a comprehensive and just equality regime', then the theoretical means need clarification. While declaring that 'vulnerability' is an inescapable human condition, Fineman roundly critiques the competing notion of 'autonomy' as mere cultural construct, noting its variance across cultures by way of support for this contention. As vulnerability is universal and constant, while our need for autonomy is not, she argues 'autonomy' should not hold inherent power as an end goal. If there is a 'universal reality'[54] that is to counter vulnerability and to act as a guide for the State when supporting citizen resilience, then it must not be a socially created notion and it must not speak to the mythologised self-sufficient, 'empowered' and 'autonomous' individual of neoliberalism. It is to alternative, collective, truths that vulnerability theorists are invited to explore, to substitute autonomous individuals as meritorious ends in themselves.

However, while the human need for autonomy might be culturally variant, our desire for it at some level is, as Cloud has convincingly argued, a universal and inescapable human impulse.[55] Faced with the recurring question of what should replace the hyper-individualised autonomy that Fineman exposes as myth, and yet not wholly persuaded that autonomy's core does not speak of universal truths, a host of academics have turned to theories of relational autonomy and the capabilities approach to see their way through the impasse. These alternative bodies of thought indicate a path that, if followed, would support prosecutors to make decisions for those who have experienced domestic abuse.[56] Relational autonomy recognises that identities are formed within the context of social relationships and are 'shaped by a complex of intersecting social determinants such as race, class, gender [and] ethnicity'.[57] Relational autonomists, while recognising that our ability to exercise choice is defined by social relations, nevertheless value our capacity and desire to exercise

53 Martha Fineman, 'The Vulnerable Subject: Anchoring Equality in the Human Condition' (n 41) 19.

54 Morgan Cloud, 'More than Utopia' (n 13).

55 Ibid, 93.

56 See, e.g., Jennifer Nedelsky, *Law's Relations: A Relational Theory of Self, Autonomy and Law* (Oxford University Press 2011).

57 Catriona Mackenzie and Natalie Stoljar, *Relational Autonomy: Feminist Perspectives on Autonomy, Agency, and the Social Self* (Oxford University Press 2000) 4.

self-determination. In a similar way, Sen and Nussbaum's capabilities approach[58] might offer a productive, well-theorised, frame that urges State responsibility to furnish its people with options from which a person can choose a life worth living. Both schools of academic thought could offer ways of conceiving how best to build the assets that promote the resilience of abused women. They offer a helpful way of focusing prosecutorial attention and of reducing the potential for paternalistic and untailored criminal pursuit of domestic abuse.[59]

In conclusion: returning to vulnerability as heuristic

Fineman has drawn back from tackling social inequality by targeting identity-based disadvantage. Her analysis of the State's obligations to citizens also, it follows, fails to promote identity-based interventions designed to target individual vulnerabilities in the manner outlined by relational autonomists and capabilities theorists. In this way, Fineman's analysis could be considered 'post-identity'.[60] Looking beyond identity and discrimination paradigms invites the State to be responsive to *vulnerability* per se. Her approach differs from perceiving women as 'at risk' or as actual or potential victims of violence. It differs from neoliberal reductionism – rendering women 'suffering bodies in need of protection'[61] and constituting them as 'wounded subjects'[62] that need to be empowered. By starting with the question of how best to assist victims of domestic abuse, the danger for Fineman is that we fall into the trap of asking the State to meet the needs of a particular vulnerable group and the identity-based approaches that Fineman derides.

Prima facie, vulnerability theory offers potential as a foundation for theoretically informed prosecutorial praxis in the area of domestic abuse. The theory offers huge promise in blasting the liberal myth of the self-determining, atomistic and fully functioning legal subject. As far as domestic abuse victims are concerned, this means that, if a victim fails to meet that standard, she ought not to be disregarded as somehow defective or unreliable. Instead, recognising the ontologically vulnerable subject, Fineman demands the State acknowledges the universality of vulnerability and respond, empathetically, by making decisions that support citizen resources and resilience. I have argued that the

58 See, e.g., Amartya Sen, *Development as Freedom* (Oxford University Press 2001); Martha Nussbaum, *Creating Capabilities: The Human Development Approach* (Belknap Press of Harvard University Press 2013).

59 For a fuller account of how relational autonomy and capabilities might assist an ethic of vulnerability, see Catriona Mackenzie, 'The Importance of Relational Autonomy and Capabilities for an Ethics of Vulnerability' in Catriona Mackenzie, Wendy Rogers and Susan Dodds (eds.) *Vulnerability: New Essays in Ethics and Feminist Philosophy* (Oxford University Press 2014).

60 Martha Fineman, 'The Vulnerable Subject and the Responsive State' (n 38) 275.

61 Alice Miller, 'Sexuality, Violence Against Women and Human Rights: Women Make Demands and Ladies get Protection' (2004) Health and Human Rights 17, 24.

62 Wendy Brown, *States of Injury: Power and Freedom in Late Modernity* (Princeton University Press 1995).

presumptions to arrest and prosecute challenge structural aspects that permit domestic abuse in line with vulnerability theory's expectations.

Yet, the chapter has argued that the theory fails to adequately illuminate *how* State actors be 'responsive' in the face of a victim whose expressed wishes are that the State withdraw. The theory does not provide an answer for the particular question in the area of prosecutorial decision-making, at least at the present time. Future scholarship might interrogate and develop Fineman's 'assets' as tools for guidance. It might further theorise the physical, human, social, ecological and existential resources – the basis of our 'resilience' – which the State has a duty to support.

Or perhaps, before we engage with these assets further, we need to recognise that Fineman's theory does not want to be shoe-horned into pre-existing structures, social models and dilemmas. Rather, her theory wants us to 'zoom out' and reconsider how society has chosen to organise itself. It is a lens through which to view our attachments to concepts such as 'empowerment', 'autonomy' and 'responsibility'. It challenges the unquestioning embrace of legal organisations such as the criminal justice system; interrogates social structural arrangements such as the allocation of power within families; asks why governments govern in the way they do, using the language of law and order and criminal justice; and enquires why the criminal justice system has become so relied upon to tackle social problems.

Vulnerability theory is not trying to be a checklist that solves specific instances of vulnerability across society. Rather, the theory's potential is its provocation of the academic community to engage, at a fundamental level, in reconceptualising our responsibilities to one another and the State's legal, political and moral obligations to its citizens. By resisting the temptation to retreat into comfortable assumptions about the benefits of concepts such as 'empowerment' through means of 'crime control', vulnerability theory challenges the legitimacy of some of society's most fundamental principles.

Vulnerability theory proposes a hugely promising foundation, but, to take this beyond mere wishful utopian thinking, the theory needs to be clear about its resistance to (relational) autonomy and develop the concepts based in alternative truths that should guide us. Vulnerability theory's greatest offering is as a heuristic that invites us to think beyond particular problems, pre-existing conceptual analyses, structures and ways of doing. Perhaps, only when we have done that work, will a return to particular legal challenges, such as the prosecution of domestic abuse, prove fruitful.

4 Vulnerability in the Irish criminal trial process

The situation of giving evidence

Liz Heffernan
Trinity College Dublin

The issue of vulnerability in the courtroom has assumed increasing prominence in law, practice and academic discourse in recent years. Responding to heightened societal recognition that giving evidence in criminal proceedings can be challenging and even harmful, states have explored and implemented policy initiatives at national and international level designed to alleviate sources of stress and trauma for witnesses.[1] In Ireland, a common law republic and EU member state, the legislature has recently strengthened a regime of special measures of support for vulnerable witnesses that dates back to the early 1990s.[2] Although innovative in its day, the original statutory scheme was limited to prescribed categories of witness, notably children and persons with certain intellectual disabilities. Moreover, because the special measures were not fully implemented nor resourced for many years, arguably, it is only in the present day that support and protection are taking root in an appreciable, meaningful sense.

Vulnerability theory offers a potentially insightful way of exploring human engagement with the criminal trial process.[3] With its emphasis on actual human experience, it encourages us to rethink the role of courts in shaping social identities. The giving of evidence in the form of courtroom testimony is a very particular form of human experience; it is exceptional in the sense that individuals are rarely if ever called to testify and in so far as it engages the specific state interest in the administration of justice. The particular vulnerability that is

1 Louise Ellison, *The Adversarial Process and the Vulnerable Witness* (OUP 2001); Jonathan Doak, *Victims' Rights, Human Rights and Criminal Justice: Reconceiving the Role of Third Parties* (Hart Publishing 2008); Adrian Keane, 'Cross-Examination of Vulnerable Witnesses: Towards a Blueprint for Re-Professionalisation' (2012) 16 International Journal of Evidence and Proof 175; David Burrows, *Children's Views and Evidence* (Bloomsbury Professional 2017); Shane Kilcommins et al., *The Victim in the Irish Criminal Process* (Manchester University Press 2018).

2 Criminal Evidence Act 1992.

3 Martha Fineman, 'The Vulnerable Subject: Anchoring Equality in the Human Condition' (2008–2009) 20 Yale Journal of Law and Feminism 1; Martha Fineman, 'Vulnerability and Inevitable Inequality' (2017) 4(3) Oslo Law Review 133; Nina Kohn, 'Vulnerability Theory and the Role of Government' (2014) 26 Yale Journal of Law and Feminism 1; Lourdes Peroni and Alexandra Timmer, 'Vulnerable Groups: The Promise of An Emerging Concept in European Human Rights Convention Law' (2013) 11(4) International Journal of Constitutional Law 1056.

DOI: 10.4324/9780429023149-5

experienced in the courtroom might be described as a form of situational vulnerability in that it is caused or exacerbated by the personal and social situation of the trial in which the individual finds herself.[4] While vulnerability theory illuminates the subject, it will be argued that the notion of universal vulnerability has limited value as a lens through which to view current developments in the Irish trial process.

The present chapter opens by exploring the issue of vulnerability in the situation of giving evidence in criminal proceedings in Ireland. It considers the role of the witness in the common law adversarial tradition and analyses the State response to vulnerability personified in the Irish legislation. Drawing on vulnerability theory, the author offers some reflections on the limits of both the current Irish law and the theory itself as applied in this context.

The witness in the trial process

The calling of witnesses to testify at trials is an essential aspect of adjudication in the Irish criminal courts.[5] A person who has information about a crime is expected to come forward and notify the Gardaí (police) and, in the event that the incident results in a prosecution, to come into court to give her evidence. The function of testifying involves answering questions put by lawyers representing the parties, and it usually takes place in open court before a judge, a jury, the media and the public.[6] The traditional case law is replete with references to the duty of citizens to give evidence in this way and the corresponding power of the State to compel them to do so. Walsh J in *Re Kevin O'Kelly* spoke about the right of a court to every person's evidence[7] and, in the subsequent case of *People v James T*, he described the judicial power to force a witness to testify as the greatest safeguard for preserving the truth.[8] Notwithstanding the evolving nature of the trial process, the contemporary law of evidence has not shaken off the depiction of testifying as a civic duty or aspect of the social contract.

Paradoxically, even the most willing of witnesses is not guaranteed an opportunity to be heard in court. A witness is not an independent, autonomous actor in the trial process and, unless she is the accused, she has neither the right to

4 Robert Goodin, *Protecting the Vulnerable: A Reanalysis of Our Social Responsibilities* (University of Chicago Press 1986) 112.

5 Liz Heffernan, *Evidence in Criminal Trials* (Bloomsbury Professional 2014); Declan McGrath, *Evidence* (3nd edn, Round Hall 2020); Caroline Fennell, *The Law of Evidence in Ireland* (4th edn, Bloomsbury Professional 2020).

6 Trials for rape and aggravated sexual assault are an exception. S6(1) of the Criminal Law (Rape) Act 1981 as replaced by s11 of the Criminal Law (Rape) (Amendment) Act 1990. In any criminal trial, the judge has the statutory authority to clear the courtroom of all non-essential personnel when a child is testifying. S257(1) of the Children Act 2001.

7 *Re Kevin O'Kelly* (1974) 108 ILTR 97.

8 *People v James T* [1988] Frewen 141. Finlay CJ in the civil case of *Mapp v Gilhooley* [1991] 2 IR 253 echoed the sentiment of the fundamental significance of viva voce evidence as a prop to adjudication.

testify nor the ability to control the decision whether she should do so.[9] In keeping with the common law tradition, a witness testifies not on her own behalf but at the behest of a party and subject only to the limited authority of the trial judge to prohibit her evidence or set conditions to its admission.[10]

The seemingly routine nature of testimony disguises the variation in the individual experience of giving evidence; the extent of the challenge may depend upon the witness's personal circumstance, her relationship with the case and the parties and her stake in the outcome of the process. The formal setting of the court and the arid language of procedure tend to obscure the reality that evidence comprises information provided directly by individuals. It includes personal stories, observations, correspondence and data. The trial process requires people to make public what may be private – to talk to strangers, including authority figures, and to speak openly about experiences that are personal and may be traumatic. Once delivered in court, a witness's evidence becomes the property of the State and may be used by any party to serve their own strategic purposes. In most cases, evidence presented in a court of law may also be publicised outside the courtroom, through traditional and social media, and beyond the control of the justice system.

Developing special measures

Courts and legislatures have increasingly acknowledged the difficulties that giving evidence presents to some individuals and, consequently, the need to protect them from the process by adapting conventional procedures. The basic response has been to provide a series of special measures that may apply to particular witnesses when they give evidence. The principal contemporary policy motivation is twofold: the need to protect and support vulnerable witnesses by minimising the distress and trauma they may experience through testifying at trial, and the related aim of enabling these witnesses to participate in the system of justice by giving their best evidence.[11] It is fair to say that, when they first

9 Most of the Irish authorities deal with the scenario of the victim as witness: *Maguire v Central Mental Hospital* [1996] 3 IR 1; *Application of Gallagher* [1991] 1 IR 31; *Re Ellis* [1990] 2 IR 291; Jonathan Doak, *Victims' Rights, Human Rights and Criminal Justice: Reconceiving the Role of Third Parties* (Hart Publishing 2008); Shane Kilcommins et al., *The Victim in the Irish Criminal Process* (Manchester University Press 2018).

10 Judicial intervention at the admissibility stage is as likely to be motivated by the need to protect the rights of another party (notably the accused) or the integrity of the adjudicative process than safeguarding the interests of the witness. The emerging construction of participatory rights for certain witnesses, such as the right of a child or a crime victim to be heard, has not yet upset this underlying common law assumption of party control. Liz Heffernan, 'The Participation of Victims in the Trial Process' (2017) 68(4) Northern Ireland Law Quarterly 491.

11 Law Reform Commission, *Report on Child Sexual Abuse* (LRC 30–1990) and *Sexual Offences Against the Mentally Handicapped* (LRC 33–1990); Liz Heffernan, *Evidence in Criminal Trials* (n 5) 60. In the case of some groups of witness, historical categorisation was grounded in the more malignant idea that these witnesses were inherently untrustworthy and consequently that the court needed to be protected from their unreliable evidence.

emerged, these policy goals were driven principally by the perceived needs of a limited number of particular categories of individuals. An intriguing question is whether they have since evolved into a broader, generalised ambition to alleviate distress and trauma within the trial process.

In Ireland, the framework for such a system of support was set down in Part III of the Criminal Evidence Act 1992, which, at the time of enactment, focused on the giving of evidence by child witnesses and witnesses with certain intellectual disabilities in trials for violent and/or sexual offences. Provision was made for witnesses coming within these categories to testify via video link[12] or through an intermediary[13] and, in more limited circumstances, to give their evidence-in-chief at an interview recorded in advance of trial.[14] These witnesses were also relieved of any obligation to identify the accused at trial.[15]

Piecemeal amendments were enacted to Part III of the 1992 Act over the years; for example, raising the age limit for child eligibility and extending the definition of sexual offences. However, the State was slow to implement the special measures in practice,[16] with the consequence that it is only in recent years that the 1992 initiative for accommodating vulnerability has begun to have meaningful effect in practice.

The statutory regime was substantially enlarged in 2017 when the Oireachtas (parliament) legislated in the Criminal Justice (Victims of Crime) Act to extend some of the special measures to crime victims who are at risk of secondary and repeat victimisation, intimidation or retaliation. The 2017 Act embodies the State's transposition of the EU Directive on the Rights, Support and Protection of Victims of Crime, an instrument that was designed, in part, to ensure minimum standards for the participation of victims in the criminal process across the member states.[17]

When amending the 1992 Act through the medium of the 2017 Act, the Oireachtas took the additional step of augmenting the range of measures that may be used to support those witnesses for whom the legislation was originally designed (i.e. child witnesses and witnesses with certain intellectual disabilities in trials for violent and/or sexual offences). Evidence may now be given from

12 S13(1)(a) of the Criminal Evidence Act 1992. The constitutionality of the section was upheld in *White v Ireland* [1995] 2 IR 268 (HC) and *Donnelly v Ireland* [1998] 1 IR 321 (SC). Video link and other special measures contained in the 1992 Act were extended to persons with 'mental handicap' by s19 as originally enacted.

13 S14 of the Criminal Evidence Act 1992.

14 S16 of the Criminal Evidence Act 1992.

15 S18 of the Criminal Evidence Act 1992.

16 Notwithstanding delays in rolling out video-link facilities across the country, its use has become increasingly routine in relation to child witnesses. In contrast, s16 was not commenced until 2008 and s14 has been invoked in only a handful of cases.

17 Directive 2012/29/EU establishing minimum standards on the rights, support and protection of victims of crime. OJ L 325/57, 14.11.2012.

behind a screen in lieu of video link in certain circumstances,[18] restrictions on the pre-recording of evidence-in-chief have been relaxed[19] and a ban on the wearing of wigs and gowns by judges and lawyers has been tightened.[20]

Legislation addressing aspects of the conduct of trials for rape and sexual assault has long been a feature of Irish law. Under the Criminal Law (Rape) Act 1981, complainants of rape or sexual assault may give their evidence in proceedings from which the public are excluded.[21] The Act also introduced a general prohibition on the cross-examination of complainants as to their sexual history subject to a procedure whereby the defence may obtain the leave of the court to put such questions.[22] Recognising the constancy of such applications and the particular trauma that cross-examination on this subject may cause, the Oireachtas subsequently afforded complainants a right to legal representation in this context.[23] The law relating to trials for rape and sexual assault was substantially strengthened in 2017 by the enactment of the Criminal Law (Sexual Offences) Act. Foremost among the provisions that acknowledge the vulnerability of a complainant is a ban on personal cross-examination by the accused.[24]

Most of the measures described above pertain to the way in which evidence is given and, for this reason perhaps, they are often referred to methods of 'accommodating' the witness.[25] This phraseology has the positive connotation of acknowledging vulnerability and re-conceptualising the function of testifying from the standpoint of the witness. Nevertheless, the notion of accommodating the witness has the potential to reinforce negative associations such as harm and dependency. It reflects an institutional assumption that vulnerability is atypical in the courtroom and that affirmative steps are required to bring the witness into line with the conventional expectations of participation at trial. Moreover, accommodation is inherently limited as an approach to reform because it does not address, much less disturb, the structure and culture of the

18 S14A of the Criminal Evidence Act 1992 as inserted by s30 of the Criminal Justice (Victims of Crime) Act 2017.

19 S16 of the Criminal Evidence Act 1992 as amended.

20 S14B of the Criminal Evidence Act 1992 as inserted by s30 of the Criminal Justice (Victims of Crime) Act 2017.

21 S6. The anonymity of complainants is protected by s7.

22 S3 of the Criminal Law (Rape) Act 1981 as amended by s13 of the Criminal Law (Rape) (Amendment) Act 1990.

23 S34 of the Sex Offenders Act 2001. The cost of such representation comes within the State scheme for criminal legal aid (s35). It is interesting to note that s21 of the Criminal Justice (Victims of Crime) Act 2017 authorises a trial judge to restrict cross-examination of a victim about aspects of her private life that are not relevant to the proceedings.

24 S14C of the Criminal Evidence Act 1992 as inserted by s31 of the Criminal Law (Sexual Offences) Act 2017 and substituted by s30 of the Criminal Justice (Victims of Crime) Act 2017.

25 Keane, 'Cross-Examination of Vulnerable Witnesses: Towards a Blueprint for Re-Professionalisation' (n 1); Emily Henderson, 'Best Evidence or Best Interests? What Does the Case Law Say About the Function of Cross-Examination' (2016) 20(3) International Journal of Evidence and Proof 183.

common law adversarial trial process, with its emphasis on party autonomy and the confrontational testing of evidence.

Identifying vulnerability

It is striking that, unlike its counterpart in England and Wales, the Irish legislation does not employ the term 'vulnerable witness'.[26] Phrases along the seam of 'vulnerability' do not form part of the formal legal lexicon of legislation and judicial pronouncements, although they do have a firm foothold in wider socio-legal discourse.

Vulnerability is defined implicitly in Irish law through a system of categorisation designed to accommodate certain groups of witness. There are some rare instances when a State actor, usually a judge, is empowered to make a subjective determination that a witness who falls outside a prescribed category should be afforded a particular special measure. For example, legislation gives trial judges the discretion to decide that an adult, who would not otherwise be eligible on grounds of intellectual disability, may be permitted to testify via video link in trials for violent and/or sexual offences.[27] However, instances in the reported case law where this authority has been exercised are rare.[28]

It might be said that the State response to vulnerability in the courtroom is the antithesis of Martha Fineman's vulnerability theory in so far as it assumes that vulnerability is not inherent or universal within the Irish trial process, but rather is particular to certain witnesses. Vulnerability is almost invariably a predetermined status designated by the State on the basis of objective criteria, such as children below a certain age or persons with particular kinds of intellectual disability. Indeed, the burgeoning of legislative special measures has not occasioned any wholesale re-conceptualisation of vulnerability. When legislating for a broader statutory regime in 2017, the Oireachtas chose to perpetuate the system of categorisation. Ireland has declined to legislate for vulnerable witnesses in general or to consider alternative ideas such as tackling vulnerability through a system of structured discretion. Whether more radical approaches are normatively or practically desirable is open to debate, but it is noteworthy that

26 Chapter 1 of Part II of the Youth Justice and Criminal Evidence Act 1999 as amended is entitled 'Special Directions in Case of Vulnerable or Intimidated Witnesses'. Nevertheless, the term 'vulnerable witness' is not itself a legal benchmark because eligibility for special measures is defined by reference to specific indicia of vulnerability such as age or incapacity. Ss16–17.

27 S13(1)(b) of the Criminal Evidence Act 1992 as amended by s30 of the Criminal Justice (Victims of Crime) Act 2017 configures this discretion in strikingly broad and unspecified terms. The subsection refers simply to the possibility that such a person may give evidence via video link 'with the leave of the court'.

28 *DPP v McManus* [2011] IECCA 32 (12 April 2011); *O'D v DPP* [2009] IEHC 559 (17 December 2009); [2015] IECA 273 (19 November 2015). The courts may exceptionally apply special measures as an exercise of their inherent jurisdiction. Caroline Biggs and Miriam Delahunt, 'Prosecutorial Challenges – Vulnerable Victims and Witnesses', 17th National Annual Prosecutors' Conference, Dublin, 12 November 2016, pp. 8–10, www.dppireland.ie (last accessed 9 December 2018).

vulnerability theory seemingly formed no part of the debate that preceded the recent, substantial reform of the law.

An accused person who takes the stand and testifies in her own defence occupies a somewhat anomalous position in the current law relating to vulnerability in the giving evidence. Much of the modern law of criminal evidence is built on the edifice of the constitutional rights of the accused – echoed in the State's international human rights commitments – which are designed to redress the imbalance of power in her relationship with the State.[29] By virtue of her entitlement to the presumption of innocence and the privilege against self-incrimination, the accused may elect not to testify in her own defence and consequently evade cross-examination at the hands of the prosecution or a co-accused.[30] This paradigm of situational vulnerability is the touchstone of the criminal process but is merely tacitly acknowledged in those terms. Its exclusion from discourse on vulnerability in the courtroom is underscored by the Oireachtas's decision to expressly exclude juvenile defendants from the realm of special measures for which other child witnesses are eligible.

It is interesting to consider whether the State system for identifying vulnerability reflects the real-world experience of individuals who give evidence within the criminal justice system. Empirical research conducted in England some years ago suggested that witnesses self-identify as vulnerable in that jurisdiction in a far broader range of circumstances and contexts than the State acknowledges.[31] The possibility of a gap between State and individual perceptions raises important questions about our understanding of the concept of vulnerability and the efficacy of the procedures that the State employs for identifying it as a basis for an appropriate social policy response.[32]

The limits of accommodation via special measures

Putting aside matters of terminology and threshold identification, reflection on the current Irish criminal trial at the level of first principles suggests that the approach to vulnerability in law and policy is controversial in a number of other respects. If one of the objectives of the current law is to equalise the situation of witnesses by levelling the courtroom's evidentiary playing field, then

29 Art 38.1 of the Constitution guarantees to a criminal defendant a trial in due course of law, and Art 6 of the European Convention on Human Rights protects the right to fair trial.

30 Art 38.1 of the Constitution; Art 6 of the ECHR; S1(e) & (f) of the Criminal Justice (Evidence) Act 1924 as amended.

31 Mandy Burton, Roger Evans and Andrew Sanders, *Are Special Measures for Vulnerable and Intimidated Witnesses Working? Evidence from the Criminal Justice Agencies* (Home Office Online Report No. 01/20, 2006); Mandy Burton, Roger Evans and Andrew Sanders, 'Implementing Special Measures for Vulnerable and Intimidated Witnesses: The Problem of Identification' (2006) Criminal Law Review 229.

32 The Victims of Crime Act 2017 contains salutary provisions that require law enforcement officers and the courts to conduct individualised assessments of the needs of crime victims in certain circumstances. S15 and s30 (inserting s14AA into the Criminal Evidence Act 1992).

it is questionable whether the special measures regime is adequate or effective in its current form.

Designating vulnerable groups has the merit that it is relatively easy to apply and consequently it is less resource-intensive than methods grounded in individual rather than collective assessments. This is particularly true of the original categories of witness within the Irish legislative scheme. For children, eligibility for particular measures is determined by statutory age limits. Persons with intellectual disabilities are eligible if they have been diagnosed as having a recognised 'mental disorder', a matter that, if disputed, may be resolved through expert evidence. Deciding whether an alleged victim of crime is at risk of secondary and repeat victimisation is likely to involve a more nuanced, subjective assessment by trial judges under the 2017 legislation.

Categorisation is also advantageous to the extent that it has the flexibility to expand or reduce the State response to complement evolving social attitudes and conditions. Thus, in recent years the State has broadened the legal understanding of vulnerability in the Irish trial process by increasing the range of supports,[33] extending the categories of witness who may be eligible and widening the contexts in which measures may apply.[34] The outgrowth of the special measures regime has had the positive, appreciable effect of opening to the door of support to far greater numbers of potential witnesses. This raises the prospect that, over time, the trend of incremental expansion may itself have a normalising effect on vulnerability and that special measures may no longer seem unusual or the preserve of restricted groups of witnesses. Indeed, the recent move to bring certain crime victims within the fold of accommodation has the potential to elevate the concept of vulnerability from the fringes to the heart of trial practice. By embracing a more generalised assumption of vulnerability, it may contribute to the 'destigmatisation' of the term.[35]

In practice, categorisation has the disadvantage of being a relatively blunt instrument for calibrating vulnerability in the situation of giving evidence. It is unduly narrow in so far as it fails to acknowledge that persons falling outside the designated categories may also be vulnerable and just as deserving of State protection. Commenting on the rules that exceptionally sanction the compellability of the spouse of an accused in order to vindicate the right of a child

33 For example, by introducing the use of screens for certain vulnerable witnesses in trials for violent and/or sexual offences, s14A of the Criminal Evidence Act 1992 as inserted by s30 of the Criminal Justice (Victims of Crime) Act 2017; and generally prohibiting the personal cross-examination of a complainant in a trial for a sexual offence, s14C of the Criminal Evidence Act 1992, as inserted by s36 of the Criminal Law (Sexual Offences) Act 2017 and substituted by s30 of the Criminal Justice (Victims of Crime) Act 2017.

34 The extension in witness eligibility and substantive context is personified by the inclusion within the special measures regime of victims of crime who have special protection needs, Part III of the Criminal Evidence Act 1992 as amended by s30 of the Criminal Justice (Victims of Crime) Act 2017.

35 Nina Kohn, 'Vulnerability Theory and the Role of Government' (n 3) 9.

victim to justice, Jackson has questioned why an elderly victim of crime should not be protected in a similar way.[36] The eligibility of persons with intellectual disabilities for special measures embodies a more patent instance of narrowing vulnerability; the legislation restricts eligibility to persons who can be classified as suffering from 'mental disorder', a term substituted by dint of recent legislative amendment for the even more antiquated phrase 'mental handicap'. Thus, it excludes persons who may struggle with conventional courtroom procedures due to issues of cognition or communication. The criticism may also be levelled at the 1992 Act that it fails to treat all members of particular categories equally. Controversially, it expressly prohibits a child defendant who gives evidence in her own defence from availing of the special measures for which other child witnesses are eligible.[37]

At the same time, categorisation may be unduly broad if it includes within the realm of special measures individuals who neither need nor perhaps desire any special accommodation. For example, an older teenager, who is presumptively entitled to testify via video link, may prefer to give her evidence viva voce in the courtroom. This overly paternalistic response on the part of the State to perceived vulnerability is arguably indicative of a broader failure to vindicate a witness's rights to autonomy and dignity.[38] It is salient to recall that Irish law does not expressly acknowledge an entitlement on the part of a witness to be heard at trial or to give evidence in a manner of her choosing.[39] Nor does the law designate procedures whereby witnesses can seek relief from the court and legal representation to advise and assist them.[40]

Given the paucity of empirical research on vulnerable witnesses in Ireland, there is no documented basis for believing that any potential over-breadth in categories of vulnerability is a pressing concern in practice; anecdotally the

36 Claire Jackson, 'Evidence – Part IV of the Criminal Evidence Act 1992: Competence and Compellability of Spouses and Former Spouses to Give Evidence' (1993) 15 Dublin University Law Journal 202, 207.

37 For example, an accused is expressly excluded from eligibility for the special measure of video link and, by extension, the special measure of an intermediary. Ss13–14 of the Criminal Evidence Act 1992 as amended. The legislation in England and Wales includes the same limitation. Ss16–17 of the Youth Justice and Criminal Evidence Act 1999 as amended.

38 *Y v Slovenia* (2016) 62 EHRR 3.

39 Art 10 of the EU Victims' Rights Directive recognises a right to be heard, which is construed to denote an opportunity to be heard at some stage in the criminal process. Liz Heffernan, 'The Participation of Victims in the Trial Process' (n 10) 491, 498 (citing references). In an Irish context, the right to participate under the Directive is apparently met where the victim is permitted to deliver a victim impact statement at a sentencing hearing. S5 of the Criminal Justice Act 1993 as amended by s31 of the Criminal Justice (Victims of Crime) Act 2017.

40 An important exception is provision for legal representation for a complainant in a trial for rape or a sexual assault offence in two instances: first, when the defence seeks the leave of the court to cross-examine the complainant about her sexual history (s3 of the Criminal Law (Rape) Act 1981 as amended by s34 of the Sex Offenders Act 2001); and, second, when the court considers the possible disclosure of a complainant's counselling records (s19A of the Criminal Evidence Act 1992 as inserted by s39 of the Criminal Law (Sexual Offences) Act 2017).

concern typically voiced is that special measures should be more widely available. In most scenarios that are relevant to the present discussion, the witness will be appearing for the prosecution and the prosecution will be assumed to look after her interests. But this is satisfactory neither from a normative nor practical perspective. Safeguarding the witness is just one of a miscellany of factors that the prosecution must juggle when representing the State at trial. Whereas in most cases there is likely to be 'a coincidence of interest' between the witness and the prosecution, situations can arise where their respective interests diverge.[41]

Finally, an obvious shortcoming in the special measures regime is the failure to protect witnesses who are deemed vulnerable from the vagaries of cross-examination, the courtroom practice most likely to interfere with their dignity and well-being.[42] It is a fundamental tenet of the common law trial that a party is entitled to test the evidence of an adverse witness through cross-examination. Moreover, in Ireland the right of an accused to cross-examine the State's witnesses is protected constitutionally and internationally as an aspect of the broader right to fair trial.[43] Exceptionally, a vulnerable witness is permitted to give her evidence-in-chief in the form of a statement made outside the courtroom prior to trial, but even in this situation the law stipulates that the witness must be available at trial for purposes of cross-examination.[44] As we have seen, there are some isolated legislative measures that seek to curb specific practices, such as the cross-examination of a complainant about her sexual history,[45] the cross-examination of a child complainant by the accused in person[46] or the unnecessary questioning of a crime victim about her private life.[47] However, beyond a general ban on irrelevant, oppressive or vexatious questioning and the broad supervisory responsibilities of the trial judge,[48] the law does not restrict the manner in which cross-examination can be conducted, including the nature and style of the questions that may be put to the witness.

41 Paul Carney, 'The Role of the Victim in the Irish Criminal Process' (2007) Judicial Studies Institute Journal 7, 11.

42 Jeff Ward, 'Vulnerable Witnesses and Cross-Examination: A Path to Reform' (2017) 7(1) Irish Journal of Legal Studies 36; Henderson, 'Best Evidence or Best Interests? What Does the Case Law Say About the Function of Cross-Examination?' (n 25); Keane, 'Cross-Examination of Vulnerable Witnesses: Towards a Blueprint for Re-Professionalisation' (n 1).

43 *State (Healy) v Donoghue* [1976] IR 325; *Maguire v Ardagh* [2002] 1 IR 385; *People (DPP) v Kelly* [2006] 3 IR 115; *Kostovski v The Netherlands* (1990) 12 21 EHRR 343; *Van Mechelen & Others v The Netherlands* (1997) 25 EHRR 647; *Al-Khawaja & Tahery v United Kingdom* (2012) 54 EHRR 23.

44 S16 of the Criminal Evidence Act 1992 as amended; s16 of the Criminal Justice Act 2006 as amended.

45 S3 of the Criminal Law (Rape) Act 1981 as amended by s13 of the Criminal Law (Rape) (Amendment) Act 1990 and s34 of the Sex Offenders Act 2001.

46 S14C of the Criminal Evidence Act 1992 as inserted by s36 of the Criminal Law (Sexual Offences) Act 2017.

47 S21 of the Criminal Justice (Victims of Crime) Act 2017.

48 Ord 36, r 37 of the Rules of the Superior Courts 1986 as amended; *People (DPP) v DO* [2006] 2 ILRM 61.

Policymakers in Ireland may glean constructive insight in this regard from recent developments in England and Wales, such as the convening of pre-trial hearings for the setting of ground rules for the fair and effective participation of vulnerable witnesses and defendants in the proceedings,[49] the giving of judicial directions to counsel at such hearings on permissible lines of questioning during cross-examination at trial[50] and the introduction of procedures for the pre-recording of cross-examination.[51]

Concluding remarks

The development of the law embodied in the 2017 Acts signals a welcome, progressive reimagining of vulnerability in the courtroom. Taken together, the panoply of legislative changes may be indicative of a nascent right on the part of vulnerable witnesses to be protected from harm caused to them by the trial process itself. At the same time, specific developments in this vein do not reflect any political or legal appetite to alter the basic structure of the common law adversarial trial. Whereas witnesses and victims may be entitled to be accommodated in certain ways when they give evidence, they continue to inhabit a forensic twilight zone without the benefit of standing, an enforceable right to be heard or any general entitlement to legal representation in proceedings.

While the time is ripe to consider and debate structural reforms that might nudge the Irish system in a more inquisitorial direction, there are significant normative and practical objections. From a legal standpoint, it is salient to recall that the emerging participatory rights of vulnerable witnesses must co-exist with the established constitutionally and internationally protected rights of the defence. The Irish Supreme Court has upheld the constitutionality of the legislation facilitating the use of video link by child witnesses,[52] and more radical, complex responses to vulnerability will require careful calibration of the delicate balance between the various rights and interests at play in the criminal trial. In the short term, there are steps that might usefully be taken to buttress the recent legislative innovations by adapting the culture of the courtroom for the benefit of all witnesses.[53]

Vulnerability theory may have a useful role to play in the future development of law and policy in so far as it prompts reflection and debate on the experience of giving evidence. By encouraging us to acknowledge the omnipresence of vulnerability, it challenges the traditional, narrower perception of the common

49 Criminal Procedure Rules 2015, para 3.9; Criminal Practice Directions [2015] EWCA Crim 1567.

50 *R v Barker* [2010] EWCA Crim 4; *R v Willis* [2012] 1 Cr App R 2 (CA (Crim Div)) paras 19–39; *R v* [2015] 1 WLR 1579 (CA (Crim Div)). Henderson, 'Best Evidence or Best Interests? What Does the Case Law Say About the Function of Cross-Examination' (n 25).

51 S28 of the Youth Justice and Criminal Evidence Act 1999 as amended.

52 *Donnelly v Ireland* [1998] 1 IR 321.

53 See nn 49–51 and n 56 below.

law trial system of who counts as vulnerable.[54] Moreover, the emphasis within vulnerability theory on the State's positive obligation to nurture individual resilience and growth[55] chimes with the idea that the trial provides an opening for victims and witnesses to participate in the justice process and an opportunity to be heard.

The potential contribution of vulnerability theory is constrained by the contextual reality that the Irish trial process eschews vulnerability as an inherent, universal human condition; it operates instead on the general premise that individuals are resilient and adequately resourced (physically, socially and emotionally) to give evidence in court. Notwithstanding the recent augmentation of the special measures regime, vulnerability remains the exception rather than the rule. Undoubtedly the exception has widened in recent years to the point where special measures are increasingly common and, in the case of video link for child witnesses, almost routine. While this gradual evolution may exert a normalising effect on societal perceptions of vulnerability, the situation of vulnerable persons giving evidence in Irish criminal courts has not reached a level of generalisation, much less the universalisation, embodied in Fineman's theory. While universal vulnerability is an attractive idea in the abstract, particularly when juxtaposed with categorised vulnerability, the giving of evidence in criminal trials is a distinct and specific aspect of social life, far distant from the settings in which the seeds of the theory of universal vulnerability were sown.

Applying a theory of universality would have certain drawbacks in the present context. Inverting the status quo and replacing it with an assumption that every witness is vulnerable could undermine the significance of individuality and obscure important differences in the nature and extent of vulnerability. Universality could run the risk of diverting State policy and resources away from those witnesses who are most in need of support and protection. Conversely, applying special measures to individuals who neither need nor desire them would undermine the values of individual dignity and autonomy. Reconciling vulnerability with the objective of positive participation implies, at a minimum, affording the witness an opportunity to influence the decision as to whether, when and how she should be heard within the process.[56]

Reflection in this vein exposes a weakness in vulnerability theory at a prescriptive level. Witnesses are vulnerable in different ways and to varying degrees, but it is not clear how this element of differentiation could and should

54 Vanessa Munro, 'Shifting Sands? Consent, Context and Vulnerability in Contemporary Sexual Offences Policy in England and Wales' (2017) Social and Legal Studies 417, 429; Lourdes Peroni and Alexandra Timmer, 'Vulnerable Groups' (2013) (n 3) 1056.

55 Martha Fineman, 'Equality, Autonomy and the Vulnerable Subject in Law and Politics' in Martha Fineman and Anna Grear (eds.), *Vulnerability: Reflections on a New Ethical Foundation for Law and Politics* (Routledge 2013) 13.

56 Greater recognition of the autonomy of witnesses might also be secured in other constructive ways, for example, by putting in place a robust State programme of witness familiarisation with the court process and exceptionally affording witnesses the possibility of legal advice and representation.

be captured and resolved. Thus, the theory of universal vulnerability sheds little light on the normative question of how to reconcile in an evidentiary setting the rights of the accused with those of victims and witnesses. The need to address the multifarious experiences of vulnerability is equally pressing as a matter of policy and practice. As Kohn points out, the theory has 'limited prescriptive value' because it provides 'little guidance as to how to prioritize among vulnerable subjects when allocating limited financial resources and political capital'.[57] By their nature, special measures for vulnerable witnesses require infrastructure, technology, personnel and training. The effective implementation of the measures in practice necessitates the allocation of financial and human resources but also a substantial investment in court time, with attendant consequences for the conduct of proceedings. The societal goal of supporting vulnerable witnesses in giving their best evidence must be achieved in harmony with the effective administration of justice. A 'whole of system' review, informed by the direct experience of witnesses, is surely an essential next step to reimagining vulnerability in the Irish criminal trial process.

57 Kohn, 'Vulnerability Theory and the Role of Government' (n 3), 13.

5 State accountability and the vulnerable individual

An Irish restorative approach

Darren McStravick
Kingston University London

Introduction

The concept of 'vulnerability' is, similar to the concept of 'community', one whose boundaries and distinct constituent parts are difficult to define.[1] The concept does, however, tend to strictly attach in theory and practice to particular groupings within a criminal law context. Conventional, court-based criminal justice processes, rules and procedures rely on certain dichotomies such as victim and offender, state and community, guilt and innocence. Indeed, Article 2 of the EU Directive 2012/29/EU, which establishes minimum standards on the rights, support and protection of victims of crime, states that the term 'victim' means 'a natural person who has suffered harm, including physical, mental or emotional harm or economic loss which was directly caused by a criminal offence'.[2] Thus, in the eyes of the EU Directive, a victim, and by proxy the concept of vulnerability, can only be represented by a person who has been directly affected by a crime.

This can, however, be viewed as somewhat simplistic when the intricacies of criminal conflicts are broken down further. The paradigm of restorative justice allows for such conflicts to be viewed with an alternative lens.[3] By way of a four-year observational and interview-led research study of two restorative-based reparation panel programmes (Restorative Justice in the Community (RJC) and Restorative Justice Services (RJS)), a newly identified meso-community of care, concern and accountability was seen to emerge as part of reparation practice and procedure.[4] These pre-diversion from prosecution programmes allowed for adults who had committed crimes, ranging from public disorder to

1 For example, see Martha Fineman, 'Vulnerability and Inevitable Inequality' (2012) 4(3) Oslo Law Review 133, 134. For one example of an analysis of problems of definition with the community concept, see Paul McCold and Benjamin Wachtel, 'Community is not a Place: A New Look at Community Justice Initiatives' in Gerry Johnstone (ed.) *A Restorative Justice Reader* (Willan Publishing 2003) 294.

2 EU Directive 2012/29/EU Article 2, 1(a).

3 Howard Zehr, *Changing Lenses: A New Focus for Crime and Justice* (Herald Press 1990).

4 Darren McStravick, 'Adult Reparation Panels and Offender-centric Meso-communities: An Answer to the Conundrum' (2018) 1(1) International Journal of Restorative Justice 96.

DOI: 10.4324/9780429023149-6

serious assault and burglary, to attend a restorative-based reparation panel with criminal justice professionals and community representatives. As part of reparation practice, the crimes would be discussed by all participating stakeholders, including the reason for the behaviour, the harm caused and the most appropriate route to successfully realising accountability, rehabilitation and reintegration. Participating offenders would sign a contract which included reparation tasks such as written apologies, community service tasks, financial and moral-based restitution and drug and alcohol dependency treatments. On successful completion of these tasks, the case would be returned to the referring judge, who would then decide on final sentence.[5]

The meso-community evolving from reparation practice and procedure was specific to the stakeholders participating within each panel case and composed of criminal justice professionals and community representatives building an individualised social care ethos into case discourses with each participating offender. This social care rationale prioritised welfare concerns and rehabilitative and reintegrative possibilities for participants. Such an individualised social and welfare-based, state-sponsored approach to managing participating wrongdoers allows for an alternative analysis of the concept of vulnerability as part of criminal conflict solving. It further allows, at least in part, a practical-based examination of a number of aspects of the theoretical vulnerability critique.

Methodology and ethical considerations

Ethical clearance was initially granted in 2012 by Dublin City University for an 'across method' triangulated research design[6] composing a desktop literature review, case study observations of restorative-based Irish reparation panel schemes and a series of semi-structured interviews with key stakeholders within the reparation process. Access was granted after meeting with programme managers and detailing the research aims in detail. Panel facilitators obtained consent from participating offenders before observations commenced. One of the principal aims throughout the observation process was not to intrude in the reparation panel process. In order to achieve this goal, the researcher sat in the corner of the room and did not participate in case discussions and outcomes. The compilation of shorthand notes was allowed during the different case studies and these were written up in full after each panel discussion.

The methodology was chosen, as a combination of observation and interview techniques allowed for a greater understanding of panel practices and procedures and also enabled insight from the perspective of the professional and

5 Most participants who successfully complete their reparation tasks are ultimately diverted from prosecution and escape a criminal record. For more analysis of the reparation models noted, see further Darren McStravick, 'Adult Reparation Panels and Offender-centric Meso-communities: An Answer to the Conundrum' (n 4), 98.

6 Norman K. Denzin, *The Research Act: A Theoretical Introduction to Sociological Methods* (3rd edn) (Prentice Hall International 1989) 244.

community representatives participating in the process.[7] In all, forty-five RJS panel-based case studies and six RJC panel-based case studies were observed. Ten semi-structured interviews were carried out in total, including a wide range of key stakeholders within the restorative justice themed process. Those stakeholders interviewed included two volunteer community representatives (RJC), two An Garda Siochána officers[8] (RJC and RJS participants), the programme managers from the two reparation programmes, two community representative caseworkers (RJS) and two Irish Probation Service panel representatives within the RJS model. Questions were designed to reveal a number of key themes around restorative justice and the nature of community involvement as part of case discourses and outcomes. Criminal justice professionals and community representatives were asked about their individual knowledge of restorative justice principles and practices, their individual backgrounds, training specifications for panel membership and their thoughts and recommendations for improving the process.

Initial data analysed the restorative quality of both programmes by way of a series of case studies examining the format of panel meetings and discourse employed within, participant backgrounds, the emotional and interactional dynamics occurring within case discussions, the crimes managed and contract terms issued. The aim was to uncover hypotheses as they arose within the data. As observations continued, it became clear that the concept of community was an increasingly utilised principle within panel discourses. This additional research theme was investigated as part of an ongoing literature review and the reparation panel data was then further analysed from a theoretical and practical 'communitarian' starting point.

Questioning the vulnerability narrative

The concept of vulnerability is one that is 'fraught with paradox' and can be 'complex, confusing, vague and ambiguous'.[9] While it can apply in either a 'universal or particular' setting,[10] for Martha Fineman the notion of vulnerability is an inevitable human condition rather than something that affects a particular marginalised group or individual. According to Fineman's vulnerability theory, the human condition is 'one of universal and continuous vulnerability', and one wherein 'the State is theorized as the legitimate governing entity and tasked with a responsibility to establish and monitor social institutions and

7 Herbert Rubin and Irene Rubin, *Qualitative Data: the Art of Hearing Data* (Sage Publications 2012) 120.

8 The Irish title for the police force in this jurisdiction is An Garda Siochána.

9 Lourdes Peroni and Alexandra Timmer, 'Vulnerable Groups: The Promise of an Emerging Concept in European Human Rights Convention Law' (2013) 11(4) International Journal of Constitutional Law 1056, 1058.

10 Ibid.

relationships that facilitate the acquisition of individual and social resilience'.[11] While this chapter is not the place to fully critically analyse the adequacy of such a theory, it can, however, be submitted that certain aspects are relevant within the fields of criminal law and restorative justice particularly and within criminological theory more generally. From a restorative justice perspective, it is important that conventional 'vulnerability' discourses are challenged. This is because the restorative paradigm generally recognises that the harm caused by a criminal act does not only attach to direct victims and that the reasons for criminal behaviour and subsequent after-effects can be multi-stranded and include offenders as indirect victims in some instances. Moreover, observations of panel practices and procedures as part of this research study provided evidence that the conventional 'victim' label could attach to a wide range of people, including the participating offender themselves and their family members. Indeed, one of the main strengths of the restorative justice paradigm is that it allows practitioners and theorists to take a broader look at the notion of victimhood, of crime and the principles of harm and remorse, and the interrelationships between the affected stakeholders.

At this point it is important to note that this broader analysis of the cause and effect of crime does link in some way to Fineman's universal approach to vulnerability. For example, it was this author's newly identified meso-community of care, concern and accountability, ably supported by criminal justice agencies and a responsive state both financially and by way of case referrals, which enabled an alternative outlook on the notion of victimhood and vulnerability. This meso-community concept derives from McCold's 'micro' and 'macro' communities analysis wherein he argues that close friends and family members of stakeholders involved in criminal events ('micro') and secondary relationships of similar stakeholders ('macro') can represent a starting point from which we can begin to understand the community concept within a criminal law context.[12] However, in contrast to McCold's theory, the meso-community identified within panel processes was illustrated by macro members, such as professional panellists and community representatives, managing participating offenders in a micro capacity; that is to say, they implemented a social-care-based, welfarist approach to participants and provided medical, financial and behavioural community-based support and advice. Furthermore, this approach originated from criminal justice professional actors acting with state-sponsored institutional support and resulted in a 'surrogate' community and communitarian bonds specific to each panel case and each participating offender. Participating offenders illustrated a vulnerability that was not in evidence at the start of proceedings. Many of the case studies involved alcohol and drug dependencies,

11 Fineman, 'Vulnerability and Inevitable Inequality' (n 1), 134.

12 Paul McCold, 'What is the Role of Community in Restorative Justice Theory and Practice?' in Harry Zehr and Barry Toews (eds.) *Critical Issues in Restorative Justice* (Criminal Justice Press 2004) 155–156.

relationship conflicts and mental health illness, while professional criminal justice stakeholders acted like community members intent on getting to the root of the offending behaviour while also offering rehabilitative and reintegrative, community-led options. The programme observations illustrated that all stakeholders can be subject to certain vulnerabilities, human limitations and frailties. Within a number of panel case meetings police officers talked of their own experiences as victims of criminal behaviour when being verbally and physically assaulted in the course of their work.

Therefore, the restorative paradigm, and reparation panel practice and procedure specifically, has allowed for practical examples of a challenge to universally held beliefs and classifications. However, such examples might also serve to reinforce the contextual and contingent nature of vulnerability in that it is only within the criminal justice and restorative justice framework that these challenges are realised. It is certainly true that such restorative frameworks and principles do allow for a greater appreciation of Fineman's vulnerability critique. However, that is not to say that these challenges cannot be transferred to other legal contexts. It has long been argued that restorative principles can help practitioners and participants to view the criminal law through a different, diametrically opposed 'reparative' lens.[13] The 'restorative lens' is one that focuses on principles such as problem solving, inclusive discourse, accountability and reparation for the harm caused to direct and indirect victims and rehabilitation and reintegration. Alternatively, it is further argued that the 'retributive lens' tends to discourage these principles and assumes a state monopoly of criminal law enforcement.[14] For Zehr, restorative justice represents a 'new paradigm' within criminal justice policy and procedure which views criminal wrongs primarily as a breakdown in relationships rather than the rule breaking of state laws by individuals.[15] Restorative justice can, as argued by Claassen, provide opportunities for recognising injustice and restoring equity between parties by managing the conflict 'at the earliest point possible and with the maximum amount of voluntary cooperation and minimum coercion, since healing in relationships and new learning are voluntary and cooperative processes'.[16]

This challenging of certain conventional criminal justice principles and labels is important in a number of ways. For example, Woolford notes that the 'victim' tag can be overly simplistic at times with many offenders having themselves been victims of crimes in the past. Also in relation to victims, he

13 Howard Zehr, *Changing Lenses: A New Focus for Crime and Justice* (n 3).

14 Ibid, 211.

15 Howard Zehr, 'Retributive Justice, Restorative Justice' in Gerry Johnstone (ed.) *A Restorative Justice Reader* (Willan Publishing 2003) 69, 81.

16 Ron Claassen, 'Restorative Justice – Fundamental Principles'. Paper presented at the National Commission for the Protection of Child Rights (NCPCR), revised May 1996 at the UN Alliance of NGO's Working Party on Restorative Justice, http://restorativejusticediscipline.com/library/RJ_Prin_w_Copyright.pdf (last visited 16 March 2020), see Principle 1.

argues that 'trauma narratives' can empower the State and 'reinforce structures of inequality'. Certain narratives can engender a sense of public fear, thus legitimising increased government surveillance and control. For Woolford, it is about 'broadening our sense of what we mean when we use these terms'.[17] Moreover, such terms can become 'corrupted' due to their frequent use within formal criminal justice systems and ideally 'restorative justice must strike out and find a new language'.[18] The reparation panels have themselves changed the discourse in this respect. For example, within the Restorative Justice in the Community (RJC) reparation project traditional 'offenders' are called 'persons who have committed an offence', while traditional 'victims' are called 'persons affected by crime'.

Within similar UK-based restorative community panel models, the 'victim' and 'offender' labels have been rebranded to 'harmed persons' and 'wrongdoers'.[19] Such rebranding can represent a renewed effort to tackle what has been seen in other jurisdictions as the 'ideological challenge' faced by restorative models generally, in which front-line police officers are more concerned with conventional criminal justice frameworks which tend to emphasise managerial targets and adversarial court-room battles between conventional 'victims' and 'offenders'.[20] It is perhaps fair to state, as Kerry and Clamp have previously outlined, that a failure to face this 'ideological challenge' head on could result in limited police referrals to restorative justice programmes generally, as well as over-zealous contract oversight.[21] Within a Sheffield-based community panel model, researchers found that a 'cultural change' was required due to a general resistance to embrace restorative justice principles within police ranks. This, it has been argued, was the result of a general perception within these ranks that restorative justice represented something of a soft option when compared to more mainstream policies. This 'cultural change' was seen to be 'one of the most challenging features of successfully implementing the community panels'.[22] A further evaluation of the South Yorkshire Restorative Justice programme, unrelated to the Sheffield-based community panel model above, uncovered concerns that police officers were being discouraged in the use of restorative justice as it was being perceived as conflicting with district targets

17 Andrew Woolford, *The Politics of Restorative Justice: A Critical Introduction* (Fernwood Publishing 2009) 112.

18 Ibid, 97. See, in particular, chapter 5 of Woolford (n 17) for a breakdown on identities within criminal justice systems.

19 Linda Meadows et al., *Evaluation of Sheffield's City Council Community Justice Panels Project* (Sheffield Hallam University 2010) 4.

20 Kerry Clamp and Craig Paterson, 'Rebalancing Criminal Justice Potentials and Pitfalls for Neighbourhood Justice Panels' (2011) 9 British Journal of Community Justice 21, 31.

21 As judges are presently the sole arbiters of whether or not an offender can participate in the reparation panel process, this concern is not directly applicable to the panel process. It might, however, become the case if the Gardaí are given increasing powers of referral in line with current juvenile diversionary and adult cautioning practices.

22 Linda Meadows et al., *Evaluation of Sheffield's City Council Community Justice Panels Project* (n 19), 27.

including sanction detection rates.[23] An interview with a Garda officer for the purposes of this research study also uncovered claims of indifference towards the restorative concept generally among colleagues, with many others seeing it as something of a 'soft option'.[24]

Thus, a challenge to the formal criminal justice narrative and an analysis and critique of the more conventional 'vulnerable victim' discourse can provide a basis for a better understanding of crime and the harm caused by illegal acts. This is relevant when considering that many participating offenders within the reparation panel process could themselves be legitimately labelled as a type of victim, with many of those referred suffering from dependency issues in relation to medication and alcohol. Others were classified as 'homeless' and living in temporary accommodation and hostels due to relational breakdowns and financial hardship. The reasons for offending were multi-stranded, with mental health disorders, debt concerns and the recent deaths of friends and loved ones all cited by participants as determining factors in their offending behaviour.

Challenging the *imitor* paradox

Observations of panel case discourses between criminal justice professionals, community representatives and participating offenders have enabled a deeper understanding of the reasons how and why criminal conflicts arise. By implementing an ethos within panel discourses wherein the participant is classed as a 'person', a 'community member', and indeed on some occasions a 'victim' in their own right, as well as simply and procedurally an 'offender', it can be argued that the concerns of a number of theorists regarding potential inherent dangers within the restorative justice paradigm are, at the very least, being acknowledged.[25] For example, Pavlich has expressed some concerns that restorative processes tend to rely on courtroom-based 'empowering identities' that can serve to limit restorative and community-led ideals.[26] This paradox is said to exist 'within two bifurcated strands of thought associated with restorative justice that amount to a paradox at the heart of its governmentality'.[27] Pavlich has outlined the paradox thus: 'On the one hand, restorative justice is presented as a distinct form of justice that exists *sui generis*, making sense of advocates'

23 Linda Meadows, Katherine Albertson, Daniel Ellingworth and Paul Senior, *Evaluation of the South Yorkshire Restorative Justice Programme* (Sheffield Hallam University 2012) 24.

24 Interview with Garda panellist, Thurles, 19 November 2014.

25 For example, some theorists have argued that restorative justice does little to protect an offender's procedural rights; see Andrew Ashworth, 'Responsibilities, Rights and Restorative Justice' (2002) 43 British Journal of Criminology 578, 585), while Cunneen has similarly argued that offenders have little choice but to participate in a restorative programme, as the only alternative is a conviction and thus the question of voluntary consent is moot; see generally Chris Cunneen and Carolyn Hoyle, *Debating Restorative Justice* (Hart Publishing 2010).

26 George Pavlich, *Governing Paradoxes of Restorative Justice* (Glasshouse Press, 2005), 98.

27 Ibid, 20.

claims that they are offering and deploying a form of justice which is ethically and practically distinct from criminal justice institutions. On the other hand, the restorative paradigm claims relevance and success by presenting itself as a component of reform within existing criminal justice systems.'[28]

For Pavlich, the former would seem to suggest 'an image of justice deliberately contra to criminal incarnations and having a coherence in its own right'. However, 'the overall effect is to generate an irresolvable, aporetic structure that simultaneously sees itself as independent of, yet is constitutively dependent upon, criminal justice'.[29] Furthermore, restorative justice continually claims to be different from state-based courtroom justice in that it deals with the aftermath of criminal wrongdoing from within the community itself. Thus, the community should then, if the pretence is logically followed, exist outside the realm of state agency influence and oversight as much as possible.[30] However, as Pavlich argues, restorative justice communities do not question what 'crime' itself is. They do not challenge the conventional image of crime, that 'founding concept of criminal justice'; and they do not challenge what a crime is, whether harm has to be always a product of crime, the question of vulnerability and whether specific definitions of crime can themselves be harmful. Furthermore, the restorative community itself can be made up of individual identities such as 'the victim' and 'the offender', identities which are already cemented in conventional criminal justice dialogue. Therefore, a paradox presents itself in which

> the image of community used to differentiate restorative from criminal justice rests on empowering identities of key figures – victims and offenders – as defined within the courtroom … [The] strength of this community is thus, paradoxically used to signal the distinctiveness of a restorative justice founded upon the active participation of such adversarial personae as victims and offenders as the basis of strong, democratic, communal formations.[31]

Alternatively, it is submitted that these mainstream criminal justice identities of 'offender', 'victim' and the question of vulnerability, and 'criminal justice professional', have evolved and been laid open to challenge within a number of reparation panel discussions. The aim of restorative justice generally should be to address the criminal behaviour and work out the best ways in which to repair the harm caused to those affected by the harm and also to prevent the recidivist tendencies of the participating offender. Reparation panels are no different in this respect. However, there has also been, within the series of cases observed,

28 Ibid.
29 Ibid.
30 Ibid, 95.
31 Ibid, 98.

a noticeable shift away from the more adversarial conventional criminal justice contest of offender versus police, 'us versus them' and the shifting of blame and the denial of guilt and accountability. Garda officers have been observed, on occasion, not wearing their uniform to meetings, thus adopting an arguably less intimidating tone to offenders, for whom the reparation process can be an intimidating process.[32] Many of those Garda representatives observed have employed elements of a 'humanistic dialogue' within case discussions.[33] Such dialogue has been said to 'rest on client empowerment, recognition of each other's humanity despite the conflict, and the building of a deeper, mutually respectful relationship'.[34]

An example of this approach was observed during one panel case managing a burglary offence. Within this case, the Garda representative detailed his own experience to the offender and others present of how his home had been burgled when he was a child and the subsequent feelings of fear that gripped his whole family. He explained how he watched his father, himself a Garda officer, leave the family home in an attempt to apprehend the offenders. He explained to the participant that he was unsure at the time whether or not his father would safely return. This type of dialogue can help to 'humanise' the policeman in the eyes of the offender. It can help to turn conventional justice labelling on its head in that the Garda officer illustrated a level of vulnerability that is rare within the offender/police dynamic.

Reparation panel discourses, therefore, illustrated examples wherein conventional criminal justice norms and labels are being challenged. The needs of participating offenders were addressed alongside the criminal deeds. Discussions within meetings represented a conversational rather than adversarial discourse. Criminal justice professionals illustrated a sympathetic tone when managing offences, while also underlining the need for reparation for the harm caused. Participating offenders have illustrated victim and vulnerability traits of their own due to addiction issues and relational breakdowns; and the reasons for the offending behaviour were shown to be multidimensional. The notion of oversimplified, mainstream criminal justice labelling has been further illustrated within other restorative mediation studies. Within one UK-based victim offender youth justice mediation model, a victim of a house burglary was surprised and relieved that the offender, on meeting him face to face, was 'no bigger than my ten year old son', thus challenging the victim's perceptions of the offender, and offender stereotypes generally.[35]

32 Many Garda officers did wear their uniform to panel meetings. However, one Garda panellist in particular was never observed wearing his uniform to a panel. He was also the most experienced of those Garda representatives, with an extensive background in juvenile restorative justice practice.

33 See Mark S. Umbreit and Mark P. Armour, *Restorative Justice Dialogue: An Essential Guide for Research and Practice* (Springer Publishing 2011) 21.

34 Ibid.

35 Aidan Wilcox and Catherin Hoyle, *The National Evaluation of the Youth Justice Board's Restorative Justice Project* (Youth Justice Board: Oxford, 2004) 42 https://restorativejustice.org.uk/sites/default/

Just as Fineman has argued that the vulnerability label should be universal and not attach to specific groups or individuals, in turn serving to ultimately destigmatise the concept, so restorative justice strives to find a new lens with which to view criminal justice conflicts and the affected stakeholders therein. The newly identified meso-community has enabled a rethink as to how we view victimhood within criminal law conflicts. Criminal justice professionals have been successfully viewing criminal justice through a 'reparative' prism where cases of offending are viewed as harmful events which can affect a wide range of local community members. Crime has, in many ways, been 'repackaged' as a breakdown in relationships between individuals and community members rather than the more conventional relationship between the prosecuting state and the accused. Locally based volunteers, panel caseworkers and programme facilitators have taken more responsibility for addressing offending behaviour by facilitating dialogue and managing reparation and rehabilitation goals within panel practices and outcomes. Both professional and community-based actors have acknowledged that vulnerability can be multi-stranded and include not only the direct victim but also other stakeholders such as participating offenders and the community as a whole. These factors have allowed for an alternative discourse to evolve from criminal disputes and have also allowed for a challenge and possible remedy to Pavlich's previously identified concerns over an over-reliance on 'adversarial personae' and principles within the broader range of restorative practices.[36]

The state-sponsored meso-community response

It can be reiterated at this point that the reparation panel process is a good example of a responsive state, backed up by community representation, taking accountability and responsibility for the management of criminal-based harms. As part of Fineman's distinct vulnerability narrative, the state and its institutions has an important role to play in that it must be 'responsive to the realities of human vulnerability and its corollary, social dependency, as well as to situations reflecting inherent or necessary inequality, when it initially establishes or sets up mechanisms to monitor these relationships and institutions'.[37] As part of ongoing practices of reparation and the utilisation of restorative principles in the reparation panel model, criminal justice professionals and community representatives have worked hand in hand with responsive state institutions in the quest for accountability, remorse, reparation and reintegration. Additionally, Fineman has viewed the state's role as one that provides a platform on which particular individuals can build 'resilience' to their inevitable vulnerability and

---

files/resources/files/National%20Evaluation%20of%20the%20Youth%20Justice%20Board%27s%20Restorative%20Justice%20Projects.pdf (last visited 16 March 2020).

36 George Pavlich, *Governing Paradoxes of Restorative Justice* (n 26), 98.

37 Martha Fineman, 'Vulnerability and Inevitable Inequality' (n 1), 134.

dependency on others. This notion of resilience is important, as it serves as a 'critical, yet incomplete, solution to our vulnerability' and is further strengthened by the resources provided by societal organisations and state institutions. In all, these resources are listed as physical, human, social, ecological or environmental and existential.[38]

The paradigm of restorative justice, and specifically the reparation panel model, increases the potential for a successful realisation of at least two of these listed resources, namely the social and human assets. For example, according to Fineman 'human' resources are those which aid and improve individual development as well as the development of material resources. This human resource, or 'human capital', is largely developed through certain state institutions and systems that help with the provision of education and knowledge, and training and experience. Social resources, or 'social capital', is that which, as Fineman describes, gives us 'a sense of belonging and community (and is) provided for through the relationships that we form within various institutions including the family, social networks, political parties and labour or trade unions'.[39]

The reparation panel programmes and, specifically, the newly identified 'meso-community of care, concern and accountability' is an important provider of both of these valuable resources. Indeed, these particular assets chime with the 'social capital' principles previously offered up by Bourdieu and Putnam. For Bourdieu, social capital involves 'transforming contingent relations, such as those of neighbourhood, the workplace or even kinship, into relations that are at once necessary and elective, implying durable obligations subjectively felt … such as feelings of gratitude, respect and friendship'.[40] In this regard, social ties are said to have an important and valuable role to play in that they can 'affect the productivity of individuals and groups … social capital refers to connections amongst individuals – social networks and the norms of reciprocity and trustworthiness that arise from them'.[41]

The importance and benefits of social support for offenders within the criminal justice system has been mooted since the early 1990s. Francis Cullen has previously argued that social support can stretch across a number of social levels and be delivered by either formal agencies or informal familial and friendship relationships. Cullen has suggested that this support can be both 'expressive' and 'instrumental'.[42] In a reparation panel context, Cullen's idea of 'expres-

38 Ibid.

39 Ibid.

40 Pierre Bourdieu, 'Forms of Capital' in John Richardson (ed.) *Handbook of Theory and Research for the Sociology of Education* (Greenwood 1993) 249–250.

41 Robert D. Putnam, *Bowling Alone: The Collapse and Revival of American Community* (New York: Simon and Schuster 2000) 19. See also, generally, Robert Putnam, *Democracy in Flux: The Evolution of Social Capital in Contemporary Society* (Oxford University Press 2002).

42 Francis Cullen, 'Social Support as an Organising Concept for Criminology: Presidential Address to the Academy of Criminal Justice Sciences' (1994) 11 Justice Quarterly 527.

sive' support, emotional support based on relationship ties, is represented by criminal justice professionals and community representatives listening to participants discuss their dependency and financial problems as part of case discourses, whereas 'instrumental support' can be seen as the reparation contract goals that participants hope to achieve, such as dependency abuse meetings, anger management classes and housing and financial support with community-based agencies.

The reparation-styled meso-community allows for these support structures to develop within case discussions and as part of rehabilitative and reintegrative contract goals. A number of the cases illustrated how the conventional vulnerability concept can be further analysed and challenged. For example, one panel case involved a participant charged with an assault offence. Initial discussions led to the discovery of an existing bipolar medical disorder. The participant was unsure how to get treatment for the disorder and outlined to the panel representatives his struggles with the illness. The medically trained community representative within the panel was able to point him in the direction of relevant services and arrange an appointment. One man referred to the panel after admitting to a charge of fraud outlined that he had suffered from depression throughout his life and admitted to suicidal tendencies. The panellists were told that these feelings had increased after he had lost his job several years ago and his personal relationships had suffered because of the mental health issues. Within another case, a single mother charged with the theft of one thousand euros' worth of clothes explained that her sister was currently in prison and that she was acting as a guardian to her two children. This, alongside caring for her own family, had considerably increased the financial and mental health pressures for her. Other offenders explained that dependency issues had led to relational breakdowns and homelessness, including a case with a young adult charged with drug offences who had been exiled from his family home because of the offence. It should be reiterated that, within all cases observed, the harm caused by each offence, and the accountability and reparation for that harm, was always highlighted and treated with paramount importance by panel members. However, relational bonds were also in evidence within each panel case as part of the welfare and social care ethos on display. Participants were redirected to relevant medical community-based support services and offered advice, encouragement and recommendations by professionals and volunteers alike. This, in turn, was illustration that panellists recognised that participants could also emit signs of vulnerability in their own right, with that vulnerability addressed and managed as part of case discourses and reparation contract outcomes.

The state-sponsored social support structures witnessed within reparation case studies have been successfully replicated in a number of other restorative programmes. For example, within a Circles of Support and Accountability restorative model managing the re-entry into society of sexual offenders after custody, the authors found that both expressive and instrumental social support was successfully observed by way of moral and emotional support, friendship, help with employment and housing, and general advice.[43] Further, Maruna and Koch have claimed that this particular notion of social support can positively influence recidivism rates among recently released inmates as well as easing their rehabilitative and reintegrative processes generally.[44] In a similar vein, social support structures resulting in surrogate relational bonds similar to those identified within reparation panel practice have been identified in a prison setting among prisoners, prison staff and volunteers as part of restorative circle processes aimed at cognitive transformation[45] and as part of an Australian restorative conferencing model made up of community representatives, victims and offenders.[46] However, the surrogate relational bonds observed within the reparative meso-community contrast somewhat with those other models listed, in that identifiable bonds were primarily moulded by criminal justice professionals, namely police and probation officers, as well as community representatives such as reparation programme actors and volunteers.

The relational meso-community bonds formed around each participating offender and specific to each panel case, are only possible due to the financial and indeed 'moral' support of the state itself. The diversionary procedure operates thanks to funding from The Irish Probation Service. Furthermore, a number of judges are supportive of the process and continue to divert cases from court prosecution to the reparation panel and the possibility of diversion from a formal criminal record. As illustrated within the case studies above, criminal justice professionals and state representatives have successfully combined with community representatives and volunteers in mapping out a social-care-based, rehabilitative response to offending behaviour. Such a 'democratic professionalised' approach[47] sees criminal justice professionals and community representatives come together to work collectively on an equal role-sharing and power-sharing basis wherein the professional expertise is directed towards 'facilitating public participation and control … they do not inevitably reduce the sphere of lay or citizen involvement, but share decision-making domains rather than monopolizing them'.[48] This illustrates one example of a responsive state pushing back against what Garland has labelled a 'culture of control'

43 Miriam Northcutt Bohmert, Grant Duwe and Natalie Kroovand Hipple, 'Evaluating Restorative Justice Circles of Support and Accountability: Can Social Support Overcome Structural Barriers' (2018) 62(3) International Journal of Offender Therapy and Comparative Criminology 739.

44 Shadd Maruna and T. Koch, 'The Impact of Imprisonment on the Desistence Process' in J. Travis and C. Visher (eds.) *Prisoner Reentry and Crime in America* (Cambridge University Press 2005) 139.

45 Damon Petrich and Brenda Morrison, 'The Alternatives to Violence Project: Using Positive Criminology as a Framework for Understanding Rehabilitation and Reintegration' in Theo Gavrielides (ed.) *Offenders no More: An Interdisciplinary Restorative Justice Dialogue* (NOVA Science Publishers 2015) 247.

46 Meredith Rossner and Jasmine Bruce, 'Community Participation in Restorative Justice: Rituals, Reintegration, and Quasi-Professionalization' (2016) 11(1) Victims & Offenders 107.

47 Susan M. Olson and Albert W. Dzur, 'Revisiting Informal Justice and Democratic Professionalism' (2004) 38 Law and Society Review 139, 142.

48 Ibid, 147.

illustrated by criminal justice policy within neoliberal societies, which has seen a shift from 'penal welfarism' and rehabilitative ideals towards a policy of risk management.[49]

Conclusion

Fineman's critique has allowed for a greater analysis and further debate of the vulnerability concept and its connection with criminal law and the criminal justice system. Although she has argued that the concept is universal rather than attaching to any specific group, the theory still retains some relevance as part of principles, policy and procedure based on restorative justice. In more conventional courtroom-based criminal justice discourses, vulnerability will always represent one particular grouping, namely victims affected by a criminal event. However, as reparation panel case observations have indicated, the vulnerability concept can also attach to participating offenders and other community-based members. In addition, Fineman's theoretical arguments of the importance of a responsive state in providing opportunities for 'resilience' with which to manage and guard against vulnerability have been practically represented to some extent within panel practice and procedures. Criminal justice professionals, ably backed by state institutions, have worked hand in hand with participants and volunteers as part of a social-care-based rehabilitative framework during case discussions and contract formulations. Participating offenders have gained in both 'human' and 'social' capital within a specific community of care, concern and accountability which recognises that vulnerability needs to be addressed as part of rehabilitative and reintegrative case management procedure. To conclude, looking at the vulnerability concept through a different lens within a particular restorative programme, and recognising and realising its intricacies, adds to the definition debate generally and provides a useful practical starting point for further theoretical analysis in the future.

49 David Garland, *The Culture of Control: Crime and Social Order in Contemporary Society* (Oxford University Press, 2002).

6 Vulnerability, resilience and the responsive state in transitional societies

Seriously injured victims of the troubles in Northern Ireland

Luke Moffett
Queen's University Belfast

Victims are often portrayed as vulnerable, helpless and passive, and can themselves play into such roles to morally motivate society to redress the harm they have suffered.[1] However, some individuals can be made more vulnerable than others, based on the violence committed against them, their own circumstances and/or the failure of the state to effectively respond to the harm in a timely and effective manner. To an extent victimhood can make individuals and communities more vulnerable, but not always so. Victims can be resilient, push back, advocate for change. Indeed, the development of transitional justice and the creation of its mechanisms and processes has been through the struggle of victims with allies in civil society, politics and even government to realise their needs for redress. In a way, victims can instrumentalise their suffering and vulnerability to gain social recognition and public attention.[2] Yet this is not a simple dichotomy of vulnerability and resilience, as it can change over time as the stress of their victimisation breaks their will or their circumstances worsen. Indeed, the vulnerability of certain victims will curtail, or at least create further barriers, their ability to claim their rights, engage in transitional justice or garner sufficient public attention to advance their redress agenda.

Despite the intersection of vulnerability and victimhood, particularly after conflict, authoritarianism or institutional abuse, there has been little analysis of its consequences on transitional justice.[3] This is notable given that transitional justice mechanisms can take years, even decades, to be established (if at all). In such time victims' needs and circumstances can change or markedly deteriorate.

1 Valerie M. Meredith, 'Victim Identity and Respect for Human Dignity: A Terminological Analysis' (2009) 91(874) International Review of the Red Cross 259–277, 262.

2 Ibid, 261.

3 See Eric Wiebelhaus-Brahm, 'After Shocks: Exploring the Relationships between Transitional Justice and Resilience in Post-Conflict Societies' in Roger Duthie and Paul Seils (eds.) *Justice Mosaics: How Context Shapes Transitional Justice in Fractured Societies* (International Centre for Transitional Justice 2017) 140–165.

DOI: 10.4324/9780429023149-7

While waiting for the state to respond, over time victims, their family and community can find ways and means to cope, both positively and negatively. This is problematic for societies transitioning from a violent past, as it embeds structural inequalities, which can be transgenerational, and compounds marginalisation by the state, abandoning individuals and communities within a society. Instead, the state under transitional justice should be building civic trust with victims and affected communities, by redressing those who bore the brunt of the violence so as to prevent its repetition.

This chapter explores vulnerability, resilience and victimhood in relation to seriously injured victims as a result of the Troubles/conflict in and around Northern Ireland and their claims for redress. These victims were blown up, shot or injured over the period of forty years, but since 2012 have been campaigning for a pension. The chapter explores the issue of seriously injured victims and their pension campaign through the lens of vulnerability and the response of the state. It begins by discussing the intersection of vulnerability, resilience and the responsive state within transitional justice. It then reflects on the campaign for a pension by seriously injured victims in Northern Ireland in light of these concepts. It finds that there is a lot to be learned from such an approach in fine-tuning transitional justice and states to be more responsive to victims' vulnerability and resilience after violence.

Vulnerability and transitional justice

Certain victims in transitional justice are often generically acceptable as vulnerable, such as women, children, the elderly and displaced persons, given that they are susceptible and exposed to certain forms of violence.[4] However, this skims over the complexities such groups may face over time, in particular the structural barriers after violence, and their engagement in transitional justice processes in their specific context. It also neglects their resilience – the fact that those who appear or are portrayed as powerless and vulnerable can also exercise 'agency, resistance and defiance'.[5] Moving away from assumptions of vulnerable groups to examine vulnerability, resilience and the response of the state can help us to understand the nuances of how transitional justice can better respond to victims and affected communities in the aftermath of violence.

4 Cécile Aptel, 'International Criminal Justice and Child Protection' in Saudamini Siegrist; Mindy Jane Roseman and Theo Sowa (eds.) *Children and Transitional Justice: Truth-Telling, Accountability and Reconciliation*, (UNICEF 2010) 67, 86; Cristián Correa, 'Reparations in Peru: From Recommendations to Implementation' (ICTJ, June 2013) 16; 2007 Nairobi Declaration on Women's and Girls' Rights to a Remedy and Reparation, www.fidh.org/IMG/pdf/NAIROBI_DECLARATIONeng.pdf (last accessed 14 December 2020) para 7.

5 Eilish Rooney and Fionnuala Ní Aoláin, 'Transitional Justice from the Margins: Intersections of Identities, Power and Human Rights' (2018) 12(1) International Journal of Transitional Justice 1, 3; Charlotte Lindsey, *Women Facing War* (ICRC 2015) 28–30.

Vulnerability has long been the concern of development studies, but there is increasing research to explore its relevance and connection to transitional justice.[6] Harwell and Le Billon warn that the failure to grasp the 'complexity and interaction of vulnerability' in transitional justice has in turn compromised the effectiveness of its mechanisms.[7] It is worth briefly outlining the scope of vulnerability in development studies to guide our analysis of its applicability to transitional justice. The ICRC defines vulnerability as 'the precarious living conditions of individuals, households or communities in the face of a threat in the form of an abrupt change in environment'.[8] The UN Development Programme (UNDP) sets out that vulnerability can be shaped in three ways: life cycle vulnerabilities, structural vulnerabilities, and group violence and insecure lives.[9] Life cycle vulnerabilities encompass the threats that individuals face at different times of their lives and that make them more susceptible to harm, whereas structural vulnerabilities are rooted in the social context of a society, such as individual and group identity and circumstances (like geographical location and gender), which may subject someone to discrimination. The final factor, group violence and insecurity, reflects the limited freedom and choice individuals and groups are subjected to in the face of violence that inhibits their development. Crises such as conflict also exacerbate health inequalities between groups in society, disproportionately increasing vulnerability.[10]

Fineman suggests that a 'vulnerability approach' is a better way to conceptualise how the state can better respond to citizen, given it is '*the* primal human condition' that we are all susceptible to changes to our well-being.[11] As such, vulnerability requires the law to be more reflexive, less concerned with equality and more with equity, to be more cognisant that power, privilege, and even the law itself, is shaped by social institutions, relationships and identities in unequal and marginalising ways.[12] This is similar to vulnerability conceived within development studies. While conflict and disaster can put individuals and groups at risk, it is also worth keeping in mind how they have the capacity and resilience to react to such changes.

6 See Pablo de Grieff and Roger Duthie (eds.) *Transitional Justice and Development: Making Connections* (ICTJ 2009).

7 Emily E. Harwell and Philippe Le Billon, 'Natural Connections: Linking Transitional Justice and Development Through a Focus on Natural Resources' in Pablo de Grieff and Roger Duthie (eds.) *Transitional Justice and Development: Making Connections*, (ICTJ 2009) 282, 285.

8 Charlotte Lindsey *Women Facing War* (n 5) 30.

9 *Human Development Report 2014: Sustaining Human Progress: Reducing Vulnerabilities and Building Resilience* (UNDP 2014) 55.

10 Ryoa Chung and Matthew R. Hunt, 'Justice and Health Inequalities in Humanitarian Crises: Structured Health Vulnerabilities and Natural Disasters' in Patti Lenard and Christine Straehle, *Health Inequalities and Global Justice* (Edinburgh University Press 2012) 197, 205–206.

11 Martha Albertson Fineman, 'Vulnerability and Inevitable Inequality' (2017) 4(3) Oslo Law Review 133, 142.

12 Ibid, 142.

For the UNDP, '[h]uman resilience is about removing the barriers that hold people back in their freedom to act. It is also about enabling the disadvantaged and excluded groups to express their concerns, to be heard and to be active agents in shaping their destinies.'[13] Whereas the World Bank characterises resilience as 'the ability of people, societies, and countries to recover from negative shocks, while retaining or improving their ability to function'.[14] Fineman more concisely suggests that resilience can be accumulated throughout life by giving 'an individual with the means and ability to recover from harm, setbacks and the misfortunes that affect our lives'.[15] However, she notes that resilience is dependent on the quality and quantity of resources (physical, human, social, ecological or environmental, and existential/spiritual) they have access to and disposal.[16] To an extent, vulnerability and resilience can been seen as two sides of the same coin, in that some individuals and groups are more likely to be exposed to some risks than to others, and that different individuals and groups cope or have capacity to deal with such risks. Between these two sides lies a space for the state to act to narrow the gap lying amidst vulnerability and resilience.

In the aftermath of violence, victims, ex-combatants and others affected by it may have differing levels of resources that can shape how they engage with transitional justice processes and manage the consequences of violence. Indeed, resilience can have subjective and objective elements, in that it may be more than structural factors or resources, but also down to the individual's mindset, as to how they cope with the aftermath.[17] Conflict, displacement and sectarian violence can have a disruptive effect on social bonds and networks, reducing victims and communities' ability to be resilient and cope in the absence of, or delayed response from, the state.[18] Moreover, long periods of conflict can reduce resources of victims and affected communities,[19] such as a person having their business destroyed, causing them to lose their home while trying to provide for their family.[20] In terms of trauma, resilience is not about being invincible, but how victims and affected communities adapt and develop in the face of adversity.[21] Without such resilience, transitional justice would not be in the position it is in today, without the struggle of victims and their allies to channel their suffering into social transformation to deal with the past.

13 *Human Development Report 2014* (n 9) 16.

14 *World Development Report 2014: Risk and Opportunity: Managing Risk for Development* (World Bank 2014) 12.

15 Fineman, 'Vulnerability and Inevitable Inequality' (n 11) 146.

16 Ibid 146–147.

17 See Javier Cabanyes Truffinoa, 'Resilience: An Approach to the Concept' (2010) 3(4) Revista de Psiquiatría y Salud Mental 145.

18 Ana María Ibáñez and Andrés Moya, 'Vulnerability of Victims of Civil Conflicts: Empirical Evidence for the Displaced Population in Colombia' (2010) 38(4) World Development 647.

19 Ibid, 647–648.

20 Focus group IR07, participant 2.

21 Javier Truffinoa, 'Resilience: An Approach to the Concept' (n 17), 146.

That said, there are particular aspects of vulnerability after mass violence that need to be addressed through a transitional justice approach. Urban Walker identifies that after mass atrocities, where impunity prevails and there is a general lack of accountability, victims face 'moral vulnerability'.[22] As moral actors, when wrongs are committed against individuals and communities the failure of the state to provide redress and allow impunity can compound victims' marginalisation in society and diminish their trust in the state. According to Walker, reparations play an important role in remedying this moral vulnerability, by society giving attention to the wrongful harm caused to a victim and requiring the responsible to publicly make good the wrong.[23] De Greiff has written on the importance of reparations in rebuilding civic trust in the state.[24] He more broadly connects moral vulnerability or impunity with the development literature and poverty, in that victimisation diminishes agency and victims' ability to aspire for better circumstances by adapting their expectations to what is feasible in the face of an impassive or abusive state.[25] This is within a broader trend in development studies that views human rights and freedoms as key priorities, beyond economic growth, to ensure human capabilities to enjoy a quality of life as a valuable indicator.[26]

A better understanding of resilience in transitional justice can shed light on how individuals and groups can have varying access to different resources, which can help in part to appreciate how urban, male elites can often dominate the shape of transitional justice within a country.[27] A greater understanding of vulnerability and resilience can assist in fine-tuning how transitional justice mechanisms enable access, engage, and shape redress and justice for victims, ex-combatants and other interested actors. For instance, how can an indigenous elderly woman who is responsible for looking after her grandchildren after the death of their parents testify at a truth commission or claim reparations? How can she find the time and money to travel, advocate or afford a lawyer that can best advance her needs?[28] A key issue here is ensuring that victims who are vulnerable are 'empowered', in the sense that sustained effort is made by the state

22 Margaret Urban Walker, 'Moral Vulnerability and the Task of Reparations', in Catriona Mackenzie, Wendy Rogers, and Susan Dodds (eds) *Vulnerability: New Essays in Ethics and Feminist Philosophy* (Oxford University Press 2014), 110, 112.

23 Ibid, 118.

24 Pablo de Greiff, 'Justice and Reparations', in Pablo de Greiff (ed.) *Handbook of Reparations* (Oxford University Press 2006) 451, 462–463.

25 Pablo de Greiff, 'Theorizing Transitional Justice' (2012) 51 Nomos 31.

26 See Amartya Sen, *Development as Freedom* (Oxford University Press 2010).

27 Christine Chung, Victims' Participation at the International Criminal Court: Are Concessions of the Court Clouding the Promise? (2008) 6(3) Northwestern Journal of International Human Rights 459, 513.

28 Eric Wiebelhaus-Brahm, 'After Shocks: Exploring the Relationships between Transitional Justice and Resilience in Post-Conflict Societies' (n 3) 152.

to ensure their inclusion and access to transitional justice processes.[29] This may be incredibly difficult without development programmes and services in place to help those on the margins of society who may be illiterate, old, disabled, sick, geographically remote, or stigmatised and silenced. Civil society has an important role to play in broadening inclusion and participation.

Transitional justice has, to an extent, been responsive to the needs of vulnerable groups, such as women, children, internally displaced persons (IDPs) and indigenous communities. This has been particularly informed by the victim-centred approach and gender inclusion, which has enabled a broader base of voices to engage in such processes.[30] That said, more work needs to be done to enable children, IDPs and those seriously injured or disabled to be able to engage with such mechanisms. There is also a large gap in the field on the role of resilience in how victims, their families and communities cope with their harm and the resulting debt or impact on these social institutions when waiting for the state to act.[31] Such a debt or impact can be negative in the sense of affecting individuals who are carers from pursuing their career or life plans, and/or have a psychological and transgenerational impact (the trauma of witnessing a loved one being injured or killed), but can also be positive in bringing a family or community together and building solidarity or a social movement for change.

Seeing vulnerability as a new lens to view transitional justice may not avoid difficult questions of how to address the past. As Wiebelhaus-Brahm suggests, with reparations – which focus on delivering reparative measures to those who are deemed to have suffered the most or need to be prioritised – it may cause resentment to other individuals or communities who are similarly vulnerable, whether through historic, economic, social or cultural violations.[32] In addition, in post-conflict countries resources are scarce, and prioritising transitional justice mechanisms over development may limit growth to more marginalised sections of society. This may be a false dichotomy, as marginalised members of society often bear the brunt of the violence and delivering reparations to such victims may mitigate transgenerational effects of impoverishment and trauma. A vulnerability and resilience lens could identify how best to prioritise reparations to those most needy, but this could risk such a reparation programme

29 Clara Sandoval, 'Reflections on the Transformative Potential of Transitional Justice and the Nature of Social Change in Times of Transition' in Roger Duthie and Paul Seils (eds.) *Justice Mosaics: How Context Shapes Transitional Justice in Fractured Societies* (International Centre for Transitional Justice 2017) 166, 189.

30 Ana María Ibáñez and Andrés Moya, 'Vulnerability of Victims of Civil Conflicts: Empirical Evidence for the Displaced Population in Colombia' (n 18) 647.

31 See Simon Robins, 'Towards Victim-Centred Transitional Justice: Understanding the Needs of Families of the Disappeared in Postconflict Nepal' (2011) 5(1) International Journal of Transitional Justice 75.

32 Eric Wiebelhaus-Brahm, 'After Shocks: Exploring the Relationships between Transitional Justice and Resilience in Post-Conflict Societies' (n 3) 156.

becoming an assistance body, rather than a remedy for the violation of victims' rights.

There is an increasing attention in transitional justice to address not only corrective justice on past violations but distributive reallocation of resources and transformation of the drivers of violence, such as inequality and poverty.[33] With reparations, while it can offer to redistribute some resources to victims, this is generally narrowly construed, concentrating on particular civil and political violations, rather than systemic marginalisation, where victims want their needs addressed instead of their rights remedied.[34] As victimisation can leave victims worse off socio-economically, a vulnerability approach could be a more informed way to connect civil and political violations with economic, social and cultural ones. Such an approach often, though not always, reflects that victimisation disproportionately affects those already subjected to structural violations, such as poverty and marginalisation, in times of mass atrocities.[35]

Although transitional justice has been focused on redressing civil and political right violations, there is a lack of consideration in how development can also complement such processes and minimise perceived and real inequalities created by such measures. Indeed, victims have a right to redress alongside the right to development, with the state responsible for both. Instead it may be more useful to think of vulnerability as an added value in a rights-based approach to transitional justice, in particular in how the state responds to large universes of victims affected by such violence, especially the elderly and disabled, and those affected by gendered aspects of violence. This requires a flexible and inclusive approach, as far as possible, to cater to their different needs and to choices that can help alleviate their suffering. At the same time, consideration should be given to the resources certain victims and communities have access to when being resilient and how this can factor into the state's responsiveness in the delivery of measures such as reparations in terms of prioritisation and comprehensiveness in dealing with the past.

The responsive state

In transitional justice the state is seen as the primary responsible actor in dealing with the past.[36] This occurs even where non-state actors, such as

33 Paul Gready and Simon Robins, 'From Transitional to Transformative Justice: A New Agenda for Practice' (2014) 8 International Journal of Transitional Justice 339, 347.

34 Lars Waldorf, 'Anticipating the Past: Transitional Justice and Socio-Economic Wrongs' (2012) 21(2) Social and Legal Studies 171, 178.

35 Rodrigo Uprimny Yepes, 'Transformative Reparations of Massive Gross Human Rights Violations: Between Corrective and Distributive Justice' (2009) 27(4) Netherlands Quarterly of Human Rights 625, 631.

36 Principle 1, *Updated Set of Principles for the Protection and Promotion of Human Rights through Action to Combat Impunity*, E/CN.4/2005/102/Add.1 8 February 2005; and Principles 15 and 16, *UN Basic Principles, and Guidelines on the Right to a Remedy and Reparation for Victims of Gross Violations*

rebel or paramilitary groups, committed most of the violence, as the state is the primary duty holder in international law. In post-conflict societies, state institutions and resources may be devastated, so the state's ability to provide for victims may be limited by other pressing priorities of the transition, such as reconstruction of infrastructure. However, in societies in transition from a violent past, victims often face an intransigent government that is unwilling to deal with the past, given the fragile peace, the perpetrators still being in power or the political elite's concern to win the next election. The state, its institutions and laws after violence can also cause further harm to victims by ignoring their claims or actively blocking their demands for redress. This can be seen as secondary victimisation, by compounding harm that increases their vulnerability by closing the opportunity for them to live their lives.

Andrieu points out that victims of political violence often lose their 'trust in the world', in that 'they cannot initially act and be active, as autonomous agents in the public sphere', and are left feeling disorientated, alone and frustrated.[37] Yet, at the same time transitional justice actors (including victims) often use victims' suffering to morally motivate the necessity of such measures to deal with the past and to rebuild trust in the state and society, there is a danger that victims become locked into their identity and own narrative of the past rather than as active moral agents. Where the state is responsive to vulnerable individuals and groups, does it risk creating social dependency on the state in the long term?[38] While dependency is often stigmatised or seen as something negative in conservative political discourses, Fineman points to its universality and inevitability for us all as 'inherent in the human condition', whether as infants, in ill health or old age.[39] Fineman suggests that there is a clear role of the state to be more than responsive, but active in redistribution.[40] Independence is achieved by providing basic resources to a person enabling them to make choice unconstrained by inequalities.[41] Moving to an active state is the role of the government in providing value to unvalued or undervalued things, such as caretaking.[42]

Andrieu proposes that transitional justice mechanisms should be aware of victims' capability and the 'existence of valid vulnerabilities without locking

---

of International Human Rights Law and Serious Violations of International Humanitarian Law, A/RES/60/147, 1 December 2005.

37 Kora Andrieu, 'Political Liberalism after Mass Violence: John Rawls and a "Theory" of Transitional Justice' in Susanne Buckley-Zistel, Teresa Koloma Beck, Christian Braun and Friederike Mieth (eds.) *Transitional Justice Theories* (Routledge 2014) 85, 100.

38 Martha Fineman, 'Vulnerability and Inevitable Inequality' (n 11) 134.

39 Martha Fineman, 'Cracking the Foundational Myths: Independence, Autonomy, and Self-Sufficiency' (2000) 8 American University Journal of Gender Social Policy and Law 13–29, 18.

40 Ibid, 26.

41 Ibid.

42 Ibid.

victims into their powerlessness'.[43] In other words, state-created transitional justice mechanisms should also be transitioning victims from being vulnerable or dependent on the state in the long term, but this requires coordination with development and services to maximise benefits and may not be possible for all victims. For transitional justice this may mean that long-term measures have to be established for victims. In Chile, Argentina and Germany, pension schemes have been put in place for victims of disappearances, torture and genocide. Such pensions, while long-term financial commitments, do offer victims financial security to shape their own future beyond their suffering.[44] These issues cut across the experience of seriously injured victims, as a result of the conflict in and around Northern Ireland, who are campaigning for a pension.

The vulnerability and resilience of seriously injured victims in Northern Ireland

The conflict in and around Northern Ireland (the Troubles) between 1969 and 1998 caused the deaths of over 3700 individuals and injured more than 47,000. Yet the debate on dealing with the past since the 1998 Good Friday Agreement has focused on those bereaved, with little attention on those seriously injured or suffering other violations.[45] While this can in part be explained by injured victims only organising themselves to advocate around their issues in recent years, it exhibits the broader marginalisation of those disabled from being included and having access to avenues that can shape policy and national discussions on dealing with the past. This is noticeable in Northern Ireland, as well over 1500 victims are seriously injured and disabled as result of the conflict, although unlike those bereaved, who are seeking truth and/or justice, they are seeking reparations through a pension. The rest of this section reflects on the aspects of vulnerability, resilience and the response of the state to seriously injured victims in Northern Ireland, and teases out these themes in the practice of a transitional society.

For seriously injured victims, their harm has compounded over time. Most were blown up in bombings, suffered gunshot wounds that shattered bones and punctured vital organs, left with shrapnel in their bodies and experience chronic or phantom pain. The effects on their bodies are still being felt and their ability to cope with infections or mobility is deteriorating as they get older. Some did continue to work where they were able to, but many faced structural vulnerability through discrimination in the job market, and were

43 Kora Andrieu 'Political Liberalism after Mass Violence: John Rawls and a "Theory" of Transitional Justice' (n 37) 101.

44 Elizabeth Lira, 'The Reparations Policy for Human Rights Violations in Chile' in Pablo de Grieff, *The Handbook of Reparations* (Oxford University Press 2006), 55, 85.

45 There remains little data on the scale of sexual violence. See Catherine O'Rourke and Aisling Swaine, 'Gender, Violence and Reparations in Northern Ireland: A Story Yet to be Told' (2017) 21(9) International Journal of Human Rights 1302.

unable to continue their intended path in life. One victim, who was paralysed in shooting, went back to university to get further qualifications and made '40 job applications [but] never got a look in'.[46] People with disabilities are also more vulnerable to 'hate crime, excluding attitudes and biased welfare reforms'.[47] Society expects them to have 'no future',[48] which further inhibits their ability to agitate for change when their agency is not respected. This corresponds with views expressed by seriously injured victims, who were made to feel inadequate and invisible when out in public. As two victims said:

P4: I remember going into the town with [his wife] for a cup of tea. I was sitting in a café and the waitress said to [his wife], 'Does he take sugar in his tea?'
P2: Aye, as if you weren't there.[49]

Other victims spoke about how their family or community treated them differently and made them feel no longer welcome. One carer, whose husband was injured in a bombing, felt no longer welcome at their church and said that his 'mother would have been embarrassed about what happened to him because I think people actually said to her, "Was your son in something? Was your son in some organisation that led him here?"'[50] Structural vulnerability also plays a part in the geography of victimhood, wherein victims' experiences were different in rural areas, where families who were targeted may have felt more isolated when being attacked or would still come across the person responsible for their suffering in their daily routine.[51]

The violence in Northern Ireland also had a gender dimension, which still reverberates, where women took on the role of sole parent and breadwinner, due to most men being killed during the Troubles. For those seriously injured, women have often become the sole carers of injured family members. As one victim caseworker said, 'their lives were shattered and they never, ever fully reclaimed them'.[52] The lack of a responsive state has meant that families have absorbed the social debt of dependency by caring for injured family members, often giving up their own careers and life plans to do so.[53] Some seriously injured victims have spoken of how their spouses have had nervous breakdowns, depression or suffered from addiction as a result of the incident and

46 Focus group IR07, participant 4.
47 Inger Marie Lid, 'Vulnerability and Disability: A Citizenship Perspective' (2015) 30(10) Disability and Society 1554.
48 Ibid, 1566.
49 Focus group IR07, March 2017.
50 Interview with IR08, May 2018.
51 *Human Development Report 2014* (n 9) 55.
52 IR16.
53 Marie Breen Smyth, *The Needs of Individuals and their Families Injured as a Result of the Troubles in Northern Ireland* (WAVE 2012), 12.

their role as carers. This vulnerability for victims and their carers has only been exacerbated as they get older. These life cycle vulnerabilities are different to those of other older persons due to their disability and suffering, which limits their ability to live their life with the dignity, and quality, they expect.[54] Getting older also causes anxiety for the injured victims, who may not know where their care is going to come from.[55] A vulnerability and responsive state approach would value the contribution of carers and include them as the beneficiaries of the victim's pension (upon their death) or provide state-funded carers.

The harm caused to seriously injured victims has also left them morally vulnerable. They are forgotten about in agreements dealing with the past or are not prioritised.[56] Instead their suffering is relegated to their private space, as greater attention is paid to the bereaved. The pension campaign is as much about financial security as it is about acknowledgement of their experience of suffering. This is perhaps beyond moral vulnerability, as prosecutions occurred and compensation was paid to some seriously injured victims, but insufficient attention to ensure their care in the long term or adequate redress.[57] Instead these victims are more socially invisible, in the sense that society does not want to see them. One victim left blinded in a bombing spoke about the day-to-day difficulties of living with the consequences and the social exclusion caused by her injuries:

> If I had known that I was going to be like this for 35 years, I would have committed suicide because it is no life. Absolutely none. You have to ask somebody, 'What's that?' if you go into a shop or even stay at home. I should be out. I was working in a [business] … to be [left] sitting in the corner. My hands were badly cut with glass, my wrists and my face … because it's not a life. Definitely not.[58]

This invisibility is particularly acute for complex victims – that is, victimised perpetrators who are seriously injured and considered *persona non grata* when it comes to discussing reparations.[59] They are seen as persons who are responsible

54 *Human Development Report 2014* (n 9) 55.

55 Marie Breen Smyth (n 53), 10.

56 See the House of Commons Northern Ireland Affairs Committee, *Consultative Group of the Past, Final Report 2009*, available online https://publications.parliament.uk/pa/cm200910/cmselect/cmniaf/171/171.pdf (last accessed 14 December 2020); Haas-O'Sullivan Proposed Agreement 2013, available online www.northernireland.gov.uk/publications/haass-report-proposed-agreement (last accessed 14 December 2020); and Stormont House Agreement 2014, available online www.dfa.ie/media/dfa/alldfawebsitemedia/ourrolesandpolicies/northernireland/Stormont-House-Agreement.pdf (last accessed 14 December 2020).

57 See Stuart Magee, *Exploring Models for the Proposal of Special Pension Provision for Those Injured in the Northern Ireland 'Troubles'* (WAVE 2011).

58 Interview with IR21, April 2017.

59 See Luke Moffett, 'Reparations for "Guilty Victims": Navigating Complex Identities of Victim–Perpetrators in Reparation Mechanisms' (2016) 10(1) International Journal of Transitional Justice 146.

for causing harm to others, thereby viewed as undeserving of redress. This causes them further social exclusion, as they are not eligible for the state criminal injuries compensation scheme and are vilified in the media. While victims can be defined as vulnerable, those responsible for violence can also claim such victimhood to justify their actions on the basis of historic and collective victimisation.[60] A moral vulnerability lens highlights that, despite suffering similar harm, their suffering is somehow less deserving of redress, but this risks creating impunity for certain crimes against certain individuals. Maybe at best the issue of vulnerability in transitional justice can better highlight the ongoing hardship such individuals suffer and build more solidarity in finding a way to nuance their responsibility and responding to their harm caused by others.

In terms of resilience, despite their suffering, seriously injured victims have been campaigning for a pension as well as raising awareness of their plight. It may take years for a victim to have the confidence or the public space to speak about their suffering and advocate for their rights. In turn, it can take time for such victims to organise themselves into groups to put political pressure on a government to change their policy or laws. For seriously injured victims, this is a more difficult process. Many of them spent years in hospital, and often decades later still have to return for further surgeries, infections and to remove shrapnel, as well as to deal with ongoing psychological trauma. That said, once they have learned to advocate, they have also been promoting other victims' issues on the Victims and Survivors Forum, such as the widow's pension, reflecting their moral leadership beyond their own suffering. As one victim caseworker said about them,

> these guys were not speaking out before they came together and started working on this issue; now they're up and they're as comfortable talking to each other as they are talking to prime ministers and first ministers and politicians up in Stormont … They absolutely know their stuff and are fantastic advocates … it has really been down to them.[61]

For many injured victims they have just got on with their lives as best they could and do not want to revisit the history of their injuries. This has meant they have had to navigate their own means of resilience to cope with their ongoing suffering. As one victim said:

> We had no idea about claiming culture [after the bombing] … It was never how somebody would give me money, for somebody to give me help. It

60 Marie Smyth, 'Putting the Past in its Place: Issues of Victimhood and Reconciliation in Northern Ireland's Peace Process' in Nigel Biggar (ed.) *Burying the Past: Making Peace and Doing Justice after Civil Conflict* (Georgetown University Press 2001) 126.

61 Interview with IR06.

> wouldn't have even occurred to us that we need help, it was just how do we rebuild. So, this is how me and my family are, it's about self-dependence and building life and being self-supportive and self- sufficient. That's how we've always been. So, all these things never even occurred to us.[62]

Nonetheless, despite this resilience, it has not been easy for many victims to live a 'normal' life, as they are reminded about their injuries every day. They can, to an extent, be dependent on the support of their family and other resources to which they have access. Victim organisations in civil society, funded by the government and the EU, have played an important part in facilitating this space, but this requires victims to associate with these organisations, which can in certain areas be aligned to a particular community.

The Northern Irish and United Kingdom governments have not been as responsive as they could be to the needs of seriously injured victims. To an extent, the government continues to treat the Troubles as an ordinary justice issue, despite the extraordinary and sectarian-driven violence. Instead of narrowing the gap between vulnerability and resilience of victims, the actions and inactions of state institutions and actors have instead exacerbated victims' vulnerability and marginalisation. This can be seen from the experience of victims claiming compensation. One victim – a teenager when a bomb exploded, causing her to lose both her legs – felt that going to court was intimidating and her barrister forced her to accept a settlement so she would not upset the judge. As she said, 'You just did not go into court. In other words, if you challenge us, we'll reduce it. That's the environment I accepted it in.'[63] One victim who lost both of his legs in a paramilitary shooting was denied compensation because he refused to help the police identify those responsible, despite him still being threatened at the time.[64] The response of the state is not always equal for all victims. There is better care and financial support for state forces compared to civilians, but there are also those on part-time or short contracts in the security forces who were left impoverished, despite being seriously injured while on duty or returning from work.

One victim, who lost one of his legs in a booby trap bomb and suffered other shrapnel wounds, spoke about how after the bombing he lost his business and home, as his insurance did not cover 'acts of war'. He was left in hospital for a year and upon release he was dependent on basic social benefits for years until he was declared medically fit to be assessed for compensation. When he went to claim compensation, it was reduced by £27,000, for the expense of the benefits he had received. He said:

> You didn't get help. Nobody came forward to say, 'We'll do that for you.' It didn't happen. They took away your dignity … I didn't even feel like a

62 Interview with IR12, April 2018.

63 Focus group IR07, April 2017.

64 'Gun victim loses appeal', *BBC News*, 9 November 2001.

> man. I couldn't earn. I couldn't go out and work. I got to a stage where I couldn't cope. I tried to commit suicide … when I think back on that, but that was when I was at my dire straits. I just wanted out of it.[65]

The insensitivity of the state to these victims caused them mental distress. This not only had an effect on the direct victim, but also their family, who became their carers for the rest of their lives. There was no mental health support, meaning people found their own positive and negative coping mechanisms to deal with the trauma.[66] One victim told how his wife opened the door to the gunmen the night he was injured. She never forgave herself, turning to alcohol to cope and dying young at the age of 51 as a result.[67] Some victims felt that as a result they had become a 'burden' on their loved ones.

While the state, through the Victims and Survivors Service, provides £1500 annually for seriously injured victims, it has to be applied for each year and claimed back with receipts. Even this amount is not enough for victims who used their criminal injuries compensation to buy a house. One shooting victim expressed how he used the money to pay his council rates on his house, leaving him with half the money and a choice between heating his house for the winter or getting physiotherapy once a month.[68] Similarly, the state was unresponsive to victims' vulnerability from ongoing or future violence. One victim, who lost both of his legs in a loyalist bombing, was placed in a loyalist estate by the Housing Executive, where he was subjected to intimidation and threats.[69] Moreover, the house was grossly inadequate for his needs, given that the toilet was downstairs from his bedroom and there were twelve steps into the house. This intersection of structural vulnerability and ongoing violence exhibits the need of the state to better understand the suffering of each individual's identity and situation to better minimise their suffering.

For the most part the pension campaign by seriously injured victims of the Troubles/conflict in and around Northern Ireland reflects their agency in seeking to redress the past. It has been their vulnerability and the unresponsiveness of the state that has left them in a position where their situation is deteriorating in the long term. In contrast to those bereaved during the conflict, seriously injured victims do not position themselves as morally vulnerable, but as structurally vulnerable. In other words, they want the dire economic straits they find themselves in to be addressed, rather than to have their harm acknowledged or those responsible held to account.[70] That said, with the inclusion of combatants who are seriously injured within the pension campaign, there remains tension.

65 Focus group IR07, participant 2.

66 There remains a campaign to set up a Mental Trauma Service that would be staffed by medical specialists. Currently CBT is provided by victim groups.

67 Focus group IR07, participant 4.

68 Focus group IR07.

69 IR21.

70 For some this is important, but secondary to remedying their harm.

In a way, seriously injured victims have become politically vulnerable in the sense that the pension issue has political capital for politicians to support, but at the same time it has become a means for politicians to point-score against the other side. This has meant that most political parties have come out in support of the pension, but the debate as to who should get it has focused on who is more deserving, or innocent, rather than on victims' continuing vulnerability.[71]

Conclusion

Vulnerability, resilience and the responsive state are important conceptual tools in developing a better understanding and practice of transitional justice. Further work is necessary to better understand how victims and affected communities cope and create their own informal mechanisms of redress to deal with the past in the face of state impassivity. In the case of those victims seriously injured due to the Troubles/conflict in and around Northern Ireland, their campaign for recognition and a pension continues. Their concern is that, while politicians and government officials express their sympathy and support, there is growing discontent among the victims that they are just waiting for them to 'die off', as already four members of the campaign group have died in the past few years.[72] This highlights the importance of transitional justice to be timely, in order to mitigate further harm to victims. For these victims, it is little comfort that they have become more resilient through this process, as over time, without a more active or responsive state, their situation will leave them more vulnerable.

71 See Luke Moffett, 'Victim Personal Statements in Managing Victims' Voices in Sentencing in Northern Ireland: Taking a More Procedural Justice Approach' (2017) 68 Northern Ireland Legal Quarterly 4.

72 Focus group IR07.

7 Responding to abuse in Ireland

What can the Catholic Church learn from the Truth and Reconciliation Commission of Canada?

Gladys Ganiel
Queen's University Belfast

Introduction

> The priest grabbed him, grabbed him by the hair, threw him down. Now, that was a cement floor where we played. And here he kicked him repeatedly. There was no stick. He had brand new boots, leather. I was sitting not too far away. I wasn't very big. I still can't forget to this day. It's like I'm still watching him. It must have been ten minutes. These were brand new boots. On the thighs and the buttocks. He bounced his boots off him as he kicked him … Now the principal said to him. 'George,' he said, 'you will kneel there until six o'clock,' he told him.[1]

These words might have been spoken by a survivor of clerical abuse in Ireland.[2] But this story is that of Adam Highway, a First Nations survivor who testified before the Truth and Reconciliation Commission (TRC) of Canada.

In 2015, the TRC released its final reports on the abuse of children in Indian Residential Schools (IRS). For more than a century, the schools were administered through a partnership between the Canadian Government and the Christian churches, including the Catholic, Anglican, United, Methodist and Presbyterian churches. The Canadian Government has estimated that about 150,000 First Nation, Métis and Inuit children were removed from their parents and communities to attend the schools, where many were physically, sexually and spiritually abused. About 3,200 died from tuberculosis, malnutrition

1 Testimony of Adam Highway, on witnessing the principal of Sturgeon Landing, Saskatchewan, beating a pupil in the 1920s. *The Survivors Speak: A Report of the Canadian Truth and Reconciliation Commission* (Truth and Reconciliation Commission of Canada 2015) 144.

2 This paper confines its discussion to the Republic of Ireland.

DOI: 10.4324/9780429023149-8

and other diseases before the closure of the last school in 1996.[3] The TRC ran over seven years, featuring seven centrepiece national events and various community-based events. It collected 6,750 individual statements, to be archived at a National Centre for Truth and Reconciliation at the University of Manitoba.[4] The TRC found that the IRS system had been part of a deliberate State–Church policy of 'cultural genocide', and made 94 recommendations in areas including health, education, justice, public inquiry, monitoring reconciliation, language, commemoration and memorials.

The TRC can be understood as part of a broader 'transitional justice' process[5] or 'culture of redress' in Canada.[6] Taken together, these measures have attempted to address human vulnerability in relation to abuse. The TRC was established as part of the 2006 Indian Residential Schools Settlement Agreement (IRSSA) between the government, churches and First Nations survivors. IRSSA was the largest class action settlement in Canadian history, and included a $2 billion compensation package. Its five components were: a Common Experience Payment (average $28,000 to each survivor, whether they had been individually abused or not); an Independent Assessment Process, through which those who experienced the most serious abuse received additional compensation payments; a commemoration fund ($20 million for national and local projects); funding for health and healing services; and the TRC. The Canadian government, Protestant churches and some of the Catholic religious congregations and orders also issued apologies. The Government apology, coming in 2008 in Parliament, was delivered by the Prime Minister and witnessed by First Nations representatives. TRCs have generally been adopted in countries transitioning from violent, internal conflicts. So the Canadian TRC is unusual, which prompted Kim Stanton to argue (emphasis mine):[7] 'The fact that the IRS negotiators decided to have a TRC in addition to and separate from these other aspects of the settlement *suggests that there is something to be gained from having the TRC process itself.*' In Canada, survivors and their allies fought for a TRC over many years, because they believed the previous efforts of the State and churches did not go far enough. The TRC was not a result of benevolence on the part of the State, churches, or the general population. As Stanton puts it:[8]

> The TRC was not created out of a groundswell of concern about IRS survivors by the public; rather it was agreed to by their government's legal

3 Susana Mas, 'Truth and Reconciliation Final Report Points to "Growing Crisis" for Indigenous Youth' *CBC News* (14 December 2015).

4 Matt James, 'On Carnival and Context: A Response to Bridget Storrie' (2015) 9 International Journal of Transitional Justice 486.

5 James Gallen, 'Jesus Wept: The Roman Catholic Church, Child Sexual Abuse and Transitional Justice' (2016) 10 International Journal of Transitional Justice 332.

6 Jennifer Henderson and Pauline Wakeham (eds) *Reconciling Canada: Critical Perspectives on the Culture of Redress* (Toronto: University of Toronto Press 2013).

7 Kim Stanton, 'Canada's Truth and Reconciliation Commission: Settling the Past?' (2011) 2(3) *International Indigenous Policy Journal* 11.

8 Ibid.

> advisers in order to settle costly litigation. Were it not for the enormous financial costs to the government of continuing to defend against the class actions, the TRC would not exist in Canada.

Canada's TRC, then, seems to have been conceived to meet the needs of survivors, which were not being met in other ways.

Like Canada before its TRC, the State and Catholic Church in Ireland (hereafter Church)[9] already have implemented a number of measures for addressing human vulnerability in relation to abuse. But again, like Canada, there is a sense that this has not been enough. This chapter builds on previous contributions in this volume, recognising the failures of the Irish State and Church in addressing human vulnerability in relation to abuse. It emphasises that the Church is widely perceived as not having responded as well as the State to abuse, and explores the reasons why.

By focusing on the Church, this chapter pushes the application of vulnerability theory beyond the State. It argues that vulnerability theory also can be a useful point of engagement for churches (or other institutions) that have been implicated in abuse. Indeed, while Fineman is known for emphasising the decisive role and responsibility of the State in protecting the vulnerable, she also has argued that the 'inevitable dependency' of the vulnerable 'should be the concern of society generally, with responsibility shared across social institutions'.[10] A focus on the responsibility of the Church in addressing the needs of the vulnerable is appropriate not only because of its history of involvement in abuse, but also because it is one of society's main providers of 'existential resources', which Fineman argues are essential for human flourishing and resilience.[11]

In that light, this chapter explores how, despite some efforts, the Church has not adequately apologised or acknowledged its responsibility in failing the most vulnerable children and women who were placed in its care. Nor has it made the structural changes that would be necessary to ensure that the most vulnerable are protected and nourished in the future. Then, the chapter asks what the Church might learn from Canada's TRC. Although it is still too early to definitively evaluate its effects and effectiveness, two key lessons stand out: 1) a 'victim-centred' TRC can meet *some* survivors' needs for recognition and acknowledgement, beyond what is offered through apologies, inquiries and reparations; and 2) Canada's TRC has *theoretically* established a basis not just for *individual* healing and reconciliation, but for *social structural change.* Its 'calls to action,' if fully implemented, could provide a basis for structural changes to address wider legacies of past abuse. It may be naïve to hope that either the Church or State would establish a TRC in Ireland, even if a Canadian-style TRC could supplement and enhance how Ireland deals with the legacy of

9 Hereafter the Catholic Church will be referred to simply as the Church. This is for simplicity's sake, and not to obscure the fact that there are other churches in Ireland.

10 Martha Fineman, 'Vulnerability and Inevitable Inequality' (2017) Oslo Law Review 139.

11 Ibid, 146.

abuse. But, given the widespread perception that the Church has not done enough, the chapter concludes by asking how activists within the Irish Church might apply lessons from Canada's TRC to the current context. While activists face significant obstacles in their efforts, vulnerability theory may provide a useful point of engagement for their work, building on emerging theologies that are already grappling with the abuse crisis.

The Church and human vulnerability: the failure to address abuse

The failures of the Irish State to address human vulnerability in the form of abuse have been detailed in this volume. In contrast, this chapter focuses on the failures of the Church, pushing the application of vulnerability theory beyond the State. This is not to say that what the State has done should be without criticism; rather, those criticisms are valid and are articulated elsewhere.[12] But there is a sense that at least the State has done *something*, whereas the Church is perceived as having done almost *nothing*. This was apparent during Pope Francis' visit to Ireland in August 2018. It was captured neatly in a speech by Taoiseach Leo Varadkar, delivered at a civic reception:[13]

> Holy Father, I believe that the time has now come for us to build a new relationship between church and state in Ireland – a new covenant for the 21st Century. It is my hope that your visit marks the opening of a new chapter in the relationship between Ireland and the Catholic Church. Building on our intertwined history, and learning from our shared mistakes, it can be one in which religion is no longer at the centre of our society, but in which it still has an important place.

Varadkar was widely praised for the speech, with one commentator calling it 'one of the finest speeches of his career and one of the best of our recent political history'.[14] Varadkar acknowledged 'the failures of both Church and State and wider society', which had 'created a bitter and broken heritage for so many, leaving a legacy of pain and suffering'. His words highlighted that Church and State were jointly responsible for abuse, signalling a need for responses from both Church and State authorities. But the very fact that it was the Taoiseach, rather than a Church leader, proposing a 'new covenant' signalled that the balance of power between Church and State in Ireland had shifted decisively. And even though Varadkar

12 Anne-Marie McAlinden, 'An Inconvenient Truth: Barriers to Truth Recovery in the Aftermath of Institutional Child Abuse in Ireland' (2013) Legal Studies 189.

13 Speech of An Taoiseach, Leo Varadkar, on the occasion of the visit of Pope Francis (25 August 2018) www.taoiseach.gov.ie/eng/News/Taoiseach's_Speeches/Speech_of_An_Taoiseach_Leo_Varadkar_on_the_occasion_of_the_Visit_of_Pope_Francis.html (last accessed 14 December 2020).

14 Simon Carswell, 'Varadkar Sets out his Blueprint for New Covenant' *Irish Times* (Dublin, 27 August 2018).

stated that Church and State should share responsibility for abuses, it seemed that Varadkar had somehow managed – albeit graciously – to place most of the blame on the Church. This was exemplified by his pleas to the pope to 'use your office and influence' to 'bring about justice and truth and healing for victims and survivors'. With this subtle shifting of blame to the Church, Varadkar failed to fully acknowledge that the dependency of vulnerable people was caused by a mutually reinforcing Church–State relationship characterised by the State's deferral to and reliance on Church authorities. In contrast, Smith has described how the State facilitated Church abuse, calling the State's outsourcing of the care of vulnerable people to the Church a 'willing abdication of responsibility'. He detailed a process in which vulnerable women and children were not protected but rather abused and/or stigmatised as sexually immoral by both Church and State, highlighting 'political discourses [that] legitimized state practices of institutionalizing many of its most vulnerable citizens'.[15] So when Fineman asks, 'does the state monitor a given institution in a way that is responsive to human vulnerability?'; the answer in the case of historical abuse in Ireland is an unequivocal 'no'.[16]

Varadkar's pleas to the Pope also reflected widespread public opinion that the Church, and Francis himself, have not done enough to address abuse, in Ireland or internationally.[17] In the build-up to Francis' visit, which was part of the international World Meeting of Families, I argued that 'the national conversation became dominated by the issue of abuse – so much so that the visit seemed to have become an unofficial referendum on the papal response to abuse'.[18] In my research on the papal visit, I found that 46 per cent of articles in the country's 'newspaper of record', the *Irish Times,* during the month of August engaged with the abuse crisis in some way. It dominated the news more than any other topic, reflecting public indignation. I also commissioned a nationally representative survey after the visit, which found that the dominant opinion (48 percent) was that Francis had not gone far enough to address abuse during his visit, with 30 per cent saying he had gone far enough and 22 per cent neither/nor or no opinion. In addition, even though Francis met privately with survivors and made an unprecedented and powerful plea for forgiveness during the penitential rite at his mass in the Phoenix Park, only 31 percent of people agreed that visit had been 'a healing time for victims and survivors of clerical sex abuse'. Finally, for those who did not attend any events associated with the papal visit, that top reason was because 'I was not interested' (51 per cent), followed by 30 per cent who did not attend because 'I disagree with how the Catholic Church has handled child sex abuse'. In what follows, the failures of the Church in addressing human vulnerability are presented in contrast to

15 James M. Smith, *Ireland's Magdalen Laundries and the Nation's Architecture of Containment* (Notre Dame, IN: University of Notre Dame Press 2007) 4–5.

16 Martha Fineman 'Vulnerability and Inevitable Inequality' (n 10) 145.

17 Gladys Ganiel, 'Negating the Francis Effect? The Effect of the Abuse Crisis in Ireland' in Giuseppe Giordan (ed.) *Research in the Social Scientific Study of Religion* (Leiden: Brill 2019) 335.

18 Ibid.

State actions, demonstrating why the State is perceived as having done more than the Church through apologies, inquiries and redress/reparations. Focusing on the Church underlines the urgent need for it to continue grappling with its responsibilities for abuse, while at the same time illustrating that it could benefit from engagement with vulnerability theory.

Apologies

Apologies 'have been repeatedly cited as one of the highest priorities of victims/survivors of institutional abuse'.[19] A large-scale, cross-national study of apologies has identified five elements that must be present if an apology is to be perceived as sincere: acknowledgement of the wrong; acceptance of responsibility; expression of regret; assurance of non-repetition; and an offer of repair or corrective action.[20] The context and setting of the apology also are important: who delivers it, what venue it is in and who else is present. Taking these criteria into consideration, in Ireland, apologies made on behalf of the State have been perceived as more sincere than those made on behalf of the Church. For example, Catterall et al. pointed out the positive qualities of an apology about the Magdalene Laundries by Taoiseach Enda Kenny in 2013, which was well received by survivors. Catterall et al. also contrasted Taoiseach Bertie Ahern's 1999 apology in the Dáil to that of Cardinal Seán Brady:[21]

> Ahern unequivocally accepted the State's complicity in the abuse and mistreatment of children in institutional care due to the 'failure to intervene, to detect their pain, to come to their rescue,' and committed to providing redress to victims/survivors. This approach sits in contrast to Cardinal Seán Brady's response to criticism over his involvement in silencing two victims/survivors of abuse by Fr. Brendan Smyth in 1975, and for not passing suspected cases of abuse to the civil authorities … [While] Brady vaguely apologised in 2010 during Easter mass for 'hurt' caused by 'any failure on my part,' he later claimed that it was not his responsibility to pass on allegations.

Ahern's apology also was accompanied by a list of 99 measures to address abuse, including a nationwide counselling service, inquiry processes, the Residential Institutions Redress Board (RIRB) and 'legislative changes to enable victims/survivors to press charges against abusers'.[22] By 2014, 94 of the measures had been implemented, demonstrating 'the State's continued commitment to repairing past wrongs'.[23]

19 Emma Catterall, in association with McEvoy et al., *Apologies and Institutional Child Abuse* (Queen's University Belfast 2018) 1, https://apologies-abuses-past.org.uk/assets/uploads/Apologies-Institutional-Abuse-Report_Sept-2018.pdf (last accessed 14 December 2020).

20 Ibid, 7.

21 Ibid, 8.

22 Ibid, 10.

23 Ibid.

The Church also has apologised for abuse in Ireland at the highest level, including an apology by Pope Benedict in his 2010 Pastoral Letter to the Catholics of Ireland.[24] Indeed, one of the 'calls to action' in Canada's final TRC report was for the Pope to apologise for the IRS. The report specifically cited the precedent of Benedict's apology to the Irish. Yet Benedict's apology was not well received in Ireland, in part because he seemed to blame secularism and a lack of faith among the Irish for the abuse. Francis' pleas for forgiveness at the Phoenix Park mass also can be understood as an apology. He was remarkably specific and contrite about the wrongs committed by the Church, seeming to meet important requirements for a sincere apology:[25]

> We ask for forgiveness for those places of exploitation of manual work, that so many young women and men were subjected to … In a special way we ask pardon for all the abuses committed in various types of institutions run by male or female religious, and by other members of the church … We ask forgiveness, for the time that as a church we did not show the survivors of whatever kind of abuse compassion, in the seeking of justice and truth, and concrete actions … We ask forgiveness for some members of the church hierarchy, who did not take charge of these painful situations and kept quiet. We ask for forgiveness for all those single mothers who were told that to seek their children that had been separated from them … that this was a mortal sin, this is not a mortal sin.

Even though this apology was regarded as significant, even unprecedented, there was disappointment that Francis did not identify specific actions on how to tackle abuse. This apology also must be seen in the wider context of all the apologies by Benedict and Irish bishops, which have been received as insincere exercises of damage limitation. As Catterall et al. concluded: 'given the repeated partial and non-apologies offered by Church leaders since the late 1990s, an additional obstacle may stem from its overuse of apologies, rendering any future meaningful apology suspect'.[26]

The negative reception of Church apologies when compared to the State may not be due solely to the substance of the apologies themselves. Fineman's argument that the 'solution' for vulnerability is 'resilience' sheds some light on other dynamics that may be at play. She identifies five 'resources or assets' on which resilience depends: physical (material and economic quality of life); human (access to education and other resources); social (family, social networks, communities); ecological or environmental; and existential – including

24 'Pastoral Letter of the Holy Father Pope Benedict XVI to the Catholics of Ireland' (2010) http://w2.vatican.va/content/benedict-xvi/en/letters/2010/documents/hf_ben-xvi_let_20100319_church-ireland.html (accessed 14 December 2020).

25 Quoted in Jack Power and Simon Carswell, 'Pope Asks for Forgiveness for Abuses and Exploitation during Papal Mass' *Irish Times* (Dublin, 27 August 2018).

26 Catterall, in association with Kieran McEvoy et al., *Apologies and Institutional Child Abuse* (n 19) 15.

systems of belief such as religion, culture or art.[27] Over the course of their lives, survivors of abuse, who may have been confined in institutions like industrial schools, Magdalene Laundries, or mother and baby homes, find it much more difficult to access any of the resources that promote resilience. The impact of this lack is cumulative over time, making survivors more likely to remain vulnerable because they have not had opportunities to acquire the resources that would enable them to gain privilege and power in other social institutions. For those with few resources and lacking resilience, even a specific, sincere apology rings hollow.

It also could be argued that the Church has failed to promote resilience in the existential domain, where it has not adequately grappled with how its beliefs and teachings enabled abuse,[28] or articulated theologies that, to use Fineman's description of a resilient belief system, 'allow us to see meaning and beauty in our existence'.[29] At the same time, while Ireland's religiosity is still high by European standards, it has experienced a rapid decline, which could indicate that the Church is not providing the kind of existential resources that are essential for resilience in the face of all types of adversity, not just surviving abuse.[30] In contrast, it could be argued that some State-led reforms (including redress for survivors and reforms stripping the Church of some of its powers in education and health) have improved access to physical and human resources among survivors and the wider society. Such reforms may have improved *some* individuals' resilience, making them more receptive to State apologies.

Inquiries

There has been a series of inquiries into abuse by the State: the Diocese of Ferns (Ferns Report 2005), the Archdiocese of Dublin (Murphy Report 2009); the Commission to Inquire into Child Abuse in reformatory and industrial schools (Ryan Report 2009), the Diocese of Cloyne (Cloyne Report 2011), the Magdalene Laundries (McAleese Report 2013), and the Mother and Baby Homes Commission of Investigation (Report 2021). The inquiries had a significant public impact, generating vast amounts of media coverage and exposing the horror of abuse over many years. But the Church seemed to fare worse than the State through the inquiries. The Vatican did not release relevant documents to the Irish State during the Ferns, Murphy and Cloyne inquiries. Citizens were reminded of all this in the weeks before Francis' visit, when former President Mary McAleese revealed that she had been approached in 2003 by

27 Martha Fineman, 'Equality, Autonomy, and the Vulnerable Subject in Law and Politics' in Martha Fineman and Anna Grear (eds.) *Vulnerability: Reflections on a New Ethical Foundation for Law and Politics* (Farnham: Ashgate 2007) 22–23.

28 Kate Gleeson and Aleardo Zanghellini, 'Graceful Remedies: Understanding Grace in the Catholic Church's Treatment of Clerical Child Sexual Abuse' (2015) 41 Australian Feminist Law Journal.

29 Fineman, 'Vulnerability and Inevitable Inequality' (n 10) 146.

30 Gladys Ganiel, *Transforming Post-Catholic Ireland* (Oxford: Oxford University Press 2016).

a Vatican diplomat who proposed a concordant between the Vatican and Irish State which would have ensured all Church documentation was denied to State investigations.[31] In 2017, the Children First Act came into effect. This also is seen as a State response to abuse, requiring mandatory reporting of child abuse for professionals across a spectrum of health, social and civic services.

In contrast, the inquiries have demonstrated that the Church has not always followed its own child protection procedures. In 1996, the Irish Catholic Bishops adopted a guidelines document, 'Child Sexual Abuse: Framework for a Church Response'. But the Cloyne investigation found that 'until 2008, there was a deliberate effort to conceal clerical abuse in the diocese – 12 years after the Framework Document was implemented'.[32] The Church also established a National Board for Safeguarding Children (NBSC) in 2006. While it seems that to an extent this body has helped to improve policy and monitor practice, the Church has on occasion denied it information. A former CEO, Ian Elliott, threatened to sue Archbishop Noel Treanor over an NBSC Report which omitted a serious case of abuse. The report instead said that Treanor's Diocese of Down and Conor had complied 'fully' with good child protection practice.[33] Some, like survivor Marie Collins, have questioned the independence of the NBSC and said that the State should assume responsibility for the safety of children in the Catholic Church.[34] In its own review in 2017, the NBSC found that three out of four of the religious orders that gave evidence in Northern Ireland's Historical Abuse Inquiry 'failed to implement any of the Board's standards'.[35] One of the few exceptions of a church leader who is perceived to be following through, at least in part, is former Archbishop of Dublin Diarmuid Martin. Martin has criticised a Vatican document which says bishops can use discretion on reporting abuse to authorities, publicly stating that all allegations of abuse must be reported to police.[36] An international victims group called End Clergy Abuse has even stated that Martin should be made the head of the Vatican's child protection commission.[37]

While it cannot be classified as an inquiry, the Church commissioned a major research project with the aims of understanding and addressing abuse. In 2000, the Irish Bishops' Committee on Child Abuse (now the Bishops' Committee on

31 Patsy McGarry, 'Vatican Has Never Co-operated with Irish inquiries into Clerical Child Sex Abuse' *Irish Times* (Dublin, 7 August 2018).

32 Catterall, in association with Kieran McEvoy et al., *Apologies and Institutional Child Abuse* (n 19) 9.

33 'Ian Elliott May Sue Catholic Bishop over Child Protection Report' *BBC News* (8 March 2014).

34 Sarah MacDonald, 'Archbishop Says it Would be "Disaster" if Church Watchdog Loses Trust' *Irish Independent* (Dublin, 10 March 2014).

35 Catterall, in association with Kieran McEvoy et al., *Apologies and Institutional Child Abuse* (n 19) 9.

36 Patsy McGarry, 'Archbishop Says all Allegations of Clerical Abuse Must Be Reported' *The Irish Times* (Dublin, 11 February 2016).

37 Simon Carswell, 'Victims' Group Calls on Pope to Name Sex Abusers' *The Irish Times* (Dublin, 25 August 2018).

Child Protection) employed the Health Services Research Centre at the Department of Psychology at the Royal College of Surgeons to study child sexual abuse by clergy. The results were published in a 2003 book.[38] This study was its first of its kind in the world, preceding the more well-known study carried out by John Jay College at the request of the US Conference of Catholic Bishops. The research consisted of a telephone survey of the general public in the Republic (N=1,081), which garnered an impressive 76 per cent response rate – clearly the Irish wanted to talk about these issues. The researchers also conducted 48 face-to-face interviews, including those who had experienced abuse (7), family members of those who had experienced abuse (3), convicted clergy (8), family members of convicted clergy (5) and church personnel (4 colleagues of clerical abusers and 20 other clergy and laypeople who worked for the church). Finally, the researchers surveyed 'all 153 diocesan and religious delegates[39] in all 44 Episcopal Conferences and retired bishops, including the Republic and Northern Ireland.[40] Among other things, the study found that the public were generally unaware of Church initiatives to address abuse. Just 33 per cent were aware of initiatives like 'financial compensation, providing counselling and making apologies', with 23 per cent aware of 'public statements, conferences and sermons'. Only 10 per cent had heard of the Irish Catholic Bishops' Advisory Committee's framework document.[41] If the general public were asked today if they had heard of this study, it is likely that the vast majority would not have heard of it or its myriad recommendations about how the Church could improve its responses to abuse. The researchers noted that this lack of knowledge could be down to a failure of the Church to communicate, as well as a lack of media coverage.[42]

Reparations

Redress or reparations payments have been distributed through the State's Residential Institutions Redress Board, established in 2002. A 2002 'congregational indemnity agreement' between the Irish Ministers for Finance and Education and the Conference of Religious in Ireland, representing 18 religious orders, ensured the State would pay most of the bill. The Department of Finance had recommended compensation be split 50:50 between the State and religious congregations. But the congregations' contributions were capped at around €128 million. The final compensation bill was about €1.5 billion.[43] The deal was finalised on the last day of government before elections, without debate in the

38 Helen Goode, Hannah McGee and Ciarán O'Boyle, *Time to Listen: Confronting Child Sexual Abuse by Catholic Clergy in Ireland* (Dublin: Liffey Press 2003).

39 Members of clergy responsible for receiving allegations of clerical child sexual abuse (including priests and religious).

40 Goode et al., *Time to Listen* (n 38) xxii.

41 Ibid, 192.

42 Ibid, 206.

43 Press Association, 'Religious Orders Have Paid Just 13% of Bill for Child Abuse Inquiry – Watchdog' *Irish Independent* (Dublin, 9 March 2017).

Dáil or cabinet approval. As McDonald put it: 'Irish taxpayers are to fund most of what is likely to be the largest payout from public funds to child abuse victims anywhere in the world.'[44] In 2010, in the wake of the Ryan Report, the government made another request to the congregations to split the payments 50:50. The congregations agreed to pay an additional €353 million, which was reduced to €226 million in 2015.[45] The average compensation payment has been just under €70,000, with a proportion of the costs paid to solicitors and barristers.[46] A separate scheme was established for survivors of the Magdalene Laundries in 2013, which featured a type of common experience payment, one which is not 'dependent on any proof of hardship, injury or abuse', but rather 'based on the duration of time spent in the Magdalene Laundries'.[47] The four congregations of nuns that operated the laundries simply refused to contribute compensation.[48] In 2017, the State's Comptroller and Auditor General found that the orders had paid only 13 per cent of the bill for inquiries, redress and compensation schemes.[49] So it is unsurprising that, in Ireland, criticism of the compensation payments centres on the fact that the Church seems to be contributing so little.

In sum, it seems that, when compared to the State, the Church has not adequately apologised or acknowledged its responsibility in failing the vulnerable children and women who were placed in its care. Further, by failing to recognise universal experiences of dependency and vulnerability, the Church has 'othered' victims of historical abuse in ways that prevent it from framing vulnerability and the opportunities for abuse it presents as potentially a current and future problem. Subsequently, it is not clear that the Church has made the structural changes that are necessary to ensure that the most vulnerable are protected and nourished in the future. Even when it has made efforts to understand abuse and to ensure that it does not happen again, the wider population remains unaware of what it has done. And, finally, the Church has been perceived as stingy in its failure to contribute larger sums for reparations.

Learning from Canada's TRC

In Canada, survivors believed that the State and churches had not done enough to address abuse. They lobbied for a TRC in part because they felt *there is something to be gained from having the TRC process itself.* This is an assumption

44 Henry McDonald, 'Dail and Church Agree €1.3bn Payout to Child Abuse Victims' *Guardian* (London, 1 January 2006).

45 Press Association, 'Religious Orders Have Paid Just 13% of Bill for Child Abuse Inquiry – Watchdog'(n 43).

46 Jim Cusack and Daniel McConnell, 'Lawyers Profit as Cost of Clerical Abuse Tops €1bn, *Irish Independent* (Dublin, 14 October 2012).

47 ICAP, 'Redress Scheme for Magdalene Survivors' (28 June 2013) www.icap.org.uk/redress-scheme-for-magdalene-survivors/ (accessed 1 September 2016).

48 'Religious Congregations Refuse to Contribute to Magdalene Redress Fund' *RTE News* (Dublin, 16 July 2013).

49 Press Association, 'Religious Orders Have Paid Just 13% of Bill for Child Abuse Inquiry – Watchdog' (n 43).

that takes a largely positive view of TRCs in general, even while recognising their limits. Specifically, it assumes that there is something about the public, symbolic and performative elements of a TRC that meet survivors' needs for recognition and acknowledgement. What follows is a short and largely benign analysis of Canada's TRC, which identifies two lessons that are relevant for the Irish context: a 'victim-centred' TRC can meet *some* survivors' needs for recognition and acknowledgement, beyond what is offered through apologies, inquiries and reparations; and Canada's TRC has *theoretically* established a basis not just for *individual* healing and reconciliation, but for *social structural change* – what Rosemary Nagy calls 'social accountability through public education', as well as reforms that address the legacies of colonisation, the IRS system and Canada's 'Indian policy'.[50]

Canada's TRC took what is called in the transitional justice literature a 'victim-centred' approach, where the priority is hearing what victims have to say. This is said to constitute a 'symbolic reversal of power relations'. In telling their stories, and having their suffering affirmed, survivors were promised that they were contributing to the writing of new versions of Canadian history, as well as giving themselves the opportunity for 'personal healing through truth telling'.[51]

Teresa Godwin Phelps has distinguished between perpetrator-centred and victim-centred approaches in TRCs, with perpetrator-centred approaches most concerned with identifying perpetrators and their misdeeds, which in some contexts may lead to prosecution. Benefits of perpetrator-centred approaches are that survivors may gain a fuller understanding of what actually happened and of their tormentors' rationale for their actions; survivors also may feel that justice has been done if perpetrators are prosecuted.[52] In Canada, there was a ban on 'naming names' at the TRC, effectively ruling out prosecutions resulting from it. But Phelps also has argued that perpetrator-centred approaches can marginalise survivors' perspectives, and as a result their stories are not valued appropriately.

As such, the very process of staging a victim-centred TRC gives survivors a greater degree of recognition and acknowledgement for their suffering than would otherwise be the case.[53] Collecting the stories of survivors through other means, such as inquiries, does not seem to achieve the same level of public recognition and acknowledgement. Unlike an inquiry, a TRC provides survivors with opportunities to tell their story in the context of a public, ritualised ceremony with symbolic fanfare. In Canada, the dedicated archive of TRC

50 Rosemary L. Nagy, 'The Scope and Bounds of Transitional Justice and the Canadian Truth and Reconciliation Commission' (2013) 7 International Journal of Transitional Justice 64.

51 Matt James, 'A Carnival of Truth? Knowledge, Ignorance and the Canadian Truth and Reconciliation Commission' (2012) 6 International Journal of Transitional Justice 195.

52 Teresa Godwin Phelps, *Shattered Voices: Language, Violence, and the Work of Truth Commissions* (University of Pennsylvania Press 2004).

53 Brieg Capitaine and Karine Vanthuyne (eds.) *Power through Testimony: Reframing Residential Schools in the Age of Reconciliation* (UBC Press 2017).

submissions and testimonies ensures that these stories are accessible. So, in Fineman's terms, we might conceive of a victim-centred TRC as a mechanism that promotes 'resiliency', to the extent that it creates a symbolic reversal of the prior dependency of survivors on Church and State. Further, by privileging survivors' stories, a victim-centred TRC also may help individuals create or access existential resources that recognise not just their suffering, but their perseverance when abused.

But there are limits to victim-centred approaches to TRCs. Some may not want to talk (or write a submission) about their abuse, and feel marginalised from the process.[54] In the absence of prosecutions or being able to compel perpetrators to appear, TRCs may appear light on justice and heavy on a type of symbolic recognition that lets those with power and authority get away with their crimes.

Indeed, over the course of Canada's TRC many scholars doubted that it would have the teeth to recommend and see through the structural changes that could take it beyond providing recognition and acknowledgement. Matt James called it a costly 'distraction exercise' that would not really get to the root of colonial legacies.[55] But the TRC issued 94 'calls to action', with some of the more hard-hitting recommendations coming as a 'big surprise', to quote James again.[56] High-profile recommendations included calling on the Canadian Government to implement the UN Declaration on the Rights of Indigenous Peoples, and establishing an inquiry into missing Aboriginal women and girls. At the conclusion of the TRC, Conservative Prime Minister Stephen Harper would not commit to implementing the calls to action. But Liberal Prime Minister Justin Trudeau, elected in 2015, pledged to implement them all. Although progress has been slower than critics would like, in May 2016 Canada adopted the UN Declaration. In August 2016, Canada launched an independent inquiry into missing and murdered indigenous women and girls, with a final report issued in 2019.[57] The report found that 'persistent and deliberate human and Indigenous rights violations and abuses are the root cause behind Canada's staggering rates of violence against Indigenous women, girls and 2SLGBTQQIA people'.[58]

The calls to action also include changes in education. There is a call to make teaching about 'residential schools, Treaties, and Aboriginal peoples historical and contemporary contributions to Canada' mandatory from Kindergarten

54 Anne-Marie Reynaud, *Emotions, Remembering and Feeling Better: Dealing with the Indian Residential Schools Settlement Agreement in Canada* (Transcript, 2017).

55 Matt James, 'Uncomfortable Comparisons: The Canadian Truth and Reconciliation Commission in International Context' (2010) 5(2) The Ethics Forum/Les ateliers de l'éthnique 26.

56 Matt James, 'Changing the Subject: The TRC and the Displacement of Substantive Reconciliation in Canadian Media Representations' 51(2) (2017) Journal of Canadian Studies 366.

57 'Ottawa launches inquiry into missing and murdered indigenous women' *BBC News* (3 August 2016).

58 National Inquiry into Missing and Murdered Indigenous Women and Girls, 'Reclaiming Power and Place' www.mmiwg-ffada.ca/final-report/ (2019).

(primary school) to Grade Twelve (secondary school)', which requires the development of new curriculum and learning resources.[59] Denominational schools should be required 'to provide an education on comparative religious studies, which must include a segment on Aboriginal spiritual beliefs and practices developed in collaboration with Aboriginal Elders'.[60] These changes would need to happen at the provincial level, reflecting Canada's federalist government structure. At third level, federal government should 'establish a national research program with multi-year funding to advance understanding of reconciliation'.[61] There are further education-themed calls to actions for churches, youth programmes, museums and archives, public servants and journalists. In Fineman's terms, these calls to action could go some way towards promoting 'resiliency' by improving both survivors and the wider society's access to education-based human resources. At the same time, there have been limits to the structural calls to action. Some First Nations people felt alienated by the TRC process because it did not address what they saw as a fundamental structural issue: the impact of broken treaties including the loss of their lands.[62]

It is too early to offer a definitive evaluation of how the TRC and its 'calls to action' are promoting structural change in Canada. But the TRC pushed beyond what the State had already offered in terms of reforms in areas like health, education, justice, public inquiry, monitoring reconciliation, language, commemoration and memorials. What's important in terms of the Irish comparison is the recognition that structural change is necessary, and that a TRC can be a useful mechanism for identifying the reforms that could bring it about.

Concluding reflections

There is much the Irish Church and State could learn from Canada's TRC; perhaps the most obvious lesson is that a victim-centred, Canadian-style TRC could complement and enhance their current responses to human vulnerability. The usefulness of a TRC hinges on its ability to promote recognition, acknowledgement and meaningful structural changes, which have been missing in the Irish context.

Yet Ireland is not unique in this regard. James Gallen has argued that, cross-nationally, Church and State responses to abuse have not modelled victim-centred approaches to human vulnerability or engendered meaningful structural changes.[63] Gallen concluded that 'transitional justice'-style approaches like those used after violent conflicts, including TRCs, could enhance the international Catholic Church's and States' responses to abuse. He seemed to envision

59 *Truth and Reconciliation Commission of Canada: Calls to Action* (Truth and Reconciliation Commission of Canada – 2015) 7.

60 Ibid, 7–8.

61 Ibid, 8.

62 Anne-Marie Reynaud, *Emotions, Remembering and Feeling Better* (n 54).

63 James Gallen, 'Jesus Wept' (n 5) 349.

an international, truth-commission-type mechanism, in which the Church assumed significant responsibilities (emphasis mine):

> A comprehensive cross-country analysis of the causes and nature of the abuse, including levels of state knowledge and consideration of the impact of Catholic theology and doctrine, *could reflect a commitment from the church to take the interests of victims/survivors seriously* ... Employing transitional justice to address this abuse offers a coherent and clarifying analytical framework to pursue these challenging and pressing goals.

While the Vatican's record of responding to abuse makes such a suggestion seem unlikely, Gallen's emphasis on the responsibility of the Church points to an expansion of vulnerability theory beyond the State. Given this focus on the Church's responsibilities, how might activists within the Irish Church apply lessons from Canada's TRC to the current context? This is a challenging question, and one which it is very difficult for churches which have been implicated in abuse to ask. After all, although in other contexts the churches have led efforts to establish a TRC, this was not the case in Canada.[64] It also is a complicated question, because the Church exists at many levels, including the laity in parishes, religious orders and congregations, diocesan clergy, bishops and the Vatican. It is unclear who could or would take responsibility for such a project. Theoretically the Irish bishops would have the most power to create such a mechanism, but in light of recent experience it may be unrealistic to expect a bold project like a TRC to emerge from that quarter.

But, if the Irish Church were to instigate structural changes that resulted in greater lay participation – for instance, by establishing a national assembly or regional synods (as recommended by activists like Irish Jesuit Gerry O'Hanlon) – it is possible that bodies like these could be inspired by Canada's TRC to propose mechanisms for victims/survivors that could promote recognition, acknowledgement and further structural changes in the Church.[65] To use Fineman's terms, such bodies could be conceived as new Church-related social institutions that provide people with access to the types of human and existential resources that promote resiliency. In 2021, the Irish Bishops Conference announced that it would hold a national synod within the next five years, but it is not certain that abuse will be addressed. In this light, it is worth noting that Canada's largest churches are engaging with the recommendations of the TRC which were directed towards them. While Hughes has highlighted the limitations of the churches' engagement – including a tendency for churches

64 Kevin Lewis O'Neill, 'Writing Guatemala's Genocide: Truth and Reconciliation Commission Reports and Christianity' 7(3) (2005) Journal of Genocide Research.

65 Gerry O'Hanlon *The Quiet Revolution of Pope Francis: A Synodal Catholic Church in Ireland?* (Dublin: Messenger Publications 2018).

to reframe themselves as co-victims of the IRS system,[66] it is still possible that the process *may* result in more radical new theologies and structural changes within these churches.[67] However, any TRC-style mechanisms would require financial resources from the Irish Church, something that cannot be taken for granted given its record on contributions to reparations.

Gallen's recommendation that analysis of abuse should include 'the impact of Catholic theology and doctrine' hints at a further area of focus for activists within the Irish Church: articulating theologies that respond to the abuse crisis. Such theologies have already emerged in Ireland, including Ethna Regan's articulation of a new 'political theology' and David Tombs' conception of Christ as a victim of sexual abuse. It is beyond the scope of this chapter to examine these theologies in detail. But both have vulnerability as a starting point, providing useful bases for engagement with vulnerability theory. Regan critiques the wider tradition of Catholic social teaching, noting that children are 'barely visible' in its key documents, an oversight of the most vulnerable which has made the Church susceptible to social, structural sin – and has resulted in abuse.[68] Tombs explores how the physical torture associated with Christ's crucifixion would have been understood as sexual abuse in the Roman context, and asks whether the identification of Christ as vulnerable in this way could serve as a transformational challenge within the Church and potential source of healing for victims.[69] While as yet untested, vulnerability theory could provide a useful framework for engagement for Irish activists and theologians. If accompanied by reforms to promote recognition, acknowledgement and meaningful structural changes, new theologies that engage with vulnerability theory could provide existential resources that contribute to human flourishing and resilience.

66 Jula Hughes, 'The New Victims: Perpetrators before the Canadian Truth and Reconciliation Commission' in Brieg Capitaine and Karine Vanthuyne (eds.), *Power through Testimony* (n 53) 177–197.

67 John Borrows, 'Residential Schools, Reconciliation, Churches and Indigenous Peoples' (unpublished paper, no date) www.iclrs.org/content/events/123/3419.pdf (last accessed 14 December 2020).

68 Ethna Regan, 'Church, Culture and Crediblity: A Perspective from Ireland' (2012) New Blackfriars 166.

69 David Tombs, 'Lived Religion and the Intolerance of the Cross' in R. R. Ganzevoort and S. Sremac (eds.) *Lived Religion and the Politics of (In)tolerance* (Cham, Switzerland: Palgrave Macmillan 2017).

8 Institutional liability, historical abuses and vulnerability

James Gallen
Dublin City University

Introduction

Revelations in recent decades regarding historical child sexual abuse in State and Church institutions have led to a significant expansion of institutional liability,[1] as victim-survivors seek to hold these institutions accountable for abuse by employees, institutional representatives or contractors. Vicarious liability operates primarily as strict liability for employers for a tort committed by employees.[2] A traditional 'course of employment' approach provides that an employer is vicariously liable both for employee acts authorised by the employer and for unauthorised acts, which were so connected with authorised acts that they could be regarded as improper modes of performing authorised acts.[3] In recent years, alternative theoretical conceptions have emerged across the common law world, imposing liability where wrongful conduct had a 'close connection' or constituted an 'enterprise risk' to the defendant employer.[4] Such efforts have occurred without a consistent theoretical justification. This chapter argues that the concept of vulnerability, developed in the work of Martha Fineman, both informs this expanded approach to vicarious liability and can guide its future development in a more coherent fashion.[5] In doing so, it offers a novel application of vulnerability theory to institutional liability across several common law jurisdictions and demonstrates that those jurisdictions with less developed jurisprudence in these areas would benefit from greater explicit consideration of the role of vulnerability.[6]

1 James Gallen, 'Jesus Wept: The Roman Catholic Church, Child Sexual Abuse and Transitional Justice' (2016) 10(2) International Journal of Transitional Justice 332.

2 Patrick Atiyah, *Vicarious Liability in the Law of Torts* (Butterworth 1967) 12; Oliver Wendell Holmes, 'Agency' (1890–1891) 4 Harvard Law Review 345; (1891–92) 5 Harvard Law Review 1.

3 John William Salmond and Robert Heuston, *Salmond and Heuston on the Law of Torts* (Sweet and Maxwell, 19th edn 1987) 521–522; *Canadian Pacific Railway Co v Lockhart* [1942] AC 591, 599.

4 Paula Giliker, 'Rough Justice in an Unjust World' (2002) 65 Modern Law Review 269.

5 Martha Fineman, 'The Vulnerable Subject: Anchoring Equality in the Human Condition' (2008–2009) 20 Yale Journal of Law and Feminism 1.

6 Jane Stapleton, 'The Golden Thread at the Heart of Tort Law: Protection of the Vulnerable' (2003) 24 Australian Bar Review 135; Carl Stychin, 'The Vulnerable Subject of Negligence Law' (2012) 8(3) International Journal of Law in Context 337.

DOI: 10.4324/9780429023149-9

Vulnerability theory, tort law and institutions

Scholarship on vulnerability to date has addressed several substantive issues, such as the legal organisation of work, public responsibility in the context of privatisation and the role of law regarding the elderly.[7] In tort law, Carl Stychin suggests that vulnerability theory can shift us away from the dominant conception of a pre-relational, self-reliant, autonomous 'reasonable person' and emphasise instead the ethical and legal connection between parties to disputes.[8] Jane Stapleton has claimed that vulnerability provides the central organising feature of the tort of negligence and that the most extreme form of vulnerability arises where 'a person is exclusively dependent on another to take care'.[9] Vulnerability has also been recognised as factor in the Australian High Court, which has employed vulnerability to situations where 'by reason of ignorance or social, political or economic constraints, the plaintiff was not able to protect him or herself from the risk of injury'.[10] In the United Kingdom, Stychin argues that, while vulnerability has not played an explicit role in tort law, there are doctrinal strands which can be drawn upon in supporting its relevance and in advocating its future application.[11]

To date, vulnerability theory has not addressed the role of secondary liability in tort law; that is, the liability of an institution or employer for the wrongful acts of another. This issue has been acknowledged elsewhere in feminist approaches to tort law. Leslie Bender argues that, unlike the injured individuals who do not know they will be injured until after tragedy strikes, institutional defendants have or should have planned for the contingency of potential litigation.[12] Margaret Hall argues that the term 'institutional liability' captures the responsibility of institutions in creating or facilitating the systemic nature of wrongdoing in instances that reach beyond a few 'bad apples' who infiltrate the workplace.[13]

Vulnerability theory may inform these concerns by focusing on the state's responsibility to use law to structure the interaction and liability of social institutions with individuals experiencing situations of dependency and universal vulnerability. To date, the role of vulnerability as a mechanism of redressing concrete

7 Martha Fineman and Jonathan Fineman (eds), *Vulnerability and the Legal Organisation of Work* (Routledge 2017); Martha Fineman, Titti Mattsson and Ulrika Andersson (eds), *Privatisation, Vulnerability and Social Responsibility* (Routledge, 2016); Martha Fineman, 'Elderly as Vulnerable: Rethinking the Nature of Individual and Societal Responsibility' (2012) 20(2) Elder Law Journal 71.

8 Carl Stychin, 'The Vulnerable Subject of Negligence Law' (n 6) 346.

9 Jane Stapleton, 'The Golden Thread at the Heart of Tort Law: Protection of the Vulnerable' (n 6) 142.

10 *Woolcock Street Investments v. CDG* (2004) 216 CLR 515 at 549.

11 Carl Stychin, 'The Vulnerable Subject of Negligence Law' (n 6) 348; *Fairchild v Glenhaven Funeral Services Ltd* [2003] 1 AC 32; [2002] 3 All ER 305.

12 Leslie Bender, 'Changing the Values in Tort Law' (1989–1990) 25 Tulsa Law Journal 759, 761.

13 Margaret Hall, 'After Waterhouse: Vicarious Liability and the Tort of Institutional Abuse' (2000) 22 Journal of Social Welfare and Family Law 159, 162.

injustices has been inadequately charted.[14] On Fineman's account, the state should play a critical role in redressing harms generated by vulnerability and dependencies, by creating mechanisms whereby individuals can 'accumulate the resilience or resources that they need to confront the social, material and practical implications of their vulnerability'.[15] Similarly, Goodin concluded that vulnerability analysis was enhanced by its ability to 'clearly finger' those who are, or should be, particularly responsible for seeing to it that a person's interests are protected.[16]

In recent years there has been a significant proliferation of investigations into historical abuse, both physical and sexual abuse, against children and others in residential settings, across several jurisdictions.[17] However, to date, no overarching framework has been employed to address the range of moral, legal, policy and psychological issues relevant to this abuse.[18] When viewing the issue of how state- and church-run institutions employed and organised individuals who abused children and other vulnerable groups holistically, a multi-layered form of responsibility can profitably be constructed that enables legal findings of not only individual criminal responsibility but also civil responsibility at institutional or state levels. Such an approach addresses Munro's concern that the concepts of vulnerability and exploitation 'are themselves vulnerable' to manipulation: 'to shift the locus of responsibility from the state to those individuals who directly "abuse" or exploit another's vulnerability, or indeed to the vulnerable individual herself'.[19] The focus on civil liability, particular non-fault-based liability of institutions, adds to existing critical tort scholarship by offering a novel application of vulnerability theory, avoids the risk of an exclusively fault-based conception of responsibility for vulnerability and can develop a more accurate (if complex) multi-layered account,[20] in the contexts of vicarious liability and non-delegable duties of care.

Vicarious liability 'on the move': comparative trends towards vulnerability

The emergence of new approaches to vicarious liability, namely an 'enterprise' risk conception in Canada and a 'close connection' test in the United

14 Alyson Cole 'All of Us Are Vulnerable, but Some Are More Vulnerable than Others: The Politics Ambiguity of Vulnerability Studies, an Ambivalent Critique' (2016) 17(2) Critical Horizons 260.

15 Martha Fineman 'Equality, Autonomy and the Vulnerable Subject in Law and Politics' in Martha Fineman and Anna Gear (eds.) *Vulnerability: Reflections on a New Ethical Foundation for Law and Politics* (Ashgate 2013) 13, 19.

16 Robert Goodin, *Protecting the Vulnerable: A Reanalysis of Our Social Responsibilities* (University of Chicago Press 1986) 117.

17 Johanna Sköld 'The Truth about Abuse? A Comparative Approach to Inquiry Narratives on Historical Institutional Child Abuse' (2016) 45(4) History of Education 492.

18 Gallen, 'Jesus Wept: The Roman Catholic Church, Child Sexual Abuse and Transitional Justice' (n 1) 334.

19 Vanessa Munro, 'Shifting Sands? Consent, Context and Vulnerability in Contemporary Sexual Offences Policy In England and Wales' (2017) 26(4) Social and Legal Studies 433.

20 Ibid, 432.

Kingdom, reflects not only a concern for the vulnerability and dependency experienced by children in institutional settings, at heightened risk of abuse by individuals, but also the degree of control and authority exercised by institutions in their provision of care. However, the use of vulnerability in tort law to date risks equating vulnerability with dependency, and risks mitigating the collective responsibility of all social institutions in lessening, ameliorating and compensating for vulnerability.[21]

Canada was first to reconsider the law on vicarious liability in light of the dependencies involved in institutional and child sex abuse. In *Bazley v Curry*, the defendant operated residential care facilities for children and unknowingly employed a paedophile to exercise its statutory authority to care for children.[22] McLachlin J concluded courts should assess whether there was a material or significant increase in the opportunities for wrongdoing created or enhanced by employer's enterprise,[23] in an 'enterprise risk' approach to vicarious liability. Particular emphasis was placed on: the extent to which wrongful acts were related to intimacy inherent in the employer's enterprise; the power conferred on the employee in relation to the victim; and the vulnerability of potential victims to the employee's wrongful abuse of their power. The Supreme Court concluded that the defendant was vicariously liable for the sexual abuse due to the opportunity for intimate private control, in activities like bathing or toileting, and the parent-like role required.[24]

Subsequent decisions emphasised the authority and control conferred by employers on an abuser over a dependent population. In *Doe v Bennett* the Court concluded that the central inquiry in vicarious liability is one of authority, especially the power and control given to the employee.[25] In *EB v Order of the Oblates of Mary Immaculate in the Province of British Columbia,* Binnie J noted the critical inquiry concerned the powers, duties and responsibilities conferred on the employee, who in this case was not in a position of 'power, trust or intimacy with respect to the children' based on his employment, leading to the dismissal of the case on this ground.[26] Christine Beuermann argues that vicarious liability has generally been limited to situations in which wrongdoing occurred 'in the apparent execution of authority'.[27]

However, *Bazley* did not result in vicarious liability where the employer's enterprise did not exacerbate a plaintiff's dependencies nor confer the authority

21 Martha Fineman, 'The Vulnerable Subject: Anchoring Equality in the Human Condition' (n 2) 13.

22 *Bazley* v *Currey* (1999) 144 DLR (4th) 45; Protection of Children Act, RSBC 1960, c 303, s 210. This section made the defendant institution the legal guardian of the children in its care.

23 Ibid, paras 41–42.

24 Ibid, paras 43–44.

25 *John Doe v Bennett* [2004] 1 SCR 436 at 446 [21].

26 *EB v Order of the Oblates of Mary Immaculate in the Province of British Columbia* [2005] 3 SCR 45 at 78 [51].

27 Christine Beuermann, 'Conferred Authority Strict Liability and Institutional Child Sexual Abuse' (2015) 37 Sydney Law Review 113–133, 121.

to the defendant, emphasising that a vulnerability analysis did not generate universal liability by state or private organisations for the abuse of children. In *Jacobi v Griffiths*, the Canadian Supreme Court did not accept that a charitable organisation providing recreational activities to children was vicariously liable for the criminal sexual assaults committed by one of its employees, in the absence of an environment that involved intimate quasi-parental control.[28] Much of the abuse occurred at Griffiths' home, outside the exercise of any conferred authority regarding the children.[29] The Canadian approach emphasises both the dependency of victim-survivors of child sexual abuse, and the control or conferred authority exercised by employers and superiors over abusive employees or subordinates, in a manner that recognises the role of institutions in creating situations of vulnerability and dependency.

The traditional English position on vicarious liability excluded liability for sexual abuse and intentional wrongdoing,[30] but in more recent years has expanded to address how institutions created and exacerbate situations of dependency, while using the language of pathogenic or situational vulnerability. In *Lister v Hesley Hall Ltd*, the House of Lords held the defendant vicariously liable for sexual assaults committed by its employee against infant plaintiffs.[31] The defendant institution was solely responsible for the care of the children under legislation.[32] The court employed a variety of approaches to impose liability.[33] Lord Steyn adopted the Canadian approach, but declined to consider the full range of relevant policy considerations.[34] Lord Clyde adopted a 'close connection' approach, emphasising liability should not be imposed based on the mere opportunity to commit abuse.[35] Lord Hobhouse concluded *Bazley* was too vague a test for vicarious liability, and that the correct approach should focus on the contractual duty of the servant towards his employer.[36] Lord Millett noted the inherent risk of harm created by the dependencies to those in residential institutions, from those placed in authority over them.[37]

In subsequent decisions, the English approach has been understood as a 'close connection' test, in a manner that emphasised liability where situations of dependency created a significant risk of wrongdoing. In *Maga v The Trustees of the Birmingham Archdiocese of the Roman Catholic Church*, Longmore LJ

28 *Jacobi* v *Griffiths* (1999) 174 DLR (4th) 71; *Reference re Broome v Prince Edward Island*, 2010 SCC 11.
29 Christine Beuermann, 'Conferred Authority Strict Liability and Institutional Child Sexual Abuse (n 27) 123.
30 *Duncan v. Findlater*, 6 Cl. & Fin. 894 (1839), para 18.
31 *Lister v Hesley Hall Ltd* [2002] 1 AC 215.
32 Children Act 1975 (UK) c 72, s 60.
33 Paula Giliker, 'Rough Justice in an Unjust World' (2002) 65 Modern Law Review 269, 276.
34 Ibid, para 28.
35 Ibid, para 45.
36 Ibid, para 55.
37 Ibid, paras 82–83.

emphasised the power and ability to exercise intimacy conferred on the perpetrator priest because of his ordination by the Church, as evidence of a close connection.[38] Subsequent cases re-emphasised the basis of vicarious liability as deriving from the combination of risks and controls of individuals arising from a given enterprise. In *Various Claimants v The Catholic Child Welfare Society (CCWS)*, members of the Society were alleged to have committed physical and sexual abuse against children.[39] The UK Supreme Court identified five elements which rendered it fair, just and reasonable to impose vicarious liability:

1. The employer has the means to compensate the victim and can be expected to be insured;
2. The tort was committed in the course of activities undertaken on behalf of the employer.
3. The perpetrator's activity was part of the business activity of the employer.
4. The employer, by engaging the perpetrator to carry out the activity, created a risk that the tort might be committed.
5. The perpetrator was, to a greater or lesser degree, under the control of the employer.[40]

The Court imposed vicarious liability, concluding that placing of teachers with vulnerable boys in a residential school greatly enhanced the risk of abuse.[41] The *CCWS* test emphasises the particular dependencies that can arise in residential institutions and aligns with the Canadian approach in prioritising control, authority of the employee/subordinate and the dependencies of vulnerable victim-survivors:

> Living cloistered on the school premises were vulnerable boys. They were triply vulnerable. They were vulnerable because they were children in a school; they were vulnerable because they were virtually prisoners in the school; and they were vulnerable because their personal histories made it even less likely that, if they attempted to disclose what was happening to them, they would be believed. The brother teachers were placed in the school to care for the educational and religious needs of these pupils. Abusing the boys in their care was diametrically opposed to those objectives but, paradoxically, that very fact was one of the factors that provided the necessary close connection between the abuse and the relationship between the brothers and the Institute that gives rise to vicarious liability on the part of the latter.[42]

38 *Maga v The Trustees of the Birmingham Archdiocese of the Roman Catholic Church* [2010] EWCA Civ 256; [2010] 1 WLR 1441 at 79–80.

39 *Various Claimants v The Catholic Child Welfare Society* [2012] UKSC 56.

40 Ibid, para 35.

41 Ibid, para 86.

42 Ibid, para 92.

Recent decisions expand the approach to vicarious liability further.[43] In *Armes v Nottinghamshire County Council*, in 2017, the UK Supreme Court further extended vicarious liability, holding the defendant council responsible for the physical and sexual abuse of the plaintiff by foster parents with whom she was placed while in the care of the defendant local authority.[44] The court held that foster parents could not be regarded as 'carrying on an independent business of their own', as the care they provided was 'integral' to the local authority's organisation of its child care services. In addition, the abuse was committed by the foster parents 'in the course of an activity carried on for the benefit of the local authority' and it was impossible to draw a sharp distinction between the activity of the local authority and that of the foster parents.[45] The local authority also maintained a high degree of control and statutory power over the foster parents.[46] The developments in English law seek to address risks and the potential control of abusive individuals that arise in the context of the creation or exacerbation of vulnerability in the interaction of individuals with social institutions, both in and beyond employment contexts. The expansionary trend in UK vicarious liability law reflects a commitment to the protection of vulnerable individuals and groups against institutional structures that can cause or exacerbate dependencies and risks of harm. Although the language of vulnerability is employed, it remains focused on a particular, albeit expanding, conception of vulnerability and sees liability as appropriate where institutions and organisations create or exacerbate situations of dependency.

The Australian position on vicarious liability is narrower than that in the UK and Canada, warrants further clarification and is surprising in light of the commitment of Australian negligence law to a principle of vulnerability.[47] In *New South Wales v LePore*, the Australian High Court was invited to follow the approaches in *Bazley* and *Lister*,[48] but divided regarding the appropriate test. *Lepore* led to a narrow treatment of institutional abuse in Australian law,[49] and was criticised as the 'general lack of appreciation of the context and nature of sexual assault in schools' revealed a 'lack of [judicial] appreciation of the role of power in child sexual assault'.[50] In particular, 'a recognition of 'power disparities and the special vulnerability of children' were mostly 'absent from the

43 *Mohamud v Wm Morrison Supermarkets plc.* [2016] UKSC 11; [2016] 2 WLR 821.

44 *Armes v Nottinghamshire County Council* [2017] UKSC 60.

45 Ibid, paras 59–60.

46 Ibid, paras 62–65.

47 Stapleton, 'The Golden Thread at the Heart of Tort Law: Protection of the Vulnerable' (n 6).

48 *New South Wales v LePore* [2003] HCA 4, 212 CLR 511.

49 *PAO, BJH, SBM, IDF and PMA v Trustees of the Roman Catholic Church for the Archdiocese of Sydney* [2011] NSWSC 1216, para 99; Kate Gleeson, 'Why the Continuous Failures in Justice for Australian Victims and Survivors of Catholic Clerical Child Sexual Abuse?' [2016] Current Issues in Criminal Justice 27; (2016) 28(2) Current Issues in Criminal Justice 239.

50 Jane Wangmann, 'Liability for Institutional Child Sexual Assault: Where does Lepore Leave Australia?' (2004) 28 Melbourne University Law Review 169.

judgments of most members of the High Court'.[51] Such criticism again reflects concern with particularised conceptions of vulnerability, in contrast to Fineman's universal and inherent conception.

The Australian High Court revisited the issue in *Prince Alfred College Incorporated v ADC*, where the claimant was a former pupil of the defendant boarding school who had been sexually abused by a housemaster.[52] The Court articulated a new test in Australian law for vicarious liability reasoning based on whether the employment provided not merely the opportunity, which is of itself insufficient, but the 'occasion' for the wrongdoing to be committed. The High Court explained that, in determining whether the test is met, particular features of the employee's role may be taken into account, including authority, power, trust, control and the ability to achieve intimacy with the victim.[53] However, Des Ryan argues it is not easy to discern any meaningful difference between the employment providing the occasion for the wrongdoing and the opportunity for it.[54] Further clarification of this approach and ongoing engagement with the jurisprudence emerging from the UK Supreme Court seems likely, with a retained particular conception of vulnerability.

In Ireland, early case law on vicarious liability rejected the possibility that an employer could be vicariously liable for acts of sexual harassment by employees,[55] but has recently joined the common law trend towards recognition of the creation of vulnerability and dependency as basis for liability. In *O'Keeffe v Hickey* the plaintiff, who had suffered child sexual abuse in an Irish primary school, claimed the state was vicariously liable.[56] The Supreme Court rejected vicarious liability and divided regarding its appropriate test. Hardiman J concluded that, having regard to the limited state control and management of school owned and operated by religious dioceses, Ireland was not vicariously liable.[57] Hardiman J concluded that approaches in Canada, the United Kingdom and Australia paid too much heed to the need to find a source of compensation.[58] Fennelly J noted that *Bazley* and *Lister* share a common test: 'the closeness of the connection between the abuse and the work which the employee was engaged to carry out'.[59] Fennelly J concluded that Ireland was not vicariously liable, as acting as school manager, the local priest, not Ireland, employed the perpetrator. He concluded that an employment relationship was required in close connection cases. Other cases

51 Ibid, 200.

52 *Prince Alfred College Incorporated v ADC* [2016] HCA 37.

53 Ibid, para 81.

54 Desmond Ryan, 'From Opportunity to Occasion: Vicarious Liability in the High Court of Australia', (2017) 76(1) Cambridge Law Journal 14, 17.

55 *Health Board v BC* [1994] ELR 27; *Delahunty v South Eastern Health Board* [2003] 4 IR 361.

56 *O'Keeffe* v *Hickey* [2009] 2 IR 302.

57 Ibid, 343.

58 Ibid, 339–340.

59 Ibid, 375.

excluded vicarious liability due to a lack of intimacy or quasi-parental role or responsibility in the relationship between perpetrator and victim plaintiff.[60] Though Irish case law had not employed the language of vulnerability, its concern for parental-like situations of dependency mirrored, albeit conservatively, trends in other jurisdictions.

In *Hickey v McGowan,* the Supreme Court aligned Ireland with the comparative trends towards expanding vicarious liability more explicitly.[61] The plaintiff was sexually abused by a Marist Brother and alleged that the Marist Order, an unincorporated association, were vicariously liable. The Supreme Court concluded that Fennelly J's adoption of the 'close connection' in *O'Keeffe* should now be taken to represent the law in Ireland on vicarious liability and that, despite the absence of a residential component to the school and the fact that the children were not vulnerable for reasons other than their youth, this test was met in *Hickey.*[62] This approach offers welcome recognition of the universal nature of vulnerability and the particular dependency of children, and the need for a comprehensive approach to vicarious liability, not exclusively focused on intimacy or residential settings. In assessing the vicarious liability of a religious order, O'Donnell J stated:

> To apply tests drawn from the relatively modern world of commerce and industry to religious organisations which have existed for centuries is in my view, to miss the sheer scale and impact of religious institutions on people's daily lives, particularly in Ireland of the first three-quarters of the 20th century. The relationship between members of an order and his or her fellow members and indeed the order itself was much more intense, constant and all pervasive than the relationship between an employer and an employee, or in the old language of the late Victorian cases, a master and his servant.[63]

This is a critical insight into the distinctive application of the principles related to vulnerability of control, risk creation and enterprise to an environment that is not primarily commercial in nature, but may generate liability where acts of abuse 'are sufficiently closely connected to the object and mission of the order'.[64] In so doing O'Donnell J reframed the 'enterprise risk' conception of *Bazley* to more accurately reflect the nature of institutional liability and vulnerabilities and dependencies involved in religious orders. O'Donnell J retained the limited and exceptional nature of vicarious liability,[65] stressing 'the mere fact of voluntary association may not create the type of intense relationship that

60 *Reilly v Devereaux* [2009] IESC 22.
61 *Hickey v McGowan* [2017] IESC 6.
62 Ibid, para 26.
63 Ibid, para 37.
64 Ibid.
65 Ibid, para 42.

justifies imposing vicarious liability in the case of a religious order'.[66] The Irish approach demonstrates an important alternative to the 'akin to employment' approach of the UK, that directly acknowledges the role of religious organisations as sites of potential vulnerability, dependency and abuse.

Constructing an account of vulnerability and institutional liability

Vulnerability, dependency and control all feature in the explanations for liability of institutions in vicarious liability, but concern remains that these concepts lack a sound theoretical foundation, are too vague and unpredictable,[67] and emerge from social convenience and rough justice.[68] Paula Giliker notes that vicarious liability may only be understood by recognising the influence not only of the conflicting policies of corrective and distributive justice, but of background factors such as insurance, the lobbying power of other stakeholders and alternative compensatory mechanisms.[69] In addition to the context of historical abuse in religious institutions from which the expanded approach to vicarious liability has been largely generated, any justification must fit the modern contexts in which the concept may apply. Phillip Morgan notes that modern multinational and multi-layered corporate structures, designed to enable judgment proofing at one end, and precarious forms of work at the other, challenge the suitability of current approaches to vicarious liability.[70]

The existing debates regarding the purpose of vicarious liability arrive at several policy justifications, which cumulatively may be necessary but are individually insufficient to describe existing case law.[71] In *Bazley,* the Canadian Supreme Court favoured the provision of a just and reasonable remedy for harm, a loss distribution function to enterprises and the deterrence of future harm as the policy grounds for vicarious liability.[72] In *CCWS,* Lord Millett favoured a loss distribution approach,[73]

66 Ibid, para 39.

67 Claire McIvor, 'The Use and Abuse of the Doctrine of Vicarious Liability' (2006) 35 Common Law World Review 268.

68 *ICI* v *Shatwell* [1965] AC 656, 685; Glanville. Williams, 'Vicarious Liability: Tort of the Master or of the Servant?' (1956) 72 Law Quarterly Review 522; Patrick Atiyah, *Vicarious Liability in the Law of Torts* (Butterworth 1967) 16; Paula Giliker, *Vicarious Liability in Tort: A Comparative Perspective* (Cambridge University Press 2013) Douglas Brodie, 'Enterprise Liability: Justifying Vicarious Liability' (2007) 27 Oxford Journal of Legal Studies 493; Jason Neyers, 'A Theory of Vicarious Liability' (2005–2006) 43 Alberta Law Review 287.

69 Paula Giliker, 'Vicarious Liability or Liability for the Acts of Others in Tort: A Comparative Perspective' (2011) 2 Journal of European Tort Law 31, 56.

70 Phillip Morgan, 'Vicarious Liability for Group Companies: The Final Frontier of Vicarious Liability?' (2015) 31(4) Professional Negligence 276–299.

71 Richard Kinder, 'Vicarious Liability: For Whom Should the Employer be Liable?' (1995) 15 Legal Studies 47–64, 56.

72 *Bazley v Curry* (1999) 174 DLR (4th) 45, 61.

73 *Various Claimants v Catholic Child Welfare Society and others* [2012] UKSC 56, [2013] 2 AC 1, [34].

while elsewhere Lord Nicholls has endorsed the justice of a remedy for victims of harms arising from an enterprise.[74] These approaches have been criticised as being conceptually open-ended,[75] with no principled limitations to liability. The idea of enterprise risk has also been used as a justification in scholarship as well as a test in case law. Modern enterprises operate as a mechanism for absorbing, controlling and spreading social and economic risks.[76] Both Irish and UK case law have embraced a conception of enterprise which includes non-commercial enterprises, such as religious orders. In reviewing these approaches, Phillip Morgan argues a better conception of vicarious liability that assesses the association between perpetrator and institution across a two-axes scale to trigger vicarious liability.[77] One axis represents the degree of day-to-day control exercised over an employee or other designate. Such control could be highly regimented, such in an army or religious congregation; or very limited, such as with a volunteer or independent contractor. The second axis addresses the discretion in how the person carries out the role, and the level of direction they receive.[78] For Morgan, as the level of discretion in role increases, more day-to-day control is required to compensate. For vicarious liability to be present where the level of discretion in role is at its highest, day-to-day control must be at an extremely high level.[79]

All of these developments have been incremental, taking twenty years across common law jurisdictions to expand the conception and role of vulnerability in vicarious liability. Such expansions remain predicated on a particularised conception of vulnerability, but also employ the language of dependency and control in more general terms. It may be possible that further case law, outside of the context of historical abuse or abuse of children, will continue to expand courts' understanding of control, dependency and institutions.

This focus on control and discretion of actors associated with an institution align with a vulnerability theory approach. For Robert Goodin,

> relationships involving inequalities of vulnerability create opportunities for more powerful persons to take unfair advantage of more vulnerable persons, particularly in situations where the more powerful exercise discretionary control over resources on which the more vulnerable are dependent and cannot obtain elsewhere or where people are unable to protect themselves or their interests.[80]

74 *Dubai Aluminium Co Ltd v Salaam* [2002] UKHL 48, para 21.

75 Jonathan Morgan, 'Vicarious Liability for Independent Contractors?'(2015) 31(4) Professional Negligence 235–258, 248.

76 Simon Deakin, 'The Changing Nature of the "Employer" in Labour Law' (2001) 30 Industrial Law Journal 72, 83.

77 Phillip Morgan, 'Recasting Vicarious Liability' (2012) 71(3) Cambridge Law Journal 615–50, 642.

78 Ibid.

79 Ibid, 643.

80 Robert Goodin, 'Protecting the Vulnerable: A Reanalysis of Our Social Responsibilities' (n 16) 195–201.

As a result, the more powerful are obliged to be particularly vigilant, not only in guarding against the misuse of their position of power, authority or privilege to take unfair advantage of others, but also in protecting those who are vulnerable to them.[81] On this account, those institutions which create or exacerbate situations of dependency, and involve inherent vulnerability, should be held vicariously liable where they maintained sufficient day-to-day control, and/or limited discretion, over potentially abusive associates. Such an approach still acknowledges the enterprise as a social institution, pursuing purposive activity which may create inherent vulnerability, dependencies or harms.

The exploitation of the vulnerable can be recognised as a process involving the responsibility of both individual abusers and the institutions and structures which led to the abuse. Fineman has been critical of a 'targeted group approach to the idea of vulnerability', as it ignores its universality and inappropriately constructs relationships of difference and distance between individuals and groups within society.[82] Such an approach 'will tend to direct critical attention to discrimination by and against individuals, not to the real or potential failures, distortion, or corruption of societal structures that affect everyone in society'.[83] An approach to institutional liability that focused merely on the control by institutional defendants on either dependent plaintiffs or potentially abusive employees or contractors would reinforce a targeted group approach and risk stereotyping both victim and perpetrator, without due regard to the role of institutional responsibility. An evaluation of institutional liability from the perspective of both control of plaintiff and perpetrator enables courts to appreciate the universal nature of dependency:

> a state of dependency is not deviant, but natural and inevitable both on an individual and a societal level. We are all, and always, dependent upon societal structures and institutions, although the degree of dependence and the specific institutions through which dependency is mediated may change over the life course.[84]

Vulnerability theory usefully clarifies the relationships between concepts such as vulnerability, dependency and control that are central to institutional

81 Catriona Mackenzie, Wendy Rogers and Susan Dodds, 'Introduction: What is Vulnerability, and Why Does it Matter for Moral Theory?' in Catriona Mackenzie, Wendy Rogers and Susan Dodds (eds.) *Vulnerability: New Essays in Ethics and Feminist Philosophy* (Oxford University Press 2014), 14.

82 Martha Fineman, 'Elderly as Vulnerable: Rethinking the Nature of Individual and Societal Responsibility' 20(2) Elder Law Journal 71–112, 85.

83 Martha Fineman, 'Feminism, Masculinities' (2013) 13 Nevada Law Journal 619, 636, 639.

84 Martha Fineman, 'Equality and Difference: The Restrained State' (2015) 66(3) Alabama Law Review 608–626, 622.

liability. When viewed holistically across areas relevant to historical abuse – for instance, criminal law, civil law and human rights law – the concept of vulnerability provides the means for an analysis and justification of a multi-layered conception of responsibility for wrongdoing at individual, institutional or structural levels.

9 Vulnerability, social and economic rights and austerity in Ireland

Claire-Michelle Smyth
University of Brighton

Introduction

This chapter considers the impact of austerity measures on society's most vulnerable through the effects they have had on the rights categorised as social and economic, which are often seen politically as easy targets in pursuit of reducing budget deficits. The chapter will first explore the legal status of social and economic rights in both international and domestic law, before examining how they have been decimated since the economic crisis. Fineman's theory of vulnerability, particularly her iteration of the 'responsive state', is considered and, should this be adopted, whether it could afford better protection to these rights by 'vulnerability proofing' rather than 'human rights proofing' budgetary decision.

What are social and economic rights?

The rights classified as social and economic (ESC) include, inter alia, housing, healthcare, social welfare, food, water and an adequate standard of living. In the modern international human rights regime (identified as post-Second World War), these rights took a subordinate post to civil and political rights.[1]

The first document containing a comprehensive catalogue of human rights, the Universal Declaration on Human Rights (UDHR), was adopted by the United Nations in 1948. However, it was merely an aspirational document, not legally binding, and attempts to relocate these rights within the legal order began in 1949. Negotiations devolved into polemics and against this backdrop attempts to transpose the UDHR into one legally binding document were abandoned.[2] Accordingly, despite the official position that the two sets of rights are universal, interdependent, interrelated and indivisible,[3] it was agreed that two separate documents would be drafted, marking the initial and persistent divide in international law between the two sets of rights. The

1 For an analysis of the theoretical perspectives relating to this, see Claire-Michelle Smyth, 'Social and Economic Rights in a Post Neo-Liberal Society' in Claire-Michelle Smyth and Richard Lang (eds.) *The Future of Human Rights in the UK* (Cambridge Scholars Publishing 2017).

2 Primarily due to pressure from the Western-dominated Commission UN Doc A2929 (1955) 7.

3 Vienna Declaration, 1993 second World Conference on Human Rights [5].

DOI: 10.4324/9780429023149-10

International Covenant on Civil and Political Rights (ICCPR),[4] containing civil and political rights, and the International Covenant on Economic, Social and Cultural Rights (ICESCR),[5] consisting of social and economic rights, were adopted by the General Assembly and opened for signature, ratification and accession on 16 December 1966.[6] The effect of this compromise cannot be overstated. The two categories of rights were set on divergent paths, with different importance being ascribed to each. Social and economic rights were to be realised progressively, subject to available resources,[7] a 'programmatic'[8] approach not applied to civil and political rights.[9] The absence of immediate and concrete obligations in the ICESCR, coupled with the lack of any complaints mechanism,[10] were powerful factors contributing to continued violations,[11] compounding the inferior status of the rights on an international scale.[12]

4 999 UNTS 171 and 1057 UNTS 407 / [1980] ATS 23 /6 ILM 368 (1967), adopted on 16 December 1966 and entered into force on 23 March 1976.

5 993 UNTS 3 / [1976] ATS 5 / 6 ILM 360 (1967), adopted on 16 December 1966 and entered into force on 3 January 1976.

6 UN Resolution 2200A (XXI). The ICESCR entered into force on 3 January 1976 and the ICCPR entered into force on 2 March 1976.

7 ICESCR Part II Article 2.1 states that 'Each State Party to the present Covenant undertakes to take steps, individually and through international assistance and co-operation, especially economic and technical, to the maximum of its available resources, with a view to achieving progressively the full realization of the rights recognised in the present Covenant by all appropriate means, including particularly the adoption of legislative measures.'

8 Henry Steiner, Philip Alston and Ryan Goodman, *International Human Rights in Context: Law Politics and Morals* (3rd edn, Oxford University Press 2008) 284.

9 International Covenant on Civil and Political Rights, (ICCPR) 999 UNTS 171 and 1057 UNTS 407 / [1980] ATS 23 /6 ILM 368 (1967), adopted on 16 December 1966 and entered into force on 23 March 1976. Article 2 (3) states that

Each State Party to the present Covenant undertakes:

(a) To ensure that any person whose rights or freedoms as herein recognised are violated shall have an effective remedy, notwithstanding that the violation has been committed by a person acting in an official capacity;
(b) To ensure that any person claiming such a remedy shall have his right thereto determined by competent judicial, administrative, or legislative authorities, or by any other competent authority provided for by the legal system of the State and to develop the possibilities of judicial remedies;
(c) To ensure that competent authorities shall enforce such remedies when granted.

10 In contrast to the ICESCR, the ICCPR contained within its first optional protocol (999 UNTS 171 adopted on 16 December 1966 and entered into force on 23 March 1976) an individual complaints mechanism to the Human Rights Committee.

11 Michael J. Dennis and David P Stewart, 'Justiciability of Economic, Social and Cultural Rights: Should there be an International Complaints Mechanism to Adjudicate the Rights to Food, Water, Housing and Health?' (2004) 98 American Journal of International Law 462; Wouter Vandenhole, 'Completing the UN Complaint Mechanisms for Human Rights Violations Step by Step: Towards a Complaints Procedure Complementing the International Covenant on Economic Social and Cultural Rights' (2003) 21 Netherlands Quarterly of Human Rights 423.

12 Catarina de Albuquerque, 'Chronicle of an Announced Birth: The Coming into Life of the Optional Protocol to the International Covenant on Economic Social and Cultural Rights – The Missing Piece of the International Bill of Human Rights' (2010) 32 Human Rights Quarterly 144; Claire-Michelle Smyth 'Social and Economic Rights and the Struggle for Equivalent Protection

Despite the fact that Ireland has ratified ICESCR, these rights do not form part of domestic law, due to the dualist nature of the state, a position clearly intended by the Constitution.[13] While it accepts international law 'as its rules of conduct in its relations with other states',[14] Ireland requires a positive act by the Oireachtas before any part of international law can be effective domestically.[15]

Thus far, with the exception of education, social and economic rights have not found their way into the Constitution's rubric of fundamental rights.[16] In 2015, the Irish government stated[17] that these rights are litigated through the Constitution and that 'the courts do not operate a rigid classification of rights which puts economic, social and cultural rights beyond their reach'.[18] However, this is at a distinct variant with the Supreme Court's interpretation of these rights. An era of judicial activism initiated by *Ryan v AG*[19] had waned by the time cases involving social and economic rights came to be considered, and the case of *TD v Minister for Education* clearly establishes the position of these rights as being non-justiciable.[20] Hardiman J was of the opinion that relief for cases such as this ought to be advanced in Leinster House and not the Four Courts.[21] In justifying this position, he states why this is so:

> Firstly, to do so would offend the constitutional separation of powers. Secondly, it would lead the courts into the taking of decisions in areas in which they have no special qualifications or experience. Thirdly, it would permit the courts to take such decisions even though they are not, and cannot be, democratically responsible for them as the legislature and the executive are. Fourthly, the evidence based adversarial procedures of the court, which are excellently adapted for the administration of commutative justice, are

---

in International Law' in Jean Quataert and Lora Wildenthal (eds.) *The Routledge History of Human Rights* (Routledge 2019).

13 Article 29.6 'No international agreement shall be part of the domestic law of the State save as may be determined by the Oireachtas.'

14 Article 29.3.

15 Article 15.2.1 'The sole and exclusive power of making laws in the State is hereby vested in the Oireachtas; No other legislative authority has power to make laws for the State.'

16 Article 42.

17 In response to Committee on Economic Social and Cultural Rights, List of Issues in relation to the Third Periodic Report of Ireland E/C.12/IRL/Q/3 17 December 2014 [3].

18 Committee on Economic Social and Cultural Rights, List of Issues in relation to the Third Periodic Report of Ireland, Addendum, Replies of Ireland to List of Issues E/C.12/IRL/Q/3/Add.1 8 April 2015 [2].

19 *Ryan v AG* [1965] IR 294, credited with creating the doctrine of unenumerated rights.

20 *TD v Minister for Education* [2001] 4 IR 259. For full analysis of this case and previous decisions leading to this, see Claire-Michelle Smyth, *Social and Economic Rights in Ireland* (Clarus Press 2017).

21 *TD v Minister for Education* [2001] 4 IR 259, 357.

too technical, too expensive, too focused on the individual issue to be an appropriate method for deciding on issues of policy.[22]

Despite some isolated cases where litigants have succeeded, the courts have been careful to base their decision on statutory obligations[23] or on obligations under the European Convention on Human Rights (ECHR) which have been transposed into national law.[24]

Austerity measures and social and economic rights

As the position is clearly established in Ireland that it is not for the courts to protect these rights, it falls to the government to do so. The financial crisis which engulfed Europe in 2008 had governments scurrying to balance their books, resulting in sweeping cuts to public expenditure, the main casualty being social and economic rights. These measures have helped to bring about mass unemployment (rising from 5 per cent to 15 per cent in Ireland), widening inequality,[25] the impact of which has been heterogenous and uneven.[26] Koldo Casla's chapter in this collection (Chapter 10) details the cuts and the impact thereof in the UK, and the situation is no less bleak in Ireland. With increasing regularity, reports have emerged in relation to the appalling living conditions of council tenants,[27] the rise of homelessness[28] and soaring poverty

22 *Sinnott v Minister for Education* [2001] 2 IR 545, 710 reiterated in *TD v Minister for Education* [2002] 4 IR 259, 361.

23 For example, see *Cronin v Minister for Education* unrep, High Court 6 July 2004; *O'Donnell v South Dublin County Council* [2015] IESC 28.

24 *O'Donnell v South Dublin County Council* [2007] IEHC 204.

25 Daniel Vaughan-Whitehead, *Work Inequalities in the Crisis: Evidence from Europe* (International Labour Organisation 2012).

26 Anton Hemreijck, *Changing Welfare States* (Oxford University Press 2013).

27 International Federation for Human Rights (FIDH) lodged a collective complaint with the European Committee on Social Rights on 21 July 2014 alleging breaches of the European Social Charter for substandard accommodation in certain council properties. Full text of the complaint is available at www.coe.int/t/dghl/monitoring/socialcharter/complaints/CC110Case-Doc1_en.pdf> (last accessed 06 January 2017). This case was declared admissible in March 2015 and we are currently awaiting a decision of the Committee. See Cianan Brennan, 'Ireland is Facing a Human Rights Case over the Awful State of Social Housing Here' *Journal.ie* (Dublin, 24 March 2015) www.thejournal.ie/social-housing-human-rights-2009407-Mar2015 (last accessed 14 December 2020).

28 Focus Ireland estimate that there are almost 7,000 people who are officially homeless in Ireland. While the highest percentage of people accessing homeless services were single adults, there has been a significant increase (40 per cent) of families staying in emergency accommodation. In November 2016, there were 2549 children living in emergency accommodation of hostels, bed and breakfasts and hotels. See www.focusireland.ie/resource-hub/about-homelessness/ (last accessed 14 December 2020). The 2016 national census also included a section on homelessness. However, at the time of writing this report has not been published.

rates.[29] Political decisions have statistically had a disproportionate effect on the poorer sections of society. Reports suggest that poverty, in particular child poverty, is still increasing: from 18.7 per cent in 2017[30] to 19.3 per cent in 2019.[31] In addition, analysis of the budget shows that gains are disproportionately favouring those on higher incomes. For example, a single person earning €25,000 overall gained €26.62 per year, while a single person earning €75,000 gained €289.23 per annum in the 2019 budget.

In its concluding observations in 2015, the Committee for the ICESCR observed: that Ireland's response to the crisis has been disproportionately focused on instituting cuts to public spending without altering its tax regime; that the austerity measures were adopted without proper assessment of their impact; and that these steps taken have had a significant impact on the enjoyment of ESC rights of marginalised and vulnerable groups. The Committee urged Ireland to ensure that austerity measures are phased out and enhanced protection is given to ESC rights, to consider reviewing its tax regime and to institute human rights impact assessments in the policymaking process.[32] Further, the latest conclusion from the Committee of the European Social Charter found that Ireland was not compliant with its obligations as a direct result of the restrictive measures taken during austerity measures.

Despite this, and calls from domestic organisations, inequality is deeply entrenched in Ireland, and without recourse to the courts those suffering have little options.

A responsive state

Fineman's recent re-conceptualisation of vulnerability is one that can be utilised to illustrate state failings in relation to protecting the more vulnerable in society in the realm of social and economic rights.[33] Fineman's early work was based on her recognition that equal treatment does not equate to substantive equality and she relates this to her research within marriage and divorce, focusing on the unequal treatment that the wife would inevitably receive. Early attempts to dismantle discrimination centred on goals of achieving parity and gender-neutral

29 Social Justice Ireland Policy Briefing, 'Poverty, Deprivation and Inequality' (July 2016) available at www.socialjustice.ie/sites/default/files/attach/publication/4471/2016-07-04-sjipolicybriefingpoverty-2016final2.pdf (last accessed 14 December2020).

30 Social Justice Ireland, 'Budget 2017 Analysis and Critique' (October 2017) available at www.socialjustice.ie/sites/default/files/attach/publication/4566/2016-10-12-budget2017responsefinalweb.pdf (last accessed 14 December 2020.

31 Social Justice Ireland, 'Budget 2019 Analysis and Critique' (October 2019) available at www.socialjustice.ie/sites/default/files/attach/publication/5500/budget2019analysisfinaled.pdf?cs=true (last accessed 14 December 2020).

32 Concluding Observations of the Third Periodic Report of Ireland, UN Doc E/C.12/IRL/CO/3 (19 June 2015) [11].

33 Martha Albertson Fineman, Vulnerability and Inevitable Inequality' (2017) 4(3) Oslo Law Review 133.

laws,[34] which, as Fineman notes, often results in entrenched inequality. To use her example of the married woman, often she is in a more vulnerable position. Women (even today) tend to be responsible for the majority of the childcare and domestic chores,[35] and resultant evidence shows that the gender pay gap widens for women after they have children.[36] Upon divorce, women will generally assume primary responsibility,[37] she will have fewer career opportunities due to the linked childcare needs, and the difficulties that women face in being granted equitable interest in the family home where they have not financially contributed to it have been played out in the courts relentlessly.[38] Here, it is clear that the equal treatment of spouses does not result in equality and Fineman advocates for unequal treatment in order to achieve parity in the outcome.

Transpose this on to the austerity measures that are discussed in this chapter. What the state has been doing thus far is imposing blanket, universal cuts to benefits or increases in taxes. As shown above, this has resulted in inequality, with those in lower socio-economic brackets suffering disproportionately.

What Fineman posits is that the state should respond with unequal treatment to be better able to respond to those in distress. Fineman concludes that in this context the state 'must be one that recognises relationships or positions of inevitable inequality, as well as universal vulnerability and dependency acting as an instrument of social justice in both its law making and enforcement functions'.[39] Fineman's theory is music to the ears of every scholar and lawyer who advocates and campaigns for justice in the realm of social and economic rights. It is abundantly clear that decisions are being taken in the name of equality which have a most discriminatory outcome.

Meaningful protection: is justiciability necessary?

Despite the clear and abundant evidence that austerity measures have exacerbated poverty and result in significant inequalities, and notwithstanding calls from international and national organisations for 'equality proofing' of budgets, little has been done. Mounting evidence shows that states will not live up to their responsibilities in the absence of legal accountability. As noted above, Ireland is a party to international (ICESCR) and regional (ESC and ECHR) treaties which place upon it the obligation of protecting and realising these rights.

34 Wendy Williams, 'The Equality Crisis: Some Reflections on Courts, Culture and Feminism' (1982) 7 Women's Rights Law Reports 175.

35 European Institute for Gender Equality, Gender Equality Index 2017 https://eige.europa.eu/gender-equality-index/2015/domain/time/IE (last accessed 14 December 2020).

36 Latest statistics in Ireland show that the gender pay gap is at 13.9 per cent www.genderequality.ie/en/GE/Pages/GenderPayGap (last accessed 14 December 2020).

37 According to the last census report (2016), 84 per cent of lone parents were female www.cso.ie/en/releasesandpublications/ep/p-cp4hf/cp4hf/fmls/ (last accessed 14 December 2020).

38 See, for example, *L v L* [1992] 2 IR 77. Somewhat ameliorated by the Family Law (Divorce) Act 1996 and the Civil Partnership and Certain Rights and Obligation of Cohabitants Act 2010.

39 Martha Albertson Fineman, 'Vulnerability and Inevitable Inequality' (2017) 4(3) Oslo Law Review 133, 149.

In response to the compelling and severe breaches of social and economic rights, the Committee on Economic, Social and Cultural Rights at the United Nations[40] observed that:

> [t]he international community as a whole continue to tolerate all too often breaches of economic, social and cultural rights which, if they incurred in relation to civil and political rights, would provoke expressions of horror and outrage and would lead to concerted calls for immediate remedial action.[41]

The adoption of the optional protocol to the ICESCR in June 2008 goes some way in approximating the rights at an international level by allowing for an individual complaints mechanism.[42] A number of complaints relating to austerity measures have been brought before the Committee, which has unfortunately taken a restrictive view. Of the 16 cases to be heard by the Committee, only 4 have been deemed admissible. Of those 4 cases, 3 of them have had violations of the Covenant Rights upheld.[43] Primarily, these followed the line of reasoning that has thus far been adopted in the ECHR, finding a violation due to the lack of procedural safeguards in place. For example, both cases that were determined against Spain involved evictions and subsequent homelessness and turned on the lack of legal safeguards for those facing eviction and the absence of alternative accommodation.

The European Committee on Social Rights (previously called the Committee of Independent Experts) oversees the enforcement of the European Social Charter, engages in legal interpretation of its provisions together with reviewing large volumes of materials to determine whether a state is in compliance with the articles to which it has bound itself.[44] The Council

40 Established in 1985 by UN General Assembly Resolution 1985/17 of 28 May 1985. Its primary function prior to the introduction of the optional protocol was to oversee the periodic review of state compliance with implementation of the rights contained within the ICESCR and also the development and issuance of General Comments to expand on the interpretation of the Covenant rights.

41 Committee Statement to the World Conference, UN Doc E/1993/22 [83].

42 Resolution of the Human Rights Council 8/2 of 18 June 2008 adopted by the General Assembly under resolution A/RES/63/117 10 December 2008. For a detailed analysis of the background to the drafting of the optional protocol, see Claire Mahon, 'Progress at the Front: The Draft Optional Protocol to the International Covenant on Economic Social and Cultural Rights' (2008) 8 Human Rights Law Review 617; Tara Melish, 'Introductory Note to the Optional Protocol to the International Covenant on Economic Social and Cultural Rights' (2009) 48 International Legal Materials 256; Scott Leckie, 'Another Step Towards Indivisibility: Identifying Key Features of Violations of Economic, Social and Cultural Rights' (1998) 20 Human Rights Quarterly 81.

43 *IDG v Spain* E/C.12/55/D/2/2014 decision dated 19 June 2015; *Marcia Cecelia Trujillo Calero v Ecuador* E/C.12/63/D/10/2015 decision dated 26 March 2018; *Mohammed Ben Djazia and Naouel Bellili* E/C.12/61/D/5/2015 decision dated 20 June 2017.

44 Holly Cullen, 'The Collective Complaints System of the European Social Charter: Interpretative Methods of the European Committee on Social Rights' (2009) 9(1) Human Rights Law Review 61, 64.

of Europe's Parliamentary Assembly has previously called for an enhancement of the Committee and recommended that a court akin to the European Court of Human Rights be established.[45] This new court would be solely concerned with social and economic rights, making the rights within the ESC enforceable in the same manner as those protected by the ECHR. This recommendation has not been met with rapturous enthusiasm and to date the Committee's role remains primarily that of a supervisory body who issues recommendations.

The collective complaints procedure was introduced as part of the revitalisation of the Charter which began in 1990 and entered into force in July 1998.[46] The explanatory report to the protocol explains that it is 'designed to increase the efficiency of the supervisory machinery based solely on the submission of government reports'.[47] While the Committee does regularly determine that states are in breach of Charter rights (as in *European Roma Rights Centre (ERRC) v Ireland*, which contends that the housing conditions and evictions of traveller families, in particular traveller children, breach articles 16, 17 and 30),[48] they have no enforcement powers, which makes such declarations merely a political statement. The Committee must strictly adhere to its powers and cannot award compensation.[49] In the limited cases where the Committee has requested that the Committee of Ministers makes a contribution to the costs of the complainant, such requests have been denied.[50] This again undermines the status of social and economic rights when compared to the European Convention, where the court can order 'just satisfaction', which is legally binding on the state concerned.

The European Court of Human Rights has had some positive impact in protecting social and economic rights, but it has stopped short of imposing positive obligations. Primarily, victories have centred on the lack of procedural safeguards (*McCann v UK*)[51] or access to justice (*Mehmet and Suna Yigit v Turkey*).[52] The closest that the court has come to imposing a positive duty can be seen in *Moldovan v Romania*, where it was found that the state had a duty to restore the living conditions of the applicants where it was complicit in the destruction of their homes;[53] or *Soares de Melo v Portugal*, where the applicant's children were removed from her care by the state on the grounds that her poverty-stricken conditions constituted neglect.[54] In finding a breach of Article

45 Recommendation 1354 of 28 January 1998.

46 Article 14(1) of the Protocol.

47 Council of Europe, Explanatory Report on the Collective Complaints Protocol [1995] COETSER 3 (9 November 1995) [1–8].

48 *European Roma Rights Centre (ERRC) v Ireland* Complaint No 100/2013 Decision on the Merits 16 May 2016.

49 *Confédération Francaise de l'Encadrement v France* Complaint No 9/2000.

50 For example, see *European Roma Rights Centre v France* Complaint No 15/2003.

51 *McCann v UK* [2008] ECHR 385.

52 *Mehmet and Suna Yigit v Turkey* [2007] ECHR 47.

53 *Moldovan v Romania* (2005) 44 EHRR 302.

54 *Soares de Melo v Portugal* App No 72850/14 (ECtHR 16 May 2016).

8 of the Convention, the court was highly critical of the fact that the state was aware of the situation in which the applicant and her children were living and did nothing to intervene or assist. However, cases brought before the court relating to austerity measures have primarily been found to be either inadmissible or unfounded, with the court generally citing proportionality, margin of appreciation and the temporary nature of austerity measures.[55] However, there have been some exceptions, and in *NKM v Hungary* the court found that the imposition of 98 per cent tax was a violation of Article 1 Protocol 1;[56] and in *McDonald v UK* the decision to remove a night-time carer for a severely disabled woman as part of austerity measures, leaving the woman instead to rely on incontinence pads, was a violation of her right to privacy.[57]

There have been a number of national decisions that have had a significant impact on curtailing governments' enthusiastic austerity measures, including the Portuguese Constitutional Court determining that the suspension of holiday pay was a breach of the equality guarantee in the Constitution[58] and that the introduction of a flat rate tax was disproportionate and unequal.[59] The Latvian Constitutional Court has also ruled that pension cuts were unconstitutional, as they were excessive.[60] In the UK, as outlined by Koldo Casla (see Chapter 10), the intervention of the court has been essential in overturning the harshest effects of benefit caps[61] and 'bedroom taxes'.[62]

In acknowledgement of the inadequacy of the current position, and in affirmation of the emerging awareness that judicial intervention is necessary, the Constitutional Convention voted in 2014 to strengthen the legal position of social and economic rights.[63] This recommendation advocates for specific inclusion of particular social and economic rights into the text

55 *Khoniakina v Georgia* [2012] ECHR 1050; *Frimu & Ors v Romania* App No 45312/07 7 February 2012; *Santos Januario v Portugal* [2013] ECHR 321; *Koufaki v Greece* App No 57665/12 7 May 2013; *Savickas v Lithuania* [2013] ECHR 328; *Mamatas & Ors v Greece* [2016] ECHR 694; *P Plaisier BV v Netherlands* App No 46184/16 7 December 2017.

56 *NKM v Hungary* [2013] ECHR 546.

57 *McDonald v UK* [2014] ECHR 141.

58 Judgment 353/2012 of the Portuguese Constitutional Court State Budget Law for 2012.

59 Judgment 187/2013 of the Portuguese Constitutional Court State Budget Law for 2013.

60 Case No 2009–43–01.

61 *R (on the application of SG and others (previously JS and others)) (Appellants) v Secretary of State for Work and Pensions (Respondent)* [2015] UKSC 16.

62 *R (Carmichael and Rourke) v. Secretary of State for Work and Pensions* [2016] UKSC 58.

63 The Convention was established by Resolution of the Houses of the Oireachtas of July 2012. The Convention was tasked with examining and making proposals on specified areas of the Constitution. However, it also had scope to receive recommendations on other issues. On 17 December 2013, the Convention announced in its press release that it would hear submissions on social and economic rights in its final sittings and make recommendations on the amendment of the Constitution to include the same. These meetings were held in February 2014. Full terms of reference can be found at www.constitution.ie/Convention.aspx#terms-of-reference (last accessed 24 November 2016).

of the Constitution.[64] This would require a referendum,[65] which does not appear to be on the political agenda.[66] Further, Scotland have recently taken legislative steps in the Social Security (Scotland) Act 2018, which is enacted around a framework acknowledging that access to social security is a human right,[67] building on their existing rights-based approach to housing and shelter.[68]

Conclusion

It is clear that social and economic rights provide an easy option when it comes to budgetary cuts. These cuts hit the most disadvantaged groups and, given the stance of the Supreme Court, only in extreme and exceptional circumstances will the court intervene. Fineman observes that the 'responsible state' encompasses a reactive state in both law and practice. However, without the legal backstop to enforce the principle, practice will continue to promulgate inequality. Ideally, Fineman's position is the superlative one; a political arm that ensures its decisions result in substantive, rather than merely formative, equality and a judiciary ready to act when this falls short.

64 This recommendation was passed by 85 per cent of the participants. The Convention also recommended specific protection for those with disabilities and recognition of cultural and linguistic rights. A full breakdown of the votes is available at www.constitution.ie/AttachmentDownload.ashx?mid=adc4c56a-a09c-e311-a7ce-005056a32ee4 (last accessed 24 November 2016).

65 Article 46.2 of the Constitution provides that any amendment by way of 'variation, addition or repeal' to the text of the Constitution can only be done by way of a referendum.

66 To date there have been three Private Members' Bills introduced to the Dáil calling for such a referendum. The Twenty-First Amendment of the Constitution (No. 3) Bill 1999 introduced by Ruairi Quinn was defeated. The Thirty–First Amendment of the Constitution (Economic, Social and Cultural Rights) Bill 2012 introduced by Kevin Humphries has not progressed and, most recently, the Thirty-Fourth Amendment of the Constitution (Economic, Social and Cultural Rights) Bill 2014 introduced by Thomas Pringle was voted down on 20 May 2015. These bills are available to view at www.oireachtas.ie/viewdoc.asp?m=&DocID=-1&CatID=59 (last accessed 24 November 2016).

67 For analysis, see Colm O'Cinneide, 'The Social Security (Scotland) Act 2018 – A Rights Based Approach to Social Security?' 23(1) Edinburgh Law Review 1.

68 Housing (Scotland) Act 2001. See also Beth Watts, 'Rights, Needs and Stigma: A Comparison of Homelessness Policy in Ireland and Scotland' (2013) 7 European Journal of Homelessness 41.

10 Social rights and situational vulnerability in the UK

Theory and practice

Koldo Casla

University of Essex

This chapter engages with the vulnerability approach to assess UK welfare reforms implemented between 2010 and 2016, and their impact on economic and social rights. The last few years (since 2019) are not covered in the following analysis, which is divided into two sections. First, it provides a theoretical reflection of the contribution of the notion of situational vulnerability to social rights understood as the material conditions of freedom in a given community or society; and second, the chapter presents how tax and social security changes since 2010 have fuelled inequalities and harmed society, increasing the risk of abuse, discrimination and disadvantage.

Introduction

A situational understanding of vulnerability can help to rethink equality and social rights. This chapter engages with the vulnerability approach to assess UK welfare reforms and their impact on economic and social rights.[1]

First, the chapter presents a brief theoretical analysis of the contribution of the notion of vulnerability to a community-based and vernacular idea of human rights. Second, using the UK as a case study, the chapter brings the theory down to earth to critique the way in which specific tax and social security policies implemented since 2010 have fuelled inequalities and damaged society, increasing the risk of harm, abuse, discrimination and disadvantage.

Vulnerability as the restriction of freedom and equality

Vulnerability is '*the* primal human condition'.[2] We are not islands. We all depend on each other. We are all vulnerable.

1 By 'economic and social rights', or simply 'social rights', I mean the rights proclaimed in international human rights law, in particular in the International Covenant on Economic, Social and Cultural Rights and in the European Social Charter. This includes the right to health, the right to an adequate standard of living (including food and housing), the right to education, the right to social security and workers' rights.

2 Martha Albertson Fineman, 'Vulnerability and Inevitable Inequality' (2017) 4(3) Oslo Law Review 133, 142.

DOI: 10.4324/9780429023149-11

When it comes to the material conditions of freedom we are not vulnerable in the same way. Socio-economic disadvantages are unevenly distributed in society. Some of us are materially speaking less autonomous than others. Taking human rights seriously means that all members of a given community share the responsibility to ensure that nobody is left to their fate. As written by Martha Fineman:

> It is human vulnerability that compels the creation of social relationships found in designated social institutions, such as the family, the market, the educational system and so on. The very formation of communities, associations, and even political entities and nation-states are responses to human vulnerability.[3]

When we become aware of our vulnerability, we become better citizens, accomplices with each other, members of the same political community. And citizenship is a strong foundation for social rights.

As eloquently put by Wolfgang Streeck, inequality reaches a morally unacceptable level when the privileged come to believe that their lives are disconnected from anybody else's:

> [Inequality has] gone so far that the rich may rightly consider their fate and that of their families to have become independent from the fates of the societies from which they extract their wealth. As a result, they can afford no longer to care about them. This becomes a problem – one of 'moral hazard' – when differences in wealth become so extensive that they give rise to a fusion of economic and political power – that is, *oligarchy*.[4]

If one is to take inequality seriously from the perspective of human rights, the argument must be built from the reciprocal responsibilities in a community or society. This idea is not alien to international human rights law. Article 29(1) of the Universal Declaration of Human Rights established clearly that, for the bill of rights to make sense, everyone must have 'duties to the community in which alone the free and full development of *his* personality is possible' (sic).

As such, human rights, and particularly social rights, become essential ingredients of citizenship, as famously formulated by T. H. Marshall at the dawning of the British welfare state.[5] For him, 'social citizenship stemmed from a specific historical and cultural context, stated in national terms, which was informed by a communitarian sensibility. Citizenship was not universal, and it

3 Ibid.

4 Wolfgang Streeck, *How Will Capitalism End?* (Verso 2017), 28.

5 T. H. Marshall, *Citizenship and Social Class and Other Essays* (Cambridge University Press 1950).

needed to be cultivated in specific ways according to particular circumstances.'[6] Marshall did not feel the need to mention the Universal Declaration of Human Rights, but if he had considered it he would have probably agreed that Article 29 had to be in there.

This communitarianism is not cultural or ethnical, but geographical, sociological and republican. The community is synonymous with society and defined by the group of individuals that coexist in a certain space and decide their future together.

Taking material equality seriously, this communitarian approach conceptualises social rights as the material conditions of freedom. The capabilities approach, developed by Nussbaum and Sen, contributes to fleshing out the meaning of material conditions of freedom.[7] The capabilities approach puts the accent on the critical conditions that enable individuals to do something or to be someone – that is, to develop their own personality. The approach is flexible enough to recognise the inherent diversity in people's choices. It also acknowledges the importance of structural and institutional triggers and constraints.

Justifying social rights as the material conditions of freedom co-opts the most characteristic liberal axiom – freedom as negative liberty – to demand a fairer distribution of resources to ensure that everyone is really free. Growing inequality within a country suggests that public authorities are not making use of *all* available resources to ensure an adequate standard of living, as required by the International Covenant on Economic, Social and Cultural Rights.[8] In this day and age, economically advanced societies already have the necessary resources to satisfy an adequate standard of living for everyone. The problem is that most of these resources are privately owned. In fact, many of these resources have been 'accumulated by dispossession'[9] during the neoliberal era through the privatisation of public services, the financialisation of housing and the progressive lowering of the tax pressure on the wealthy. Taking equality seriously in social rights research and advocacy must grasp the nettle of this regression. Society must empower the State to intervene over those resources that are privately owned but necessary to advance in the progressive enjoyment of social rights.

The resources to protect, promote and progressively fulfil economic and social rights are generally available in advanced economies. Not making use of them to ensure an adequate standard of living is a political choice. Poverty and inequality are the product of policy decisions that increase the risk of vulnerability, understood – in the words of Britain's Equality and Human Rights

6 Julia Moses, 'Social Citizenship and Social Rights in an Age of Extremes: T. H. Marshall's Social Philosophy in the *Longue Durée*' (2019) 16 Modern Intellectual History 155, 158.

7 Martha Nussbaum, 'Capabilities and Human Rights' (1997) 66(2) Fordham Law Review 273; Amartya Sen, 'Elements of a Theory of Human Rights' (2004) 32(4) Philosophy & Public Affairs 315.

8 Articles 2(1) and 11.

9 David Harvey, 'The "New" Imperialism: Accumulation by Dispossession' (2004) 40 Socialist Register 63.

Commission (EHRC) – as 'the risk of harm, abuse, discrimination or disadvantage' for groups and individuals.[10]

The following section will show how austerity policies implemented in the UK since 2010 increased individuals' vulnerability by fuelling material inequality and curtailing the welfare state.

Equality and UK welfare reforms between 2010 and 2016

As a party to the International Covenant on Economic, Social and Cultural Rights, the UK must take steps, to the maximum of its available resources, to achieve progressively the realisation of economic, social and cultural rights, including the right to social security.[11] To comply with human rights standards, policy adjustments in times of economic crisis must be: temporary, necessary and proportionate; must be adopted after meaningful engagement with those most affected by them; must not be discriminatory; must mitigate inequalities; and ensure that the rights of the most disadvantaged people are not disproportionately affected.[12] These are the human rights principles of non-retrogression.

The most significant changes to the UK's social security were introduced through the Welfare Reform Act 2012 and the Welfare Reform and Work Act 2016, and include: (a) benefit cap, (b) the introduction of Universal Credit, bringing most welfare support into a single benefit, (c) replacing the Disability Living Allowance with personal independence payments, (d) tougher sanctions in case of breach of requirements, (e) a freeze on benefits and (f) the limitation of the Child Tax Credit and Universal Credit awards to two children.[13]

The UK's Office for Budget Responsibility observed in 2016 that 'the scale and sustained nature of the welfare spending cuts seen over the current and previous Parliaments are in some respects unprecedented'.[14] The UK made

10 Equality and Human Rights Commission, *Measurement Framework for Equality and Human Rights* (Equality and Human Rights Commission 2017) 48.

11 Articles 2(1) and 9.

12 UN CESCR, *Letter by the Chairperson of the CESCR to States parties to the ICESCR*, 12 May 2012. See also CESCR, *Public Debt, Austerity Measures and the ICESCR: Statement by the CESCR*, 24 June 2016, UN doc: E/C.12/2016/1, para 4.

13 This section is based on two submissions to the UN Special Rapporteur on Extreme Poverty and Human Rights, Philip Alston, from September 2018: one from Just Fair supported by 15 other organisations, Just Fair, 'Visit by the UN Special Rapporteur on Extreme Poverty and Human Rights, Philip Alston, to the UK from 5 to 16 November 2018: Written Submission' http://justfair.org.uk/wp-content/uploads/2018/09/Just_Fair_15_Alston_Submission-FINAL.pdf (last accessed 20 December 2020); and another from Newcastle University, supported by Newcastle City Council, 'Visit by the UN Special Rapporteur on Extreme Poverty and Human Rights, Philip Alston, to the UK from 5 to 16 November 2018: Written Submission' https://research.ncl.ac.uk/article22/outputspublications/NCL%20submission%20to%20Philip%20Alston%20Sep2018%20final.pdf (last accessed 14 December 2020). The author of this chapter was the coordinator of both submissions.

14 Office for Budget Responsibility, *Welfare Trends Report* (October 2016) 12 available online http://obr.uk/wtr/welfare-trends-report-october-2016/ (last accessed 14 December 2020).

remarkable savings at the expense of welfare expenditure. Reforms introduced since 2010 saved around £26 billion by the end of 2017, roughly 10 per cent of what welfare spending might otherwise have been, and the greatest savings came from tax credits (£4 billion lower) and child benefits (22 per cent lower).[15]

The UK's public deficit reached 2 per cent in the year ending March 2018,[16] but this figure does not reflect the economic cost of poverty in terms of public services, healthcare, achievement gap in schools, adult social care, housing and homelessness, and police and criminal justice. The cost of UK poverty was estimated at £78 billion per year in 2016.[17]

The EHRC has shown that, between 2010 and 2022, public spending per head is forecast to fall by 18 per cent in England, 5.5 per cent in Wales and just over 1 per cent in Scotland.[18] Cash losses for lower income households are larger in England than in Wales or Scotland. Households where adults are under 55 experienced larger losses from public spending changes, and the effects were particularly noteworthy in households where the adults are aged 18–24. Households with children suffer larger losses particularly due to cuts to school spending. Lone parents (9 in 10 of which are women) lose more than any other type of family in all three countries: 18.7 per cent in England, 10.5 per cent in Wales and 7.6 per cent in Scotland.

One of the requirements of the human rights principle of non-retrogression is that the implemented measures must be necessary and justifiable. In other words, to comply with human rights standards, they must be fit for the intended purposes. They must work.

The UK government justified welfare reforms as a lever to encourage, 'including through benefit sanctions where appropriate, those who can work to find and keep work and to increase their earnings rather than relying on benefits'.[19]

However, the UK Statistics Authority cast doubt on any possible causal relationship between welfare reforms and the labour market: 'The available numerical evidence does not demonstrate a particularly strong causal link between the benefit cap and the decisions made by individuals about moving into work.'[20]

15 House of Commons Library, *Welfare Savings 2010–11 to 2020–21* (July 2016) https://commonslibrary.parliament.uk/research-briefings/cbp-7667/ (last accessed 14 December 2020).

16 Office for National Statistics, *UK Government Debt and Deficit: March 2018* (July 2018) www.ons.gov.uk/economy/governmentpublicsectorandtaxes/publicspending/bulletins/ukgovernmentdebtanddeficitforeurostatmaast/march2018 (last accessed 14 December 2020).

17 Glen Bramley, Donald Hirsch, Mandy Littlewood and David Watkins, *Counting the Cost of UK Poverty* (Joseph Rowntree Foundation 2016).

18 Equality and Human Rights Commission, *The Cumulative Impact on Living Standards of Public Spending Changes* (Equality and Human Rights Commission 2018).

19 UK Government Ministry of Justice, *National Report to the UN Universal Periodic Review* (February 2017) para 50.

20 Letter from the Chair of the UK Statistics Authority to Jonathan Portes (December 2014) www.statisticsauthority.gov.uk/archive/reports---correspondence/correspondence/letter-from-sir-andrew-dilnot-to-jonathan-portes-171214.pdf (last accessed 15 May 2020).

The National Audit Office disclosed that neither they nor the Department of Work and Pensions were confident it would ever be possible to measure whether the economic goal of increasing employment has been achieved.[21] It is true that welfare reforms and historically low levels of unemployment have happened at the same time, but correlation and causation are two separate things.

In March 2015, the Supreme Court said that 'it cannot possibly be in the best interests of the children affected by the (benefit) cap to deprive them of the means to provide them with adequate food, clothing, warmth and housing, the basic necessities of life'.[22] In November 2016, the Court ruled that adults with a disability who cannot share a room with another person should not have their housing benefit reduced.[23]

The House of Commons Public Accounts Committee denounced the 'unexplained variation' in the use of benefit sanctions in different parts of the country.[24] Reflecting on the role of sanctions in getting more people to work, the Work and Pensions Committee concluded that, 'at best, evidence on the effectiveness of sanctions is mixed, and at worst, it shows them to be counterproductive'.[25] Both this Committee and the National Audit Office criticised the government for not doing enough to assess the impact of sanctions on people on low incomes.[26]

The tax and welfare cuts had a regressive effect on social protection. The cumulative impact assessment by the Equality and Human Rights Commission showed that key human rights requirements have not been met – namely, the principle of proportionality, non-discrimination, protection of most disadvantaged groups and independent review. The largest cash gains from changes to income tax and National Insurance contributions were enjoyed by the wealthiest 30 per cent.[27] As a result of changes to benefits and tax credits, households in the second and third deciles lost more than twice as much as those in the top 20 per cent. It was estimated that, at this pace, by 2022, 1.5 million more

21 National Audit Office, *Rolling out Universal Credit* (June 2018) 10 www.nao.org.uk/report/rolling-out-universal-credit/ (last accessed 14 December 2020).

22 *R (on the application of SG and others (previously JS and others)) (Appellants) v Secretary of State for Work and Pensions (Respondent)* [2015] UKSC 16, para 226.

23 *R (Carmichael and Rourke) v. Secretary of State for Work and Pensions* [2016] UKSC 58.

24 House of Commons Public Accounts Committee, *Benefit Sanctions* (February 2017) 3, 5, 7 https://publications.parliament.uk/pa/cm201617/cmselect/cmpubacc/775/775.pdf (last accessed 14 December 2020).

25 House of Commons Work and Pensions Committee, *Benefit Sanctions* (October 2018) 18 https://publications.parliament.uk/pa/cm201719/cmselect/cmworpen/955/955.pdf (last accessed 14 December 2020).

26 Ibid, 19; National Audit Office, *Benefit Sanctions* (November 2016) 7 www.nao.org.uk/report/benefit-sanctions/ (last accessed 14 December 2020).

27 Equality and Human Rights Commission, *Cumulative Impact of Tax and Welfare Reforms* (March 2018) www.equalityhumanrights.com/en/publication-download/cumulative-impact-tax-and-welfare-reforms (last accessed 14 December 2020).

children would live in poverty, the child poverty rate for lone parent households (90 per cent of whom are women) would increase from 37 to 62 per cent and households with at least one disabled adult and a disabled child would lose 13 per cent of their income. Lone mothers will lose almost one fifth of their annual income.

Four UN Special Rapporteurs – the Committee on the Rights of the Child; the Committee on Economic, Social and Cultural Rights; the Committee on the Rights of Persons with Disabilities; and the European Committee of Social Rights – expressed serious doubts about the compatibility of 'welfare' reforms with the UK's international human rights obligations.[28]

After a two-week mission to the UK in November 2018, the UN Special Rapporteur on Extreme Poverty and Human Rights, Professor Philip Alston, issued a damning report.[29] Alston labelled poverty levels as 'patently unjust and contrary to British values'.[30] He accused the government of remaining 'determinedly in a state of denial',[31] and concluded 'that the driving force (behind welfare reforms) has not been economic but rather a commitment to achieving radical social re-engineering'.[32]

> British compassion for those who are suffering has been replaced by a punitive, mean-spirited, and often callous approach apparently designed to instil discipline where it is least useful, to impose a rigid order on the lives of those least capable of coping with today's world, and elevating the goal of enforcing blind compliance over a genuine concern to improve the well-being of those at the lowest levels of British society.[33]

Even without considering the impact of Covid-19, inequality is projected to rise in the coming years, with sluggish growth across much of the distribution

28 UN Special Rapporteurs on Housing, on Rights of Persons with Disabilities, on Extreme Poverty, and on the Right to Food, 'Joint Letter to the UK Government', UN doc. AL GBR 1/2016, April 2016, 12; Committee on the Rights of the Child, *Concluding Observations: UK*, July 2016, UN doc. CRC/C/GBR/CO/5, paras 66 and 69–70; Committee on Economic Social and Cultural Rights, *Concluding Observations: UK*, July 2016, UN doc: E/C.12/GBR/CO/6; paras 40–42 and 47–48; Committee on the Rights of Persons with Disabilities, *Inquiry Concerning the UK*, 2016, UN doc. CRPD/C/15/R.2/Rev.1; European Committee of Social Rights, *Conclusions XXI-2 (2017) United Kingdom*, January 2018. See also British Institute of Human Rights et al., *Joint Civil Society Report to the UN Universal Periodic Review of the UK (3rd Cycle)*, 2016, 20–23 www.bihr.org.uk/Handlers/Download.ashx?IDMF=899c9202-602e-4244-b776-52ddaf6e79d3 (last accessed 14 December 2020).

29 UN Special Rapporteur on Extreme Poverty and Human Rights, 'Statement on Visit to the United Kingdom' (16 November 2018) www.ohchr.org/EN/NewsEvents/Pages/DisplayNews.aspx?NewsID=23881&LangID=E (last accessed 14 December 2020).

30 Ibid, 1.

31 Ibid.

32 Ibid, 2.

33 Ibid, 3.

and a 'leaving behind' of those at the bottom.[34] Wealth inequality contracted in the decade prior to the financial crisis, but it is now rising in part because of the decreasing accessibility of home ownership and the decoupling of land value and economic growth.[35]

Inequality is closely linked to the poverty premium – that is, the fact that poorer people pay more for essential goods and services. Lower income households have to assign a greater share of their food budget to basic groceries and, relative to their disposable income, they spend approximately three times as much in electricity, gas and other fuels than those with the highest income.[36]

In his end of mission statement, the UN Special Rapporteur also lamented that, in his 2018 Budget, the Chancellor could have ended the benefit freeze, and instead chose to change the income tax thresholds in a way that benefits particularly those who are better off.[37] 'Choice' is the keyword here. The UK has the means to end poverty and reduce inequalities. It is a matter of political choice not to do so.

Austerity's tentacles reached beyond tax and social security; it directly affected the resources made available to local authorities. According to the National Audit Office, government funding for local authorities fell in real terms by 49.1 per cent between 2010 and 2018.[38] The Institute for Fiscal Studies estimated that the local authorities that received the largest share of their funding from government grants in 2009 experienced most significant cuts to their service spending. The 10 per cent of authorities most dependent on grants in 2009 received an average cut of 33 per cent, compared to 12 per cent for the 10 per cent of authorities that are less dependent on grants.[39]

34 Resolution Foundation, *The Living Standards Outlook* (February 2018) 65 www.resolutionfoundation.org/publications/the-living-standards-outlook-2018/ (last accessed 14 December 2020); Institute for Fiscal Studies, *Living Standards, Poverty and Inequality in the UK: 2017–18 to 2021–22* (November 2017) www.ifs.org.uk/publications/10028 (last accessed 14 December 2020).

35 Resolution Foundation, *Britain's Increasingly Unevenly Shared Property Wealth is Driving up Inequality after a Decade-Long Fall* (June 2017) www.resolutionfoundation.org/media/press-releases/britains-increasingly-unevenly-shared-property-wealth-is-driving-up-inequality-after-a-decade-long-fall/%20I (last accessed 3 March 2020); The Progressive Policy Think Tank, *Capital Gains: Broadening Company Ownership in the UK Economy* (December 2017) www.ippr.org/research/publications/CEJ-capital-gains (last accessed 14 December 2020.

36 Office for National Statistics, *Family Spending in the UK: Financial Year Ending March 2016* (February 2017) www.ons.gov.uk/peoplepopulationandcommunity/personalandhouseholdfinances/expenditure/bulletins/familyspendingintheuk/financialyearendingmarch2016 (last accessed 14 December 2020).

37 UN Special Rapporteur on Extreme Poverty and Human Rights, 'Statement on Visit to the United Kingdom' (16 November 2018) 13 www.ohchr.org/EN/NewsEvents/Pages/DisplayNews.aspx?NewsID=23881&LangID=E (last accessed 14 December 2020).

38 National Audit Office, *Financial Sustainability of Local Authorities* (March 2018) www.nao.org.uk/report/financial-sustainability-of-local-authorities-2018/ (last accessed 14 December 2020).

39 Neil Amin Smith, David Phillips and Polly Simpson, *Council-Level Figures on Spending Cuts and Business Rates Income* (Institute for Fiscal Studies, November 2016) www.ifs.org.uk/publications/8780 (last accessed 14 December 2020).

Councils' spending on adult social care fell by 10 per cent in real terms between 2009 and 2015, and it was budgeted to be 3 per cent lower in 2018 than in 2009.[40] The Campaign for Better Transport calculated that local spending on buses in England was cut by £172 million in real terms since 2010/2011, a reduction of 46 per cent.[41] According to the Social Market Foundation, since 2015 over 47,000 children were in the care of local authorities deemed by Ofsted (Office for Standards in Education, Children's Services and Skills) to have inadequate children's services or services that require improvement.[42] Figures obtained by a freedom of information request showed public spending on residential rehab and detox treatment in England had fallen by 15 per cent since 2013/2014, when the government removed the ring fence that had required local authorities to spend certain amounts on drug and alcohol treatment.[43] The impact of local government funding cuts in England was unevenly distributed across regions: 97 per cent of the reductions in local spending on social care, children and homelessness between 2011 and 2018 took place in the fifth most deprived councils.[44]

The damaging effects of these cuts were also disproportionately distributed in society. Minority ethnic groups were more likely to live in deprived areas, and cuts to local authority spending led to cuts in local services many women rely on, such as social care, public transport, services for children and voluntary sector organisations.[45]

The socio-economic duty contained in Section 1 of the Equality Act 2010 would require public authorities to actively consider how they can reduce inequalities of outcome derived from socio-economic disadvantage. However, successive governments have failed to bring the duty to life in England.[46] Although it would only apply to public authorities and not private actors, the implementation of the socio-economic duty would constitute a significant step forward in terms of transparency, accountability and evidence-based

40 David Phillips and Polly Simpson, *Changes in Councils' Adult Social Care and Overall Service Spending in England, 2009–10 to 2017–18* (Institute for Fiscal Studies, June 2018) www.ifs.org.uk/publications/13066 (last accessed 14 December 2020).

41 Campaign for Better Transport, *Buses in Crisis: A Report on Bus Funding across England and Wales 2010–2018* (June 2018) https://bettertransport.org.uk/buses-in-crisis-2018 (last accessed 14 December 2020).

42 Matthew Oakley, *Looked After Children* (Social Market Foundation, 2018) www.smf.co.uk/publications/looked-after-children/ (last accessed 14 December 2020.

43 UK Addiction Treatment Centres, *Our Campaign Reveals Cuts to Addiction Treatment Funding, as Drug Deaths Rise* (August 2018) www.ukat.co.uk/addiction-treatment/ukat-campaign-reveals-cuts-addiction-treatment-funding-drug-deaths-rise/ (last accessed 14 December 2020).

44 Lloyds Bank Foundation and New Policy Institute, *A Quiet Crisis: Local Government Spending on Disadvantage in England* (September 2018) www.npi.org.uk/files/7715/3669/7306/A_quiet_crisis_final.pdf (last accessed 14 December 2020).

45 Women's Budget Group and Runnymede Trust, *Intersecting Inequalities: The Impact of Austerity on Black and Minority Ethnic Women in the UK* (October 2017) www.intersecting-inequalities.com/ Last accessed 14 December 2020).

46 The duty has been in force in Scotland since 2018 and in Wales since 2021.

policymaking at all levels of government. However, the UK government has refused to use this tool precisely when it was most needed.

Conclusion

Ideological austerity eroded some of the fundamental pillars of a fair society. Welfare reforms and local government funding cuts disproportionately affected those who need society's protection the most. The government failed to prove that austerity policies meet the human rights threshold.

Specific public policies put more people at higher risk of harm, abuse, discrimination and disadvantage. The socio-economic duty could have helped address some of the worst causal links between misplaced policies and negative consequences. However, the government refused to bring it into effect, thereby taking away a device that could have been very useful in holding public authorities accountable.

A vulnerability approach contributes to bringing the idea of human rights closer to home, from a global and individualist perspective to a more local and communitarian one. This chapter has advocated a conceptualisation of social rights as the material conditions of freedom within a given community or society. This frame can go hand in hand with the vulnerability approach. Everyone is entitled to social rights, but public policy must prioritise those that are struggling the most because of their material circumstances in light of rising power, income and wealth inequalities.

11 Is marriage a cure for all ills?

Vulnerability and LGBTQ communities in the wake of the Marriage Referendum

Fergus Ryan
Maynooth University

2020 was the fifth anniversary of the passage in Ireland of the 2015 marriage referendum[1] and of the Gender Recognition Act 2015. Both measures significantly improved the social and legal position of LGBTQ[2] people in Ireland. In particular, the marriage referendum and the subsequent Marriage Act 2015 extended civil marriage (and the associated status and protection flowing from marriage) to same-sex couples. The Gender Recognition Act 2015 allows adults easy access to legal recognition of their gender identity, with minimal preconditions.[3]

These measures represent the culmination of a human rights revolution which has seen Ireland move from being a state in which (in 1990) consensual adult homosexual activity (between males) was an offence to one where (in 2020) couples of the same sex may marry, and where robust protections against sexual orientation discrimination apply.[4]

This chapter nonetheless highlights how, notwithstanding the momentous changes that Ireland has recently experienced, various points of legal and social vulnerability remain for LGBTQ individuals, families and couples. While vulnerability theory posits that vulnerability is a universal phenomenon, the chapter argues that the heteronormative and patriarchal nature of society pose residual challenges for LGBTQ populations, particularly where intersectional factors such as age, ethnicity and gender are considered.

1 The Thirty-Fourth Amendment of the Constitution Act 2015. See Fergus Ryan 'Ireland's Marriage Referendum: A Constitutional Perspective' *DPCE Online (Diritto Pubblico Comparato Ed Europeo)* 2015–2 http://mural.maynoothuniversity.ie/8934/ (last accessed 14 December 2020).

2 Stands for 'Lesbian, Gay, Bisexual, Transgender and Queer/Questioning'.

3 For more on the Act, see Tanya Ní Mhuirthile, 'Gender Identity, Intersex and Law in Ireland' in Lynsey Black and Peter Dunne (eds.) *Law and Gender in Modern Ireland: Critique and Reform* (Hart Publishing 2019), 191–207.

4 See further Fergus Ryan, 'Mapping a Transformed Landscape: Sexual Orientation and the Law in Ireland' in Lynsey Black and Peter Dunne (eds.) *Law and Gender in Modern Ireland: Critique and Reform* (Hart Publishing 2019).

DOI: 10.4324/9780429023149-12

A personal reflection on vulnerability

2020 also marked 25 years since I first came out as gay. The Ireland of the time was much more conservative than today, although significant legal and social change was already afoot. Brave, seemingly fearless role models led the way; locally, nationally and internationally, gay and lesbian people were coming out in increasing numbers. LGBTQ literature and media provided enormous support, as did LGBTQ community organisations.

That is not to say that coming out was then or even is now an easy process. In common with many of my peers, there was a painful, lonely gap of several years between coming out to myself and coming out to others. The act of revealing one's sexual orientation, even to a sympathetic audience, provoked a sense of profound vulnerability at what then felt like an uncomfortable leap of faith.

As one discovers over time, coming out is an ongoing process. The heteronormative assumption of straightness is less pronounced today than it was in 1995, though it remains the case that gayness usually requires revelation; straightness is typically assumed. That revelation nowadays requires less explanation and provokes fewer questions. Nonetheless, even today, in a vastly transformed Ireland, the words 'I am gay' still stick involuntarily in my throat. I often instinctively strain to avoid pronouns in discussing my partner among strangers, and I remain cautious of revealing my sexual orientation in certain contexts. My partner and I do not hold hands in public places, and avoid public displays of affection. Despite the considerable privilege that I enjoy in other respects, a residual sense of vulnerability, of caution and discretion, remains. The work of Kenji Yoshino resonates in this context: he speaks in a similar vein of the practice of 'covering', where otherwise openly LGBTQ people 'downplay' their sexual orientation as a mechanism of social survival, 'making it easy for others to disattend [one's] sexual orientation'.[5]

Sexuality and vulnerability theory

It would, of course, be entirely wrong to suggest that people who are LGBTQ have a monopoly on vulnerability. Nor is every LGBTQ person vulnerable in precisely the same way. An analysis that highlights the challenges faced by LGBTQ populations must account for a diversity of experiences and situations, of cross-cutting factors and identities. Clearly, certain segments of the LGBTQ population are more marginalised and vulnerable than others.

As Martha Fineman argues, vulnerability is a universal phenomenon, an inevitable feature of the human condition.[6] As corporeal beings, all humans

5 Kenji Yoshino, 'Covering' (2002) 111 Yale Law Journal 769, 772.

6 Martha Albertson Fineman, 'The Vulnerable Subject: Anchoring Equality in the Human Condition' (2008) 1 Yale Journal of Law and Feminism 1.

are vulnerable to illness, disease and, ultimately, to death. At various points in our lives, humans are inevitably dependent, particularly as infants and at times of illness and infirmity. Fineman cogently argues that acknowledging this universal vulnerability challenges the liberal claim that humans are (or should be) autonomous, independent and self-sufficient. In highlighting our common shared vulnerability, Fineman argues that a stronger case can be made for appropriate state supports within an expansive welfare state, bucking the neoliberal degradation of the welfare philosophy. Acknowledging the commonality of vulnerability strengthens the case for robust social supports and challenges neoliberal laissez-faire approaches that presuppose self-dependence.

Fineman's position poses challenges for analyses of vulnerability that focus on the experiences of specific identity groups. She argues cogently against '[t]he conception of vulnerability as belonging only to certain groups or "populations" of people'.[7] An analysis focusing on sexual and gender identity ignores the universal experience of vulnerability as an inevitable human condition. Such an identarian analysis may understate the vulnerability of heterosexual subjects as well as the role of risk factors common to LGBTQ and straight populations. As Fineman observes: 'asserting that individuals within a population have significant differences from the general population obscures the similarities they inevitably share with members of the larger society'.[8] She adds that approaches that seek to distinguish between people based on a particular identity 'can undermine political effectiveness and impede coalition building. It can also distort our understanding of the true nature and extent of certain social problems.'[9] She notes: '[t]he groups that traditional equal protection analyses recognize include some individuals who are relatively privileged notwithstanding their membership in these identity groups'.[10]

In segmenting society 'so that only some groups or individuals are designated as vulnerable', Fineman highlights how those 'outside of the constructed vulnerable population' may be wrongly perceived as invulnerable.[11] The implication that some are invulnerable 'undermines a sense of social solidarity and works to erode empathy and diminish sympathy for those who are in need'.[12]

A monolithic approach to LGBTQ vulnerability also potentially ignores the wide variation of experiences within the LGBTQ population. As Fineman observes, 'Clustering individuals into what is conceptualized as a cohesive subpopulation based on one or two shared characteristics masks significant differences among those individuals.'[13] This is particularly true of LGBTQ

7 Martha Albertson Fineman, 'Vulnerability, Resilience, and LGBT Youth' (2014) 23(2) Temple Political & Civil Rights Law Review 307, 315.

8 Ibid, 316.

9 Ibid.

10 Martha Fineman, 'The Vulnerable Subject' (n 6) 4.

11 Martha Fineman, 'Vulnerability, Resilience, and LGBT Youth' (n 7) 316.

12 Ibid, 316.

13 Ibid.

populations; LGBTQ people individually have widely different experiences of marginalisation, depending on various intersectional factors. For example, a married gay white man living in a comfortable suburb and a single black lesbian woman living in direct provision share an alternative sexual orientation but do not experience vulnerability in the same way. Factors outside the context of sexual orientation may privilege or undercut the security each enjoys.

Fineman nonetheless acknowledges that social conditions can exacerbate vulnerability among particular social groups:

> Lest anyone be concerned about setting aside identities and antidiscrimination approaches for a more universal approach, specific identity categories, such as sexuality, gender, and race have an important place in vulnerability theory. While it is important to recognize that vulnerability is a fundamental and universal part of the human condition, it is also necessary to simultaneously recognize that vulnerability must be understood *as particular, varied, and unique on the individual level.*[14]

While she leans against analysing vulnerability by reference to specific identity categories, she nonetheless seems to acknowledge that these classifications are relevant in determining 'how law and policy should address discrimination or the disadvantage directed at LGBT individuals'.[15] What is notable in Fineman's analysis, however, is how she highlights the 'serious limitations' in the anti-discrimination paradigm in tackling the subordination of LGBTQ people. Most notably, she observes perceptively, 'in situations of disadvantage in which overt discrimination is not an issue, the characterization of vulnerability as individualized and attached to only certain groups can obscure various forms of structural inequality'.[16]

Heteronormativity and LGBTQ populations

Nonetheless, it is difficult to avoid the conclusion that, because of social factors relating to the treatment in society of LGBTQ populations, such populations (and especially particular segments of the LGBTQ community) are indeed vulnerable in various identity-specific respects. Many LGBTQ people experience discrimination, marginalisation, poverty, poor health outcomes and exclusion, and in a way that is specifically related, in whole or in part, to our sexuality and gender identity. This is not because of any innate condition unique to LGBTQ people. It arises rather from the fact that, even in this age of greater tolerance and acceptance, social practices remain predominantly heteronormative. Heteronormativity presupposes that heterosexuality is the normal, default, 'natural'

14 Ibid, 316–317, emphasis added.
15 Ibid, 314.
16 Ibid, 315.

sexual orientation, the preferred way of being in the world.[17] Heteronormativity is underpinned by and underpins a worldview that one's biological sex determines one's social destiny, that the manner in which one behaves, dresses and expresses oneself, one's gender identity, the social roles one plays, and the persons to whom one is attracted and with whom one falls in love are all determined definitively by one's birth sex. From an early age, human beings learn (sometimes painfully) the lesson that transgressing the boundaries of gendered expectations evokes social penalties. Society valorises the boy who plays rugby; the boy who favours ballet is ridiculed.[18] The man exposing his chest hair is virile; in 2017, by contrast, a female model received rape threats after showing her unshaven legs in a photo.[19]

Social, cultural and legal responses to variations in sexual orientation and gender identity have placed people who are LGBTQ at various stages in time in a position of vulnerability that (while not unique) takes on particular and specific forms. The hegemonic force of heteronormativity privileges heterosexuality at the expense of alternative and more fluid experiences of sexual and emotional attraction. For many centuries, that hegemony was reinforced by laws that penalised even consensual male homosexual sexual acts, and by other social rules, formal and informal, that penalised deviation from sexual norms, particularly in relation to appropriate gender roles. These laws and practices often accentuated vulnerability not simply in what they did but also in what they did not do. The former long-standing refusal to recognise and protect relationships between same-sex couples placed such couples in a precarious position, particularly at times of crisis such as illness and death, and in circumstances where one of the parties was not an EU national.[20] Legal reforms and social change have greatly alleviated that precarity, though it would be a mistake to imagine that the challenges of the past have entirely dissipated.

No sex, please – we're Irish

In common with many other jurisdictions, Ireland inherited Victorian-era laws that penalised a wide range of male homosexual sexual acts, with no exemptions for consensual private adult sexual activity.[21] Even among those

17 On the different interpretations of 'heteronormativity', see Joseph Marchia and Jamie M. Sommer, '(Re)defining Heteronormativity' (2019) 22 Sexualities 267.

18 'Lara Spencer Apologizes for "Insensitive?" Remark on Prince George's Ballet Lessons' *Guardian* (26 August 2019).

19 Haroon Siddique, 'Swedish Model Gets Rape Threats after Ad Shows Her Unshaved Legs' *Guardian* (6 October 2017).

20 On the gaps in protection for same sex couples at the turn of the twentieth century, see the discussion in John Mee and Kay Ronayne, *The Partnership Rights of Same-Sex Couples* (Equality Authority 2000).

21 See the Offences against the Person Act 1861, ss 61–62 and the Criminal Law Amendment Act 1885, s 11.

who were not directly prosecuted or threatened with prosecution, these laws created a chilling effect and exposed many gay and bisexual men to blackmail. Socially, although there were pockets of tolerance and resistance, negative attitudes towards homosexuality remained widespread right up to the late 1990s. In 1996, Mac Gréil reported how 'the level of homophobia in the Irish population is still very high and quite disturbing'.[22] In a study he conducted at that time, 25.8 per cent of respondents said that they would have denied citizenship to gay people; only 12.5 per cent would have accepted a gay person into their family.[23] These attitudes and laws did not operate in a vacuum. Arguably, these phenomena were part of an intricate tapestry sewn together by social and religious forces that sought to police gender roles and punish perceived deviations from what was considered appropriate gender behaviour. This social conservatism weighed most heavily on women, manifesting itself in strict legal restrictions on abortion and contraceptive access coupled with the stigmatisation and penalisation of unwed mothers and their children.[24]

Legal and social reform

In the space of 30 years, however, Ireland has experienced a social and human rights revolution, transforming the legal, social and cultural landscape around gender, sexual orientation and gender identity. Arguably, this sea change was not organic or inevitable; it is, rather, the product of serious and sustained resistance to socially conservative norms on multiple fronts. Such transformation required struggle, strategy and determination, spearheaded by a multitude of individual and collective acts of bravery.

In 1993, the Oireachtas changed the law to permit consensual homosexual activity where both parties were aged 17 or over.[25] The verdict of the European Court of Human Rights in *Norris v Ireland*[26] (finding the former ban to be contrary to Article 8 of the European Convention on Human Rights) helped pave the way, although it is arguable that by the early 1990s the prevailing conservative social values were beginning to wane. Various measures at Irish and EU level spanning from the late 1980s through to the early 2000s prohibited discrimination and ill treatment based on sexual orientation, in particular in the context of employment and the supply of goods and services.[27]

22 See Mícheál MacGréil, *Prejudice in Ireland Revisited* (St Patrick's College 1996), 451.

23 Ibid, 343. See also Diarmaid Ferriter, *Occasions of Sin, Sex and Society in Modern Ireland* (Profile Books 2009), who notes (at 509) how 'research conducted in twenty-four countries between 1999 and 2002 suggested Ireland was one of the most homophobic countries in the western world, with almost one-third of its people having problems with the idea of living next to gay neighbours'.

24 See also Article 41.2 of the Constitution of Ireland 1937.

25 Criminal Law (Sexual Offences) Act 1993.

26 (1988) 13 EHRR 225.

27 See the Department of Finance Circular 12/88, the Prohibition of Incitement to Hatred Act 1989, the Unfair Dismissals (Amendment) Act 1993, the Health Insurance Act 1994, the Employment

Nevertheless, there remained until the late 2000s a marked legislative reluctance to recognise and protect same-sex relationships.[28] As recently as 2004, for instance, the Oireachtas passed social welfare legislation that precluded the recognition of same-sex couples for the purposes of various social welfare administrative schemes.[29] The vulnerability of same-sex couples in the face of these legal gaps was most obvious in the contexts of immigration, illness, succession and taxation. The inability to formalise a relationship meant that the social benefits of marriage were denied to same-sex couples, and protection was denied at times of crisis, such as relationship breakdown, illness and death.

In *Zappone and Gilligan v Revenue Commissioners*,[30] the High Court affirmed that marriage in Irish law (as of 2006) was exclusively a heterosexual union. Even so, the high-profile nature of the case, together with the introduction of civil partnership in the UK in 2004,[31] helped bring to the fore the issue of legal recognition for same-sex couples. The impetus for reform initially saw the enactment in Ireland in 2010 of a civil partnership law, allowing same-sex couples to form a union that conferred most (though not all) of the same rights and responsibilities as attached to marriage.[32] 2015 saw the passage (by referendum) of a constitutional amendment entrenching a new constitutional provision that expressly permits marriage between two persons 'without distinction as to their sex'.[33] This opened up marriage to same-sex couples: as O'Mahony observed, 'The wording makes it a constitutional principle that the sex of the parties may not be a basis for restricting access to marriage.'[34]

The referendum result was powerful and transformative. By opening up marriage to same-sex couples, the referendum signalled that LGBTQ people were equal (socially and legally) with our straight and cisgender counterparts, full citizens of a diverse Republic.[35] One might argue that the referendum also offered a majority of the Irish people an opportunity to distance themselves from the socially conservative mores of a past Ireland, firmly drawing the curtains on a past Ireland that oppressed and marginalised many who stepped outside the boundaries of what was considered 'respectable'. It signalled a firm

Equality Act 1998, the Equal Status Act 2000, and the Equality Act 2004. On a European Level, see also the Council Directive 2000/78/EC of 27 November 2000 establishing a general framework for equal treatment in employment and occupation. See also the Refugee Act 1996 and its successor the International Protection Act 2015.

28 See the discussion in John Mee and Kay Ronayne, *The Partnership Rights of Same-Sex Couples* (n 20), and in Judy Walsh and Fergus Ryan, *The Rights of De Facto Couples* (Irish Human Rights Commission 2006).

29 Social Welfare (Miscellaneous Provisions) Act 2004, s 19.

30 *Zappone and Gilligan v Revenue Commissioners* [2006] IEHC 404.

31 Civil Partnership Act 2004 (UK).

32 Civil Partnership and Certain Rights and Obligations of Cohabitants Act 2010.

33 See Article 41.4 of the Constitution of Ireland 1937, as inserted by the Thirty-Fourth Amendment to the Constitution.

34 Conor O'Mahony, 'Same-Sex Marriage Referendum: A Legal Review' *Irish Times* (22 January 2015).

35 Compare *PP v Judges of the Dublin Circuit Court* [2019] IESC 11.

end to the image and identity of Ireland as monochrome and homogenous, and firmly sundered the widespread perception of Ireland as a devoutly Catholic place subservient to the will of Rome. The message was clear and resounding: we are open; we are diverse; we are modern.

The post-referendum picture

The post-referendum picture, however, is more complex and nuanced than a linear model of progress might suggest. Despite considerable legal and social progress, certain categories of LGBTQ people (particularly young people, seniors, bisexuals, people who are transgender, intersex or non-binary) remain especially vulnerable. That vulnerability is perhaps more difficult to discern (and easier to ignore) given recent legal progress and social change. An overview of some of the most notable gaps follows.

Gender recognition

For transgender people, the Gender Recognition Act 2015 was admittedly groundbreaking. It effectively allows any adult to self-declare his or her gender without any medical diagnosis, hormonal or surgical treatment, or any evidence of transition. This process permits the applicant to be legally recognised as being of their preferred gender. While this affirmation of the self-determination/self-declaration model placed Ireland in the vanguard of states in relation to legal recognition of gender identity, the position for transgender people in Ireland nonetheless remains challenging in certain respects. Most notably, notwithstanding the ease with which most transgender adults can access legal recognition, healthcare options for trans persons seeking gender-affirming treatment in Ireland remain woefully inadequate. Trans people typically face long delays and significant barriers in accessing such treatments. Equality laws protect transgender people who plan to undergo or have undergone 'gender reassignment', leaving some doubt about the precise scope of protection for those who do not meet this criterion.[36]

In addition, the 2015 Act still cleaves to a binary model that rejects the possibility of gender-fluid and non-binary identities. It presupposes a fixed, binary gender identity of either man/woman and does not cater well to gender fluidity.[37] Younger people (under the age of 16) are also left in limbo by the Act's age restrictions, which limit access to legal recognition to those aged 16 and over.[38] For 16- and 17-year-olds, recognition is contingent on court approval, which

36 C-13/94 *P v S and Cornwall County Council* ECR I-2143.

37 Compare *R (Christie Elan-Cane) v Secretary of State for the Home Department* [2018] EWHC 1530 (Admin).

38 Gender Recognition Act 2015, s 9(2) confines recognition to persons aged 18 or over, but s 12 allows applications from persons aged 16 or 17 on foot of a court order.

in turn is predicated on obtaining parental consent.[39] Formal confirmation from two medical practitioners is also required for 16- and 17-year-olds. They must certify that the young person is sufficiently mature to make the decision, is acting freely and with full information and 'has transitioned or is transitioning into his or her preferred gender'. Although the Act does not require any physical transition, requiring two doctors to certify a transition arguably risks medicalising the process of recognition for younger people. The Report of the Gender Recognition Act Review in 2018 recommended multiple improvements to law and practice to alleviate these gaps in protection; the Government's lukewarm response to the report, however, suggests that progress in the short term is likely to be modest.[40]

LGBTQ parenting

A key feature of civil partnership legislation as enacted was its near-complete exclusion of all but the most marginal recognition for children being raised by civil partners. The ring-fencing of civil partnership as a child-free zone was largely remedied by the groundbreaking Children and Family Relationships Act 2015. That Act expanded the responsibilities of persons in respect of the children of their civil partners, largely remedying the former gap in the recognition of children as members of households headed by civil partners.[41] The Act also modernised and expanded child law to allow a greater range of persons to act as parents and guardians of children. The Act allows the spouse, civil partner or cohabitant of a parent to seek guardianship (which confers the rights and responsibility to make key decisions about a child's upbringing) or custody (the responsibility to care for a child on a day-to-day basis) by means of a court order, subject to certain conditions.[42] Likewise, the Adoption (Amendment) Act 2017 now allows civil partners and cohabiting couples (as well as spouses) to apply jointly to adopt a child as a couple (previously only married couples could apply to jointly adopt a child). The 2017 Act also makes it easier for a step-parent to adopt their spouse's, civil partner's or cohabitant's child such that, if the adoption is approved, the couple can jointly act as parents to the child. Same-sex married couples have been able to apply to adopt children as a couple since 2015.

Parts 2 and 3 of the 2015 Act address the position of children born following donor-assisted human reproduction (DAHR) procedures carried out by

39 Ibid, s 12.

40 *Review of the Gender Recognition Act 2015* (June 2018) www.welfare.ie/en/downloads/GRA%20Review%20Report.pdf; and the Minister for Social Protection's response, *Gender Recognition Act 2015: Report to the Oireachtas under Section 7 of the Act* (November 2019) www.welfare.ie/en/downloads/GenderRecognitionAct2015MinistersReportUnderSection7.pdf.

41 Children and Family Relationships Act 2015, Part 12.

42 Ibid, s 49, inserting a new s 6C into the Guardianship of Infants Act 1964, and s 57, inserting a new s 11E into the 1964 Act.

medical professionals. Subject to certain conditions, a child born as a result of a DAHR procedure involving a donation of sperm, eggs or an embryo is treated in law as the child of the mother (the person who gives birth to the child) and (subject to their consent) of the mother's spouse, civil partner or cohabitant. Provided they consent to the arrangement, the donors will not be treated as the child's parents. What this means is that a mother and her spouse or partner will be treated together as the parents of a child, including where both are female. The Act also allows the mother to be the sole parent if she has no partner or if the latter does not consent to being a parent.

Despite these changes, same-sex couples continue to experience challenges in regularising parenting arrangements. Most notably, Parts 2 and 3 of the 2015 Act did not come into operation until 4 May 2020, over five years after their enactment.[43] The painfully slow passage towards commencement left many lesbian couples, in particular, in a legal limbo. This had knock-on effects for some lesbian couples seeking passports for their children, as the law prior to May 2020 did not recognise the mother's wife or partner as a parent. Although there is a facility in the Act for retrospective recognition of couples who went through a DAHR process before May 2020, some lesbian couples will not be treated as parents under these provisions.[44] Notably, the retrospective provisions do not apply where the donor is known to the couple.

The guardianship provisions, while welcome, are also limited. Unless a judge determines otherwise, the type of guardianship conferred on spouses and partners of parents by the 2015 Act is restricted in various respects, the default being to exclude decision-making power in respect of matters such as residence, consent to adoption, and passports. The conferral of guardianship and custody in such cases is contingent on co-parenting for at least two years. Guardianship ends when the child reaches 18, and does not confer any right to succession, for instance, on intestacy.

Although the DAHR and guardianship provisions of the 2015 Act are now in operation, long delays to proposed surrogacy legislation[45] have sustained the long-standing legal precarity around same-sex parenting, condemning some same-sex couples who parent to uncertainty and vulnerability around their parental status.

Although the Gender Recognition Act affirms that the parental status of a person who has a child before legal recognition of gender is not altered by such recognition,[46] uncertainty still remains over the status of trans people

43 See S.I. No. 541/2019 Children and Family Relationships Act 2015 (Parts 2 and 3) (Commencement) Order 2019.

44 Sections 20–22 of the 2015 Act.

45 A General Scheme of the Assisted Human Reproduction Bill was published in 2017, but has seen slow legislative progress since.

46 S 19 of the Gender Recognition Act 2015: '[t]he fact that a gender recognition certificate is issued to a person shall not affect the status of the person as the father or mother of a child born *prior* to the date of the issue of the certificate'.

who parent children post-recognition. A recent English court decision suggests that a trans man who gives birth to a child will still be treated as his child's mother (despite the fact that a trans man with a gender recognition certificate is generally treated for all purposes as a man).[47] While the court affirmed that a mother can legally be a man, the outcome arguably serves to undermine trans identities. Although this specific point has not yet been addressed in an Irish court, the Supreme Court has affirmed that a 'mother' for the purpose of birth registration under the Civil Registration Act 2004 is a person who physically gives birth to a child.[48] Abortion legislation also places the pregnant trans man in a precariously uncertain position: the Health (Regulation of Termination of Pregnancy) Act 2018 applies solely to a woman, defined in section 2 as a 'female person of any age'.

Younger and older people

The intersection of age and sexual orientation poses notable challenges for younger and older people who are LGBTQ. Various studies have identified the particularly vulnerable position of such older persons, especially in care environments where LGBTQ identity is at risk of negation.[49] Even in a context where sexual minorities enjoy significant legal protections, the intersection of age and sexual orientation can give rise to profound vulnerability.[50] The point can be made equally forcefully in respect of younger persons. Despite profound social change, LGBTQ youth continue to experience disturbing levels of bullying and abuse in schools and other social contexts. It is no surprise, then, that younger LGBTQ people face particularly acute challenges in this context, with the *LGBT Ireland Report*[51] recording high average levels of anxiety, self-harm and suicidal ideation among younger LGBTQ respondents (in some cases, worse than in previously recorded studies). Their precarious situation is compounded by the ambivalent regime in many schools run in accordance with a religious ethos where a well-meaning concern to support LGBTQ students may clash with the school's characteristic spirit. Laws that exclude under-16s from legal gender recognition further exacerbate the situation. The government recently rejected recommendations from the Gender Recognition Act Review Group proposing legal gender recognition for under-16s.

47 *Re TT and YY* [2019] EWHC 1823 (Fam).

48 *MR and DR v An tArd-Chláraitheoir* [2014] IESC 60.

49 Agnes Higgins et al., *Visible Lives: Identifying the Experiences and Needs of Older Lesbian, Gay, Bisexual and Transgender People in Ireland* (GLEN 2011).

50 A very specific example of such vulnerability at the interface of age and sexual orientation arises from the CJEU decision in C-443/15 *Parris v TCD*, 24 November 2016, although the outcome of that case is ameliorated in part by the Social Welfare, Pensions and Civil Registration Act 2018, s 27, inserting a new Part VIIA into the Pensions Act 1990.

51 Agnes Higgins et al., *The LGBT Ireland Report: National Study of the Mental Health and Wellbeing of Lesbian, Gay, Bisexual, Transgender and Intersex People in Ireland* (GLEN/Belongto 2016).

Ethnicity and asylum seekers

Irish law expressly recognises that for the purposes of asylum law 'a particular social group may include a group based on a common characteristic of sexual orientation'.[52] This means that, depending on the circumstances in the relevant jurisdiction, a person may claim refugee status in Ireland 'owing to a well-founded fear of being persecuted' on the basis of sexual orientation in his or her country of nationality or place of former habitual residence. Nonetheless, the landscape for LGBTQ asylum seekers remains unenviable in Ireland. Such persons face steep challenges establishing a case for asylum in a system that seems sceptical of such claims.[53] In the interim, the direct provision system of housing for asylum seekers often accommodates vulnerable LGBTQ people alongside asylum seekers with conservative views on issues of sexual orientation and identity, leading to a form of secondary victimisation of the already traumatised victims of homophobia and transphobia. LGBTQ Travellers also face heightened isolation and exclusion on two fronts – from settled people because of their Traveller status, and often from within their own (still relatively conservative) community.

Mental and physical health, personal safety

With the advent of modern anti-retroviral medication, the spectre of HIV as a death sentence has thankfully abated, although challenges remain in the field of sexual health. Incidents of HIV contraction in Ireland remained high throughout 2018,[54] although the government's belated roll-out of PrEP coverage for men who have sex with men may hopefully reduce transmission among those at risk.[55] The stigma attached to HIV-positive status remains, compounding distress, anxiety and depression, even as HIV medication greatly improves prospects of living a full, healthy life, reducing viral loads to a point where HIV is undetectable and untransmittable.[56]

In the field of mental health, steep challenges also remain. The *LBGT Ireland Report*[57] indicated a hierarchy of risk in this context, with bisexual, transgen-

52 International Protection Act 2015, s 8(1)(d).

53 See Patricia Brazil, 'Applications for Asylum by Lesbian, Gay, Bisexual, Transgender and Intersex (LGBTI) Persons', paper presented to the RIPN (25 January) www.ecoi.net/site/assets/files/1952/the-researcher-march2011-vol6-issue1-corr.pdf; and Brian Collins, 'Representing LGBT Applicants for Protection: The Experience of the Irish Refugee Council Independent Law Centre' (2019) 5(3) Legal Ease 44–50 www.legalaidboard.ie/en/policy-and-guidance/newsletters/legal-ease/volume-5-issue-3-november-2019.pdf

54 Ed O'Loughlin, 'Ireland Diagnosed Record Number of HIV Infections in 2018, Health Data Suggests' *New York Times* (25 February 2019).

55 Jack Power, 'PrEP Programme to be Rolled out in Health Service from Next Month' *Irish Times* (20 October 2019).

56 Bach Xuan Tran et al., 'Understanding Global HIV Stigma and Discrimination: Are Contextual Factors Sufficiently Studied?' (June 2019) 16(11) *International Journal of Environmental Research and Public Health* 1899.

57 Agnes Higgins et al., *The LGBT Ireland Report* (n 51).

der and intersex people reporting higher levels of poor mental health outcomes than their monosexual and cisgender counterparts. The Report also highlighted profoundly high levels of distress, anxiety and self-harm among younger LGBTQ persons. Because of a heightened risk of exclusion from the family home, young LGBTQ people experience higher levels of homelessness on average than their cis and straight counterparts. A Williams Institute study suggests that a high proportion of homeless youth in the United States are LGBTQ: 43 per cent of drop-in clients; 30 per cent of street outreach.[58]

Despite considerable social change, LGBTQ persons (particularly younger people) remain vulnerable to physical attack in the public domain because of their sexual orientation or gender identity.[59] While such attacks are clearly unlawful, Ireland lacks hate crime laws requiring judges to regard a homophobic or transphobic motivation as an aggravating factor in sentencing.

Financial vulnerability

The myth of the pink pound[60] notwithstanding, research indicates that some sectors of the LGBTQ community on average experience significantly higher levels of financial vulnerability. In a 2013 study from the United States, Badgett, Durso and Schneebaum identified higher rates of poverty for some LGBT people and families when compared to equivalent non-LGBT people.[61] The study highlights how intersectional factors – race, gender, education, location – can compound the likelihood of poverty when combined with a minority sexual orientation. A 2016 study by Brown, Romero and Gates likewise demonstrated how LGBT adults in the United States were more likely to experience food poverty and insecurity than their heterosexual counterparts.[62] Levels of food insecurity were not evenly distributed, with higher rates of food insecurity being recorded among women, younger people, racial and ethnic minorities, and people who were rural-based, non-college educated, unmarried, as well as those raising children.

58 Laura E. Durso and Gary J Gates, *Serving Our Youth: Findings from a National Survey of Service Providers Working with Lesbian, Gay, Bisexual and Transgender Youth Who Are Homeless or At Risk of Becoming Homeless* (Williams Institute 2012).

59 For a recent example, see Conor Lally, 'Gardaí Suspect "Vicious" Train Station Stabbing was Hate Crime' *Irish Times* (2 February 2020).

60 As early as 1998, the BBC described how '[b]ecause of family circumstances (or more precisely lack thereof) the gay community tends to have much more disposable income to spend', BBC News, 'Business: The Economy: The Pink Pound' http://news.bbc.co.uk/2/hi/business/142998.stm; *Financial Times*, 'The Power of the Pink Pound' www.ft.com/content/a3a5d9be-0788-11e2-92b5-00144feabdc0.

61 M. V. Lee Badgett, Laura E. Durso and Alyssa Schneebaum, *New Patterns of Poverty in the Lesbian, Gay, and Bisexual Community* (Williams Institute 2013).

62 Taylor N. T. Brown, Adam P. Romero and Gary J. Gates, *Food Insecurity and SNAP Participation in the LGBT Community* (Williams Institute 2016).

For these financially vulnerable populations, relationship recognition (through access to marriage and civil partnership) is arguably of less significance than for middle-class and wealthier LGBTQ populations. As Ruth Colker has perceptively observed: '[f]or poor people marriage may offer few economic advantages. It should not surprise us that marriage is a less popular institution in poor communities than in middle-class communities.'[63] For instance, many of the tax and pension benefits that flow from marriage in Ireland are of more benefit the more wealth one possesses, but are of limited value to poorer persons with limited assets and those in precarious, low-paid employment.

Indeed, legal recognition can sometimes work to the distinct disbenefit of same-sex couples of limited means. The inception of civil partnership and equalisation of cohabitation rules in 2011 saw the formal recognition of same-sex cohabitation in social welfare law.[64] Although this worked to same-sex couples' benefit in some cases, rules such as the requirement to include the income of a partner when means testing could potentially result in lower overall payments to a couple. Where a couple are entitled to certain social welfare payments, the combined payment can be lower than that paid to two unconnected individuals. Recognition of gay couples also resulted in some lesbian mothers losing out on lone parent supports to which they were previously entitled.

Marriage and LGBTQ liberation

This raises difficult questions about the appropriateness of foregrounding marriage as a central goal for LGBTQ liberation. Several commentators have robustly challenged this approach as diverting attention away from wider injustices experienced both by LGBTQ people and in wider society, suggesting that the energy devoted to accessing the institution of marriage could have been better expended in tackling poverty, marginalisation and prejudice.[65]

Others fairly question the privileging of marriage over other manifestations of family life. Notwithstanding the prominence of themes of equality and diversity in family life in the narrative of the Yes campaign, the 34th Amendment left wholly intact the privilege associated with marriage under the Irish Constitution. While Article 41.4 opens up marriage to same-sex couples, Article 41 has consistently been interpreted by the Supreme Court as confining constitutional recognition of families exclusively to the family based on marriage.[66] Unions outside that framework of marriage therefore continue to

63 Ruth Colker, 'Marriage' (1991) 3 Yale Law Journal of Law and Feminism 321, 326.

64 Social Welfare and Pensions Act 2010.

65 See Ryan Conrad (ed.), *Against Equality: Queer Critiques of Gay Marriage* (Against Equality Press 2010); and Paula Ettelbrick, 'Since When Is Marriage a Path to Liberation?' in William Rubenstein (ed.) *Lesbians, Gay Men and the Law* (New Press 1993).

66 See, for instance, *State (Nicolaou) v An Bord Uchtála* [1966] IR 567, *G v An Bord Uchtála* [1980] IR 32 and *JMcD v PL and BM* [2010] 2 IR 199.

be constitutionally subordinated. Although legislation has improved somewhat the position of non-marital cohabitants,[67] the 34th Amendment did nothing to enhance legal support for the diversity of arrangements outside of marriage. Arguably, the discourse of the marriage referendum further entrenched the privileged status of marriage. Furthermore, while the extension of marriage to same-sex couples in England and Wales and Northern Ireland led to civil partnerships being kept for same-sex couples and opened up to opposite-sex couples,[68] the opposite has happened in Ireland. In Ireland, marriage equality saw civil partnership being closed to new entrants; those who entered into civil partnerships prior to May 2016 are still recognised as such,[69] but since that date new civil partnerships cannot be formed.[70]

While cohabitation legislation has somewhat improved the position of financially vulnerable long-term cohabitants, marriage retains its central and privileged constitutional position. Despite a significant growth in alternative forms of family life, marriage retains its gold standard status, implicitly signalling that non-marital families (in particular non-marital lone parent families) are less worthy, less valued, 'second-class' citizens.

Conclusion

None of this is to suggest that the social and legal position of LGBTQ people in Ireland has not improved. There is no doubt that the social and legal landscape has transformed in this context. Law reform on its own is only part of the solution, although an important part in helping shape culture and empowering minorities. Nonetheless, many LGBTQ people remain vulnerable and marginalised in various ways, as illustrated by this chapter.

LGBTQ people may contribute unintentionally to this marginalisation. Commentators suggest that LGBTQ subjects and couples can exhibit 'homonormativity' – a phenomenon that, in Duggan's words, 'upholds and sustains' rather than contests 'dominant heteronormative assumptions and institutions … while promising the possibility of a demobilized gay constituency and a privatized, depoliticized gay culture anchored in domesticity and consumption'.[71] This highlights the importance of maintaining a keenly political, critical lens with an eye to ensuring solidarity with marginalised, less 'conventional' and more vulnerable LGBTQ populations.

67 See Pt 15 of the Civil Partnership and Certain Rights and Obligations of Cohabitants Act 2010.

68 See *Steinfeld and Keidan v Secretary of State for International Development* [2018] UKSC 32, the Civil Partnerships, Marriages and Deaths (Registration etc) Act 2019 (E&W), and the Northern Ireland (Executive Formation etc) Act 2019 (UK).

69 However, a person may also marry his or her civil partner, thus dissolving the prior civil partnership.

70 Marriage Act 2015, Part 4.

71 Lisa Duggan, *The Twilight of Equality: Neoliberalism, Cultural Politics, and the Attack on Democracy* (Beacon Press 2003) 50.

12 Transgender children and young people in Ireland

Socio-legal challenges to self-identification and expression of gender

Máire Leane and Fiachra Ó Súilleabháin
University College Cork

Introduction

'Transgender' is a term that refers to a person whose gender identity and/or gender expression differs from the biological sex assigned to them at birth. Some individuals do not identify with a specific gender role, as a boy or a girl, a man or a woman, and may have a gender-fluid or a non-binary identity. Those who identify as non-binary may self-identify as neither exclusively male or female or may self-identify as having gender identities which move between or are not captured within the existing gender categories of male and female. There are multiple terms used to describe this, and in this chapter the term 'trans' is employed as an inclusive umbrella term, which covers the diversity of gender identities expressed by those who do not conform to the binary of male and female. Estimates suggest that between 0.03 and 0.05 per cent of the population are transgender,[1] with recent research in New Zealand indicating that 1 per cent of adolescents report being trans and 2.5 per cent are unsure about their gender.[2] There is no prevalence data regarding trans people in Ireland. However, the Transgender Equality Network Ireland (TENI) was contacted eighty-five times in 2014 in relation to family support for trans or gender-variant children under 18 years and the issue of gender identity is receiving increased attention in Ireland.[3]

Medical recognition and responses to gender nonconformity began in early 1900s, but surgical and hormonal interventions which allowed trans people to alter their bodies to align with their gender identities were not widely accepted

1 Keith J. Conron, Gunner Scott, Grace Sterling Stowell and Stewart J. Landers, 'Transgender Health in Massachusetts: Results from a Household Probability Sample of Adults' (2012) 102(1) American Journal of Public Health 118.

2 Terryann C. Clark et al., 'The Health and Well-Being of Transgender High School Students: Results From the New Zealand Adolescent Health Survey' (2014) 55(1) Journal of Adolescent Health 93.

3 www.teni.ie (accessed 14 December 2020).

DOI: 10.4324/9780429023149-13

until the late 1960s.[4] Gender nonconformity was constructed as a medical disorder and included in the *Diagnostic and Statistical Manual of Mental Health Disorders* in 1968.[5] In 2013, the *Diagnostic and Statistical Manual of Mental Health Disorders* (5th edition) replaced the condition of Gender Identity Disorder with that of Gender Dysphoria, described as the distress caused by incongruence between gender identity and biological sex.[6]

Since 2007, the UN Convention on the Rights of the Child has included gender identity under the non-discrimination provision encoded in Article 2 of the convention.[7] However, extensive challenges exist in the realisation of the human rights of trans children and youth in the international context. Very little data have been collected about their experiences, with most professions, institutions and legal and administrative structures lacking the evidence base required to respond successfully to their needs.[8] The national and international evidence available indicates that their rights to determine their gender identities are constrained by legal, medical, social, educational and familial factors and they experience discrimination and exclusion in multiple ways and in multiple contexts.[9] Many are rejected by their families, resulting in withdrawal of emotional and financial support.[10] They can encounter high levels of violence, often from someone known to them,[11] and they are significantly more likely to experience depression, anxiety, suicidal ideation, suicide attempts, self-harm than non-trans peers.[12] Safety and acceptance in school settings are also com-

4 Jaclyn M. White Hughto, Sari L. Reisner and John E. Pachankis, 'Transgender Stigma and Health: A Critical review of Stigma Determinants, Mechanisms, and Interventions' (2015) 147 Social Science & Medicine 224.

5 White Hughto et al., 'Transgender Stigma and Health' (n 4) at 224.

6 Ibid.

7 Michael N. Barron, *Background Paper to the Thematic Session: Non-discrimination of Lesbian, Gay, Bisexual, Transgender and Intersex (LGBTI) Young People*, Sofia, Bulgaria, Conference on the Council of Europe Strategy for the Rights of the Child (2016–2021), 5–6 April 2016.

8 Ibid, at 5.

9 Samantha J. Gridley et al., 'Youth and Caregiver Perspectives on Barriers to Gender-Affirming Health Care for Transgender Youth' (2016) 59(3) Journal of Adolescent Health 254; Daniel E. Shumer, Natalie J. Nokoff and Norman P. Spack, 'Advances in the Care of Transgender Children and Adolescents' (2016) 63(1) Advances in Pediatrics 79; Joseph G. Kosciw, Emily A. Greytak, Adrian D. Zongrone, Caitlin M. Clark and Nhan L. Truong, *The 2017 National School Climate Survey: The Experiences of Lesbian, Gay, Bisexual and Transgender Youth in our Nation's Schools* (GLSEN 2018); Helen Keeley, Fiachra Ó Súilleabháin and Máire Leane, 'Sexual and Gender Minority Populations and Suicidal Behaviours' in Danuta Wasserman (eds.) *Oxford Textbook of Suicidology and Suicide Prevention* (Oxford University Press 2021).

10 Rhonda J. Factor and Esther Rothblum 'A Study of Transgender Adults and Their Non-transgender Siblings on Demographic Characteristics, Social Support and Experiences of Violence' (2008) 3(3) Journal of LGBT Health Research 11.

11 Rebecca L. Stotzer, 'Violence Against Transgender People, a Review of United States Data' (2009) 14(3) Aggression and Violent Behaviour 170.

12 Shumer et al., 'Advances in the Care of Transgender Children and Adolescents' (n 9); Agnes Higgins et al., *LGBTIreland Report* (GLEN and BeLonG To 2016).

promised for many trans children and youth.[13] In the Irish context, research has highlighted similar experiences of discrimination, bullying, negative health outcomes and challenges to well-being experienced by LGBTI children and youth.[14] Drawing on Fineman's theory of vulnerability, this chapter critically appraises the ways in which the Irish Gender Recognition Act (2015) creates vulnerabilities for trans children and youth and considers what legal and statutory responses are required to provide this cohort with resources that scaffold resilience.

Legal responses to trans identities and expressions in Ireland: a failure of recognition

While the concept of gender has been the subject of scholarly and activist interrogation since the twentieth century, the vast majority of legal systems in the West are built on the dominant framing of gender as binaries of man/woman, male/female and masculine/feminine. This has resulted in a prevailing hegemony that presumes clarity of biological sex at birth; presumes one's gender identity correlates with one's natal sex; supposes heterosexuality and a preference for marriage, pronatalism and marital fecundity. This is very much the case in Ireland, where post-colonial desires for solidarity and cohesion, underpinned by Catholic social teaching, resulted in the othering of those who did not conform to this view of Irishness. O'Carroll[15] has commented that the fledging Irish state focused on integration as a means of developing a 'nation' identity. Quite literally, identities become 'battlegrounds',[16] where those people who do not conform are denigrated and designated as potentially polluting, contaminating and risky.[17]. These gendered expectations are an artefact of the patriarchal dichotomisation of gender and have profound consequences for trans people.[18] What has resulted in Ireland is an 'apart-

13 Kosciw et al., *The 2017 National School Climate Survey* (n 9).

14 Bernie Collins, Seline Keating and Mark Morgan, *All Together Now! Pilot Project on Homophobic and Transphobic Bullying In Primary Schools Final Report* (St Patrick's College Dublin and BeLong To 2016); Higgins et al., *LGBTIreland Report* (n 12); www.teni.ie (n 3); Peter Dunne and Cearbhall Turraoin, *'It's Time to Hear Our Voices': National Trans Youth Forum Report 2015* (TENI 2015); Jay Mc Neil, Louis Bailey, Sonja Ellis and Maeve Regan, *Speaking from the Margins: Trans Mental Health and Wellbeing in Ireland* (Transgender Equality Network Ireland/TENI 2013); Orlaith O'Sullivan (ed.), *Touching the Surface: Trans Voices in Ireland* (TENI 2012); Paula Mayock, Audrey Bryan, Nicola Carr and Karl Kitching, *Supporting LGBT Lives: A Study of the Mental Health and Well-being of Lesbian, Gay, Bisexual and Transgender People* (GLEN and BeLonG To Youth Service 2009).

15 J. P. O'Carroll, 'Cultural Lag and Democratic Deficit in Ireland: Or, "Da's Outside de Terms of d'Agreement"' (2002) Community Development Journal 37(1) 11.

16 Jeffrey Weeks, 'Necessary Fictions: Sexual Identities and the Politics of Diversity' in J. Weeks, J. Holland and M. Haites (eds.) *Sexualities and Society: A Reader* (Polity Press 2003).

17 Deborah Lupton, *Risk* (Routledge 1999).

18 Petra L. Doan, 'The Tyranny of Gendered Spaces – Reflections from Beyond the Gender Dichotomy' (2010) 17(5) Gender, Place and Culture 634.

heid of sex'[19] and a 'polarization of gender'[20] that has an enduring impact for trans people and particularly trans children and youth. The legal system is one particular space where trans people experience what Doan has described as a 'tyranny of gender', rendering them vulnerable, because they dare to challenge the hegemonic expectations for appropriately gendered behaviour in Irish society.[21]

Ní Mhuirthile has discussed the importance of the 'recognisable body' in legal systems,[22] because one must be defined in a manner which the law can comprehend. People are divided into male/female binary categorisations before the law in Ireland (Civil Registration Act, 2004, Schedule 1). There have been dramatic changes to the legal landscape in the past two decades in Ireland for trans people who wish to permanently change their legal sex from one of the binary categorisations to the other (i.e. male to female, or female to male). These changes stemmed from an initial civil action taken by a Dr Lydia Foy (*Foy v An tArd Chláraitheoir & Ors (No1)* ([2002] I.E.H.C. 116), who sought to have her birth certificate changed from male to female in order to correspond with her preferred gender identity. Dr Foy's first application to the High Court was not upheld for a number of reasons, including the Court's assertion of the State's legitimate interest in operating a functioning system of registered births which conveys on to citizens other rights (such as marriage, succession and guardianship/motherhood).[23] Thus, Dr Foy's true gender identity was not recognised by the State, with natal sex recorded as a 'snapshot of matters on a particular day'[24] seen at that time as more important than an individual's self-identification of their gender for effective functioning of a national birth registration system. Following the introduction of the European Convention on Human Rights Act 2003 in Ireland, and a finding before the Strasbourg court where the United Kingdom had been in breach of Article 8 of the ECHR[25] by failing to allow for a trans person to change their birth certificate in a case strikingly similar to that of Dr Foy, the High Court declared that was also in breach of Article 8 in *Foy v An tArd Chláraitheoir & Ors (No2)* ([2007]). It took another eight years for the legislature to introduce gender recognition legislation.

The Gender Recognition Act 2015 allows adults (aged 18 years or over) a gender based on self-declaration. Under this landmark piece of legislation,

19 Martine A. Rothblatt, *The Apartheid of Sex: A Manifesto on the Freedom of Gender* (Crown Publishing 1995).

20 P. Doan, 'The Tyranny of Gendered Spaces' (n 18).

21 P. Doan 'The Tyranny of Gendered Spaces' (n 18) at 635.

22 See Chapter 13 of this volume; also Tanya Ní Mhuirthile 'Legal Recognition of Preferred Gender Identity in Ireland: An Analysis of Proposed Legislation' in M. Leane and E. Kiely (eds.) *Sexualities and Irish Society: A Reader* (Orpen Press 2014).

23 T. Ní Mhuirthile, 'Legal Recognition of Preferred Gender Identity in Ireland' (n 22) at 133.

24 *Foy v An tArd Chlá;raitheoir & Ors (No 1)* [2002] IEHC 166, para 170.

25 *Goodwin v United Kingdom* appl. no. 28957/95 [2002] 35 EHRR 447 (ECtHR).

transgender adults can simply make a declaration to the Department of Social Protection of their 'settled and solemn intention' to live in a preferred gender in order to access a gender recognition certificate. On receipt of a gender recognition certificate, an individual can then get a new birth certificate, passport and driving licence which correspond with their preferred gender identity. Successful lobbying by experts through experience (trans people themselves), trans organisations (Transgender Equality Network of Ireland/TENI) and allies resulted in the removal of the need for supporting testimony from medical and psychological/psychiatric experts before declarations can be made. The successful passing of the 34th Amendment to the Irish Constitution (also known as the marriage equality referendum) in May 2015 allowed for same-sex marriage, which further supported gender recognition legislation, because it allows a trans person to self-declare their gender and remain married to a person of the same sex if they so wished. At the time, the gender recognition legislation was seen as putting Ireland 'in the small vanguard of countries that provide true equality to their transgender citizens and residents'.[26]

While the introduction of gender recognition legislation does offer profound transformative opportunities for adults who wish to permanently declare a gender not assigned to them at birth, there are significant limitations. First, gender self-declaration is not possible for individuals under 18 years of age. Children under 16 years are not granted any rights or mechanisms to identify as trans or gender-expansive. Adolescents aged between 16 and 18 years have a very restricted capacity for gender recognition, which involves a Circuit Family Court application, is contingent on parental or next-friend (guardian) consent and requires two supporting medical reports. This significantly restricts the autonomy of trans youth, because the process is complex, medicalised and legal in nature. This means that the gender of trans youth is mediated through adults, while children under 16 years are not afforded any rights at all to identify their gender. The current legislation reifies the vulnerability of their legal positioning (despite the 31st Amendment of the Irish Constitution, which proactively asserted children's rights and the right of the State to take child protection measures) and reinforces the notion of childhood as a transitionary period where young people's self-knowledge and self-awareness is considered incomplete, lacking sophistication and vulnerable. The current legislation serves to prohibit the affirmation of trans youth identities and significantly detracts from the life quality of trans youth.[27] However, Dunne and Turraoin aptly note that 'refusing to acknowledge a child's preferred gender does not erase or lessen that child's

26 Mark Kelly, 'ICCL Welcomes Commencement of Gender Recognition Act 2015', Irish Council of Civil Liberties press release (4 September 2015) www.iccl.ie/?s=gender+recognition (last accessed 14 December 2020).

27 P. Dunne and C. Turraoin, *'It's Time to Hear Our Voices'* (n 14) at 1.

self-identification. Trans young people exist in Ireland; They are a vibrant, diverse and active community.'[28]

Second, the current gender recognition legislation in Ireland reinforces the traditional male/female dichotomy – one can only be recognised as male or female, as man or woman. This reasserts a binary that fails to recognise gender as diverse, fluid, embodied and performative. Intersex people and people who do not define themselves as either exclusively male or female are obliged to fit within a gender dichotomy even in an era when one can self-declare a gender. Gender fluidity, expansive conceptualising of gender and other forms of gender nonconformity challenge prevailing gender and power processes in a society that is structured around two specific socially accepted gender identities and expressions.[29] It is hardly surprising that legal systems have entrenched dichotomous views of gender when binaries are enshrined in principles of justice – good vs bad, guilty vs not guilty, right vs wrong. Grappling with gender variance and expansion beyond male and female poses real challenges to a legal system when that system itself forms an integral part of a structural 'regulatory regime'[30] that enforces the 'tyranny of gender'.[31]

The limitations of current Irish gender recognition legislation have been reviewed at the request of the Minister for Employment Affairs and Social Protection. The review group reported in June 2018[32] with specific recommendations to expand legal gender recognition to children and to provide for the legal recognition of gender fluidity. The review group have favoured an administrative process for legal gender recognition for children *of any age* with a straightforward revocation process. They also recommended that gender recognition processes for children and youth should only enter court/judicial processes when there is a conflict between parents about consent or it is not possible or safe to obtain consent from parents.[33] While these recommendations offer potential to further depolarise gender mechanisms in Ireland, they remain to be implemented. Doan has argued that 'Gender de-polarization would undermine the social reproduction of male power that thrives on the separation and segregation of the sexes and thereby would

28 Ibid.

29 P. Doan, 'The Tyranny of Gendered Spaces' (n 18) at 639; Stephen Whittle, 'Gender Fucking or Fucking Gender: Current Cultural Contributions to Theories of Gender Bending' in R Ekins and D. King (eds.) *Blending Genders: Social Aspects of Cross-dressing and Sex-changing* (Routledge 1996).

30 Michel Foucault, *The History of Sexuality,* vol. 1, *An Introduction* (Random House 1978).

31 P. Doan, 'The Tyranny of Gendered Spaces' (n 18).

32 Department of Employment Affairs and Social Protection, *Review of the Gender Recognition Act 2015* (June 2018) www.welfare.ie/en/downloads/GRA%20Review%20Report.pdf (last accessed on 14 December 2020).

33 Ibid, at 109.

provide transgendered individuals greater freedom to express the range of their gender identity positions.'[34] It could be equally argued that gender depolarisation would reduce the existing vulnerabilities trans youth endure before the law in Ireland.

Redefining the parameters of justice: acknowledging vulnerabilities and scaffolding resilience

Martha Fineman's examination of the relationship between human vulnerabilities, and the State's responses to them, provides an insightful framework for examining and understanding the experiences of young trans people in Ireland. Fineman argues that acknowledgement of the vulnerability we all experience at different stages of life challenges liberal notions of individualised independence and self-reliance and highlights the key support which family-based care provides to the well-being of State and society.[35] She argues, however, that justice cannot be achieved if responsibility for addressing such vulnerability is seen as the responsibility of the individual or the family. Rather she argues that the State and its institutions must also shoulder responsibility for ensuring well-being, particularly in situations where inequality is created or exacerbated by the failure of the State to acknowledge and respond to the institutionally sanctioned vulnerabilities experienced by some individuals. The failure of the Irish Gender Recognition Act (2015) to legally recognise those individuals who self-identify as gender variant, and for whom the designation of male or female is experienced as inaccurate or inauthentic, is a clear example of how the law can render an individual vulnerable. Gender-variant people who have no legal mechanism for officially recording or gaining recognition for their self-expressed identities are placed outside of socially sanctioned gender identities and, in the case of trans children and youth, are rendered particularly vulnerable in their interactions with other State institutions such as education and healthcare, within which the gender binary is an organising pillar. Fineman understands the differentiated engagement that trans children and youth have with the legal, social, cultural and economic institutions of the State as a form of embedded vulnerability.[36] The value of a vulnerability lens is that it incites critical exploration of the particular manifestations of vulnerability as experienced by individual embodied subjects in their engagements in social relationships and with social institutions, and in so doing it highlights the role which the State plays in creating or alleviating these vulnerabilities.[37]

34 Petra L. Doan, 'Queers in the American City: Transgendered Perceptions of Urban Space' (2007) 14(1) Gender, Place and Culture 57–74, 58.

35 M. Fineman, 'Vulnerablity and Inevitable Inequality' (2017) 4(3) Oslo Law Review 133–149.

36 Ibid, at 145.

37 Ibid.

The limited Irish research on the experiences of trans children and youth clearly demonstrates the multiple ways and multiple contexts in which they are rendered vulnerable. The National Trans Youth Forum Report 2015, which surveyed 161 young people,[38] revealed the multiple and overlapping vulnerabilities experienced by respondents. In the sphere of education, the survey indicated that most trans youth faced significant obstacles in freely expressing their preferred gender in second-level schools. Only a quarter of survey respondents felt their gender was acknowledged, with staff resistance to recognising their gender being cited as the most common obstacle. In relation to medical care, the survey identified significant structural barriers and knowledge deficits, which limit care options for young people who wish to medically transition. More than half the respondents (53 per cent) reported that medics' awareness of trans healthcare was such that, when seeking medical support, they educated a health provider about elements of trans care. Lack of integration between the various components of a medical transition pathway was also frequently identified as a barrier to a comprehensive medical response. In short, the findings of the Forum Report provide clear evidence that the 2015 Gender Recognition Act, by not paying adequate attention to the structural and functional implications of its provisions, in effect contributes to the ongoing embedded vulnerability of trans children and youth.

The value of a vulnerabilities approach in informing responses to trans children and youth is called into question by commentators who highlight what they perceive to be a psycho-medicalised construction of gender-variant youth as an at-risk cohort with elevated levels of self-harm and suicidality.[39] Roen, while acknowledging the mental health and self-harm challenges experienced by some gender-variant youth and welcoming legislative, policy and service responses to support this cohort, argues that discourses which link gender-variant youth with pathology and risk reduce opportunities for more complex readings of what self-harm might mean in the lives of these young people.[40] She, along with other critics of a vulnerabilities focus, such as Bryan and Mayock,[41] calls for a more nuanced analysis of the multiplicity of intersecting factors that can impact on the well-being of gender-variant youth. Fineman's critique of neoliberal constructions of vulnerabilities as inadequacies of the individual or the family or community unit to which they belong, and her emphasis on identifying the resources that will support resilience in cohorts experiencing particular vulnerabilities, addresses these concerns.[42] In this regard she places responsibility for action not on the individual but on the wider social and legal

38 P. Dunne and C. Turraoin *supra* n 14.

39 Katrina Roen, 'Rethinking Queer Failure: Trans Youth Embodiments of Distress' (2019) 22(1–2) Sexualities 48; Audrey Bryan and Paula Mayock 'Supporting LGBT Lives? Complicating the suicide consensus in LGBT mental health research' (2017) 20(1–2) Sexualities 65.

40 K. Roen, 'Rethinking Queer Failure' (n 39).

41 A. Bryan and P. Mayock, 'Supporting LGBT Lives?' (n 39).

42 M. Fineman, 'Vulnerablity and Inevitable Inequality' (n 35) at 141.

institutions, systems, practices and discourses which create and shape situations that render gender-variant youth particularly vulnerable. It is vital, however, that any work which seeks to map and name these vulnerabilities is informed in large part by the accounts of gender-variant children and youth. Rooke cautions that some professionals, particularly medical and legal personnel, have the potential to render trans subjectivities invalid or inauthentic.[43] Dominant psycho-medicalised discourse of distress may limit policy and service responses which support the agentic capacities of gender-variant youth and are informed by the ways in which they are resisting and reshaping hegemonic norms. It is imperative that self-articulated accounts of what they have experienced (at what level, in what situations, through what practices or interactions, with what outcomes) must inform a mapping of the operationalisation of vulnerability in the lives of trans and gender-variant youth. This will aid both the identification of the mediators and moderators that shape it and the design of interventions to address it.

Conclusion

In Ireland, the State can work towards the development of resilience among trans and gender-variant youth by proactively addressing the structural systems that create and sustain vulnerabilities. The adoption and implementation of the recommendations of the recommendations made by group who reviewed gender recognition legislation would enable legal gender transition to children of all ages, provide for a clear revocation process and give legal recognition to gender fluidity. Legal changes also need to be reinforced by affirmative actions, including full government support of *The LGBTI+ National Youth Strategy* and the expansion of nationwide publicly available and responsive social, health and medical services.[44] Professional bodies and educational settings should ensure the inclusion of gender identities and expressions on curricular programmes for social, health, legal, civil and medical professionals who are employed in public sector service provision. An integral component of such affirmative curricular development should recognise the expertise that lived experience give trans and gender variant people through strategic partnerships with advocacy/activist groups who have been championing the right to self-declare gender identities and expressions.[45] Generating and embedding gender-affirmative cultures and practices in all public offices, services and institution would provide an opportunity to validate trans and gender-expansive subjectivities. Public

43 Alison Rooke, 'Trans Youth, Science and Art: Creating (Trans) Gendered Space' (2010) 17(5) Gender, Place and Culture 655.

44 Department of Children and Youth Affairs, *The LGBTI+ National Youth Strategy* (DCYA 2018–2020).

45 Such as Transgender Equality Network Ireland (TENI), Gender Rebels, Cork Transgender Peer Support Group, Limerick Transgender Peer Support Group, UP Cork Youth Group, IndividualiTy (run by BeLonG To Youth Services) and TransParent CI group.

statements supporting gender identity that are openly displayed in public spaces and buildings would provide clear markers of 'recognition' for trans and gender-variant youth. Making trans and gender-variant youth feel less vulnerable in the public spaces they occupy in their daily lives serves to dismantle the tyranny of gender dichotomies that impact everyone's life experiences.[46] Those who transgress gender norms are particularly vulnerable in public spaces, because they live outside the hegemonic 'bipolar gender world'.[47] The introduction of hate crime legislation would work towards addressing violent and discriminatory behaviour towards trans and gender-variant young people and the prevailing distrust among sexual and gender minority populations towards policing and justice systems.[48] These responses reflect the physical, human, social, ecological or environmental, and existential, resources that Fineman has identified as resources that the State can provide in response to vulnerability.

Applying Fineman's theory of vulnerability to analysis of the Irish State's response to trans and gender-variant young people underscores the limitations of the current legal and social response to providing social justice for this cohort. The responsibility for exploring, identifying and responding to the vulnerabilities of gender-variant youth lies with the State and the institutions and service provision organisations it overseas. Scaffolding equality and social justice for this cohort requires systemic State-led inquiry informed by consultation with gender-variant children and youth, and those that care and advocate for them, into all elements of the socio-legal structures and practices that shape the embodied vulnerabilities experienced by this cohort. Critical reflection informed by Fineman's vulnerability theory can facilitate a redefinition of the parameters of justice for this vibrant and growing section of society. It will require critical reflection among professionals, and within and between the institutional structures where they work, and must be underpinned by an openness to learning and to including new knowledges generated from the subjectivities and lived experiences of gender-variant children and youth.

46 P. Doan, 'The Tyranny of Gendered Spaces' (n 18) at 649.

47 P. Doan, 'Queers in the American City' (n 34) at 60.

48 European Union Agency for Fundamental Rights, *LGBT Survey* (FRA 2012); Amanda Haynes and Jennifer Schweppe, *Life-Cycle of a Hate Crime* (Irish Council of Civil Liberties 2018); Amanda Haynes and Jennifer Schweppe, *Gendered Policing and Policing Gender: The Trans Community and An Garda Síochána* (Transgender Equality Network Ireland/TENI 2018).

13 Recent reforms in law on LGBT rights in Ireland

Tightening the tourniquet in the rights of vulnerable intersex people

Tanya Ní Mhuirthile
Dublin City University

Introduction

'Intersex' is a general term that refers to the state of being born with biological sex characteristics that vary from what is typically thought of as exclusively male or female.[1] Intersex bodies are healthy bodies and, save in cases involving salt-wasting congenital adrenal hyperplasia,[2] there is no medical urgency involved that requires immediate intervention to safeguard the life or physical health of the person with the intersex variation. Yet intersex bodies are transgressive, in that they do not adhere to the conventional norm of biological human bodily configuration as expected by society and accepted by law. Thus, interventions are permitted on bodies with intersex variations that are explicitly prohibited on other bodies,[3] in order to facilitate the restructuring of the intersex body so that it more closely resembles the acceptable norm. This chapter argues that it is in this moment of intervention that the intersex body is rendered vulnerable. The protections and safeguards that people with an intersex variation might ordinarily expect to enjoy by virtue of their humanity are denied once law 'sees' the intersexness of their bodies. A visceral example of this is demonstrated in the decision of *In the Marriage of C and D (falsely called C)*.[4] Here the Brisbane

1 The author would like to acknowledge funding from the Irish Research Council under the COALESCE 2019 scheme. 'Intersex' is a highly contested term. Since 2006, medical professionals have employed the term 'disorders of sexual development' or 'DSD'. Peter A. Lee, Christopher P. Houk, Ieuan A. Hughes and S. Faisal Ahmed, 'Consensus Statement on Management of Intersex Disorders' (2006) 118(2) Pediatrics e 488. However, the use of the term 'DSD' has not found favour with some intersex activists and patients: see Elizabeth Reis, 'Divergence or Disorder: The Politics of Naming Intersex' (2007) 50(4) Perspectives in Biology and Medicine 535; and Georgiann Davis, *Contesting Intersex: The Dubious Diagnosis* (New York University Press 2015).

2 Gerard S. Conway and Pierre D.E. Mouriquand, 'Congenital Adrenal Hyperplasia' in Adam H. Balen, Sarah M Creighton, Melanie C. Davies, Jane Macdougall and Richard Stanhope *Paediatric and Adolescent Gynaecology: A Multidisciplinary Approach* (Cambridge University Press, 2004), 310.

3 Criminal Justice (Female Genital Mutilation) Act 2012.

4 *In the Marriage of C and D (falsely called C)* (1979) 35 FLR 340.

DOI: 10.4324/9780429023149-14

Family Court annulled the marriage of the parties on the basis that under *Hyde v Hyde*[5] marriage is the union of one man and one woman. The putative husband in this case being 'neither man nor woman but a combination of both' was found to be incapable of contracting a valid marriage.[6] This chapter contends that adopting a vulnerability approach would enable the creation of spaces within the legal order wherein the innate human dignity and rights of people with intersex variations can be vindicated.

The importance of a recognisable body

In order to come *sui juris*, one must be legally recognisable as either male or female. This binary conception of corporality is evident in the list of required particulars of which the State must be informed when registering a birth. In Schedule 1 to the Civil Registration Act 2004, sex features as the third item for notification before name of the child or details of the parents. Thus, official recognition of sex is of primary importance in establishing legal identity. Sex has assumed this importance in relatively recent times. Writing in the 1600s, Coke CJ noted that '[e]very heire is either a male, or female or an hermaphrodite, that is both male and female. And an hermaphrodite … shall be heire, either as male or female, according to that kind of the sexe which doth prevaile'.[7] This historic acknowledgement of intersex variations contrasts sharply with the virtual invisibility of intersex in the twentieth century.[8] This disappearance of intersex from public and legal consciousness was necessitated by the prioritisation of heteronormativity.[9] In promoting the social and legal acceptability of heterosexuality, people whose bodies did not adhere to strict understandings of male and female, or whose sexuality did not orientate in a heterosexual manner, were outcast.[10]

Against this background, it is not surprising that the birth of a child with visibly ambiguous genitalia would be regarded as a 'social emergency'.[11] Legal definitions of male and female were formally stated by Ormrod J in *Corbett v Corbett*,[12] where it was held that legal sex and gender were determined by the

5 *Hyde v Hyde* (1866) LR 1 P&D 130.

6 *In the Marriage of C and D (falsely called C)* (n 4).

7 Sir Edward Coke, *The First Part of the Institutes of the Law of England* (Robert H. Smith 1853), 225.

8 Alice Domurat Dreger, *Hermaphrodites and the Medical Invention of Sex* (Harvard University Press 1998).

9 Tanya Ní Mhuirthile, 'Building Bodies: A Legal History of Intersex in Ireland' in Jennifer Redmond, Sonia Tiernan, Sandra McAvoy and Mary McAuliffe, *Sexual Politics in Modern Ireland* (Irish Academic Press 2015) 154. See also Anne Fausto-Sterling, *Sexing the Body: Gender Politics and the Construction of Sexuality* (New York: Basic Books 2000).

10 Offences Against the Person Act 1861 and the Criminal Law (Amendment) Act 1885. Homosexual behaviour between consenting adults was finally decriminalised in the Criminal Law (Sexual Offences) Act 1993.

11 American Academy of Pediatrics, 'Evaluation of the Newborn with Developmental Anomalies of the External Genitalia' (2000) 106 Pediatrics 138.

12 *Corbett v Corbett (Otherwise Ashley)* [1970] 2 All ER 33.

congruence of the chromosomes, gonads and genitals at the moment of birth.[13] Notwithstanding this formal legal test, in reality gender assignment, and the recording of this information of a birth certificate, is a presumption determined by the appearance of the genitalia and investigations as to an individual's chromosomal and gonadal make-up only occur where there is genital ambiguity.[14] Thus, when a baby is born with ambiguous genitalia, social, medical and legal expectations are confounded such that the baby becomes culturally unintelligible. We have no pronouns in the English language to encapsulate this situation. To refer to such a child by the gender-neutral pronoun 'it' is to dehumanise that child. Viewed from this perspective, bodies with intersex variations may be considered grotesque.

Shabot argues that the grotesque body is one that is has an open subjectivity that defies clear definitions and borders.[15] As such it is unrepresentable by any system of knowledge governed by rational principles that aims for a clear framing of the objects of research. A postmodern realisation of the embodied subject, Shabot contends that the 'grotesque body is inherently ambiguous: it is not an isolated body, but at the same time it does not lose itself in the homogeneity of undifferentiated wholeness'.[16] Thus it is, in Bakhtin's words, incomplete.[17] According to this understanding of grotesque bodies, they are completed by their interactions with the outside world. It is when the grotesque body touches the outside world through childbirth, defecation, eating and drinking that it becomes complete – this is a fleeting achievement, as the grotesque body is ever unfinished and ever creating.[18] Thus Shabot argues that acknowledging the grotesque inherently creates anxiety, as the grotesque world is one which is 'a fragmentary, complex reality … where clear hierarchal relations derived from well-defined binary oppositions are not viable'.[19] Prior to interrogating law's response to the intersex body, this chapter will first explore the manner in which intersex variations are medicalised.

Pathologisation of intersex bodies

It is difficult to assess with precision the rate of intersex variations in society. This is partly due to the tendency to 'hide' the intersex diagnosis and partly due

13 Ibid, at 48.

14 Tanya Ní Mhuirthile, 'Foy v An tArd Chláraitheoir' in Máiréad Enright, Julie McCandless and Aoife O'Donoghue (eds.) *Northern/Irish Feminist Judgments: Judges Troubles and the Gendered Politics of Identity* (Oxford: Hart Publishing 2017) 587, 292–293.

15 Sara Cohen Shabot, 'The Grotesque Body: Fleshing Out the Subject' (2007) 15 Thamyris/Intersecting: Place Sex and Race 57.

16 Ibid, at 59.

17 Mikhail Bakhtin, *Rabelais and His World* (Bloomington: Indiana University Press 1984) 317.

18 Ibid, at 26.

19 Shabot, 'The Grotesque Body' (n 15) at 60.

to the lack of diagnostic labels to cover every possible permutation of intersex corporeal configuration. A study published in 2000 of eleven different intersex diagnoses estimated that approximately 1.7 per cent of the global population are intersex to some degree.[20] Of these, Lee et al. estimate that 1 in 4,500 births evidence genital ambiguity.[21] This is a problematic statistic, as there is no agreement as to what constitutes unambiguous genital appearance.[22] In the absence of an agreed standard, any decision on ambiguity is inevitably entangled with cultural and aesthetic preconceptions of how the genitalia should look and function. As Kessler puts it, ambiguity depends not only on how the genitals look, but on who is doing the looking.[23] There is no universal medical or surgical treatment protocol for engaging with a body with intersex variations. It is worth restating that there is nothing inherently problematic or dangerous about a body configured intersex.

Early surgical interventions have been subject to criticism, as they do not exclusively impact upon the body with intersex variations but also have far-reaching consequences in terms of that person's development and life experience.[24] They have been the subject of much commentary: the physical aspects are much discussed in medical writings, whereas the psychological/emotional harm is more commonly discussed by sociologists, intersex support groups and intersex activists.[25]

A variety of surgical interventions are routinely performed on children with intersex variations to create gendered genitals. Such procedures include: clitoroplasty, phalloplasty, vaginoplasty, labioplasty and gonadectomy. The side effects of these interventions can include: pain, scarred tissue, pain during erection,[26] loss of sexual sensation,[27] blood clots,[28] colitis,[29] the elimination of the natural con-

20 Melanie Blackless et al., 'How Sexually Diamorphic Are We? Review and Synthesis' (2000) 12 American Journal of Human Biology 151.

21 Lee et al., 'Consensus Statement on Management of Intersex Disorders' (n 1) at e 488.

22 K. W. Feldman and D. W. Smith, 'Fetal Phallic Growth and Penile Standards for Newborn Male Infants' (1975) 86(3) Journal of Pediatrics, 395; S. E. Oberfeld et al., 'Clitoral Size in Full-Term Infants' (1989) 6(4) American Journal of Perinatology 453; and Susanne Kessler, *Lessons from the Intersexed* (Rutgers University Press 1998).

23 Kessler, *Lessons from the Intersexed* (n 22) at 44–46.

24 Dreger, *Hermaphrodites and the Medical Invention of Sex* (n 8); Fausto-Sterling, *Sexing the Body* (n 9); Kessler, *Lessons from the Intersexed* (n 22); M. Diamond and H. K. Sigmundson, 'Management of Intersexuality: Guidelines for Dealing with Persons with Ambiguous Genitalia' (1997) 151(10) Archives of Pediatric and Adolescent Medicine 1046.

25 Ida Ismail and Sara Creighton, 'Surgery for Intersex' (2005) 5 Reviews in Gynaecological Practice 57; Sharon E. Preves, *Intersex and Identity: The Contested Self.* (New Brunswick, NJ: Rutgers University Press 2003); Kessler, *Lessons from the Intersexed* (n 22).

26 Ian A. Oyama, Adam C. Steinberg, Adam S. Holzberg and Joseph L. Maccarone, 'Reduction Clitoroplasty: A Technique for Debulking the Enlarged Clitoris' (2004) 17 Journal of Pediatric and Adolescent Gynecology 393.

27 Ismail and Creighton 'Surgery for Intersex' (n 25).

28 Ibid.

29 Ibid.

tour and pigmentation of the labia minora[30] and infertility. As a result of complications such as these, frequently bodies with intersex variations will require more than one surgical intervention to correct the after-effects of previous surgeries.

Commentary on intersex variations is not confined to the physical impact which gender assignment surgery but the physical impact of gender assignment surgery on the lives of people with intersex variations is also much discussed.[31] In particular, criticisms centre on the sense of shame and stigma evident in personal narratives from those with intersex variations. In her study, Preves reports that repeated 'corrective' medical and surgical interventions decreased their sense of autonomy and undermined the development of a solid sense of self, and that those with intersex variations felt treated as objects of medical research, and as a result they felt freakish. Finally, she notes that medical interventions impaired their ability to engage in healthy sexual relationships due to both physical and psychological trauma.[32]

The second criticism of the medical approaches centres on the guidelines medical professionals use to determine gender assignment. These guidelines, which have developed organically through the publication of results of various surgical attempts in peer-reviewed journals, are prescriptive. Meyers-Steifer and Charest identify the three criteria underpinning the guidelines: 'the potential for (1) an ambiguous appearance of the genitalia before and after puberty, (2) adequate sexual functioning, and (3) fertility'.[33] Of these three criteria, it is the appearance of genitalia which garners most commentary, as Hendricks states: '[i]n truth, the choice of gender still often comes down to what the external genitals look like'.[34] This could be because the indicia of success in the creation of female genitalia might be held to a lower standard than those for the creation of male genitalia. An analysis of the guidelines reveals that what is important is that, once fertility has been preserved if possible, female genitalia can function as a site for heterosexual intercourse.[35] However, for males, it is important that the penis can function properly, i.e. permit urination while standing and engage in penetrative intercourse, but appearance is also prioritised.[36] Thus, if the phallus is deemed to be too small, the child will be assigned female.[37]

30 S. M. Maas and J. J. Hage, 'Functional and Aesthetic Labia Minora Reduction' (2000) 105(4) Plastic and Reconstructive Surgery 1453.

31 Katrina Karakazis, *Fixing Sex: Intersex, Medical Authority and Lived Experience* (London: Duke University Press, 2008); Kessler, *Lessons from the Intersexed* (n 22); Preves, *Intersex and Identity* (n 25).

32 Preves, *Intersex and Identity* (n 25) 62.

33 C. H. Meyers-Steifer and N. J. Charest, 'Diagnosis and Management of Patients with Ambiguous Genitalia' (1992) 16(5) Seminars in Perinatology 332, 336–337.

34 M. Hendricks, 'Is It a Boy or a Girl?' (1993) (November) Johns Hopkins Magazine 10, at 15.

35 Oberfeld et al., 'Clitoral Size in Full-Term Infants' (n 22); Kessler, *Lessons from the Intersexed* (n 22).

36 K. W. Feldman and D. W. Smith, 'Fetal Phallic Growth and Penile Standards for Newborn Male Infants' (1975) 86(3) Journal of Pediatrics, 395; S. Y. C. Tong, K. Donaldson and J. M. Hutson, 'When is Hypospadias not Hypospadias?' (1996) 164 (5 February) Medical Journal of Australia 153; Kessler, *Lessons from the Intersexed* (n 22).

37 Kessler, *Lessons from the Intersexed* (n 22).

Response of law to issue of surgeries on those with intersex variations

Law is largely silent on the issue of surgical interventions on intersex children. There has never been a case on this point in Ireland or the United Kingdom. A case directly on point is currently *sub judice* before the North Carolinan courts.[38] Were such a case to come before the Irish courts, it is unlikely that a complainant would be successful.[39] This is not true of all interventions on the genitalia of children. The Criminal Justice (Female Genital Mutilation) Act 2012 ('FGM Act') specifically outlaws the cutting of genitalia of girls and women in any cultural context. The protection created by this legislation does not extend to those with intersex variations.[40] Recently, various UN bodies have specifically addressed the issue of interventions on intersex bodies and like the case of FGM have repeatedly considered them to amount to torture.[41] It is difficult to defend the accusation that domestic laws which do not protect the rights of intersex people to choose whether, how and when their bodies should be cut tacitly collude in the violation of their rights.

When introducing the Gender Recognition Act 2015 ('GRA'), the then Minister for Social Protection hailed it as guaranteeing the rights of intersex people.[42] Although the GRA has been welcomed for divorcing legal rights from medical treatment pathways, it does not implode the binary gender paradigm that underpins the recognition of people before the law. Rather, it further entrenches the primacy of the categories 'male' and 'female' by confirming they are the only acceptable ones. The scheme established by the GRA pertains to adults only. There is an exemption to the minimum age criterion for young people between the ages of 16 and 18 pursuant to an application to the Circuit Court and supported by medical evidence of transition.[43] However, the

38 *M.C. vs. Medical University of South Carolina*, filed 14 May 2013 in County of Richland Common Pleas http://interactadvocates.org/wp-content/uploads/2016/03/050714_Crawford_Complaint_Release_FINAL_FINAL.pdf.

39 According to *Dunne v National Maternity Hospital* [1989] IR 91 and *Bolitho v Hackney Health Authority* [1998] AC 232, once evidence can be adduced that a reasonable body of professionals would use the same technique/approach, then a medical practitioner will not be found to have been negligent.

40 Nancy Ehrenreich and Mark Barr, 'Intersex Surgeries, Female Genital Cutting, and the Selective Condemnation of "Cultural Practices"' (2005) 40(1) Harvard Civil Rights – Civil Liberties Law Review 71; Isabelle R. Gunning, 'Arrogant Perception, World-Travelling and Multicultural Feminism: The Case of Female Genital Surgeries' (1992) 23 Columbia Human Rights Law Review 189.

41 UN Committee on the Rights of the Child, *Concluding Observations on the Combined Third and Fourth Periodic Reports of Ireland* (Geneva: United Nations 2016) UN Doc: CRC/C/IRL/CO/3–4, paras 39 and 40; UN Committee on the Elimination of Discrimination Against Women, *Concluding Observations on the Combined Sixth and Seventh Periodic Reports of Ireland* (Geneva: United Nations 2017) UN Doc: CEDAW/C/IRL/CO/6–7, paras 24 and 25.

42 Press Release, 'Minister for Social Protection Publishes Revised General Scheme for Gender Recognition Bill 2014' (Dublin: Department of Social Protection, 18 June 2014) www.welfare.ie/en/pressoffice/Pages/pr180614.aspx (last accessed 14 December 2020).

43 Section 12 of the Gender Recognition Act 2015.

GRA contains no provision for the under-16s; thus, it does nothing to alleviate pressure on parents to consent to procedures on their intersex children. As an alternative, intersex people might seek to use the provisions contained in Section 63(2) of the Civil Registration Act 2004 ('the 2004 Act') to correct a clerical error or an error of fact in the recording of a birth. The question then becomes whether such an amendment would be permissible. Consideration of this section in *Foy v An tArd Chlaraitheoir (No 2) (2007)* suggests that, as the system of birth registration is a matter of historic importance and not intended to establish the present identity of any person interacting with the law in Ireland, it cannot. Being, then, a snapshot of 'observable characteristics of the newborn' as they appeared at the moment the birth was registered, it seems unlikely that the 2004 Act would permit an alteration of the record.[44]

Neither the GRA nor the 2004 Act overtly exclude people with intersex variations. Yet, read together, this is the net effect. These statutes control how a person comes *sui juris*. In order to avail of the protections of law and to fully enjoy inalienable human rights, one must present oneself to the State as either male or female. Where one's body inherently defies such categorisation, law delays active protection of one's rights as in the case of interventions on intersex bodies. The protection of the FGM Act 2012 to guard against non-consensual genital surgeries does not extend to those with intersex variations. Neither does law intervene to prevent or to limit parental proxy consent to such surgeries. Yet it could by adopting the approach in *Re J (Child's Religious Upbringing and Circumcision)*, where the Court refused to permit the circumcision of a boy on the basis that the procedure was not medically indicated, would cause pain and distress, was irreversible and the immediate harm to the child outweighed the speculative future benefits should he subsequently identify as Muslim.[45]

Sharpe convincingly argues that homophobia is the unconscious subconscious of law.[46] Despite the introduction in 2015 of both gender recognition and marriage equality,[47] this criticism, refined to heterophilia, continues to be valid. The categories of male and female are limited and cannot encapsulate the entirety of human existence. Intersex bodies are inherently ambiguous. They are at their most grotesque when questions of medical or surgical interventions arise, as this is the moment when they 'touch' the outside world. They demonstrate the non-viability of the oppositional binary gender paradigm underpinning law. Law uses its internal dogma to look the other way and does not activate protections for the rights of those with intersex variations. From a doctrinal perspective all aspects of formal equality have been met: parents give

44 *Foy v An tArd Chlaraitheoir (No 2)* (2007) IEHC 470, at para 73.

45 *Re J (Child's Religious Upbringing and Circumcision)* [2000] 1 FCR 307. Tanya Ní Mhuirthile, *Realising Gender Recognition: Rendering the Vulnerable Visible or Further Vulnerabilising the Invisible?* UCD Working Papers in Law, Criminology and Socio-Legal Studies, Research Paper no. 41/2010 http://ssrn.com/abstract=1680899 (last accessed 14 December 2020).

46 Andrew N. Sharpe, *Transgender Jurisprudence. Dysphoric Bodies of Law* (Cavendish Publishing 2002).

47 Marriage Act 2015.

lawful proxy consent, children may be too young to participate meaningfully, interventions are construed as being in their best interests and, if necessary, the child can activate rights under the GRA at a later stage in life. Thus for the rational, reasonable man the correct procedures have been followed. The vulnerability thesis advanced by Martha Fineman and others offers a way to disrupt this doctrinal dominance and consider the question from a fresh perspective, one that might enable the activation of the protections of human rights law for those with intersex variations.[48]

Adopting a vulnerability approach

For Fineman, vulnerability is not an exceptional disadvantage. Rather, it is a universal experience which may be occasional or enduring. It arises 'from our embodiment, which carries with it the ever present possibility of harm, injury, and misfortune from mildly adverse to catastrophically devastating events whether accidental, intentional or otherwise'.[49] Thus we are all interdependent: this is the foundation of society. She argues that 'It is the recognition and experience of human vulnerability that brings individuals into families, families into communities, and communities into societies, nation states and international organisations.'[50] Consequently, she contends that there is an obligation on the State to reduce, ameliorate and compensate for vulnerability.[51] The need to make institutional change to arrangements that create privilege and perpetuate disadvantage is evident when viewed through the lens of vulnerability theory.

Fineman argues that the liberal subject is at the centre of lawmaking.[52] The liberal subject is always an adult,[53] and thus the laws produced reflect only a percentage of embodied human experience and do not account for moments of vulnerability such as dependency or childhood.[54] Kohn identifies three ways that vulnerability theory helps to support and further understanding of social policy.[55] First, articulating the universal condition of vulnerability highlights the importance of the role of the State in this regard and justifies the interventions necessary for the State to discharge that obligation – for example, introducing social welfare provisions. Second, the focus on a universal vulnerability helps to reduce the stigma experienced by members of particular

48 Martha A. Fineman, 'The Vulnerable Subject: Anchoring Equality in the Human Condition' (2008) 20(1) Yale Journal of Law and Feminism 1.

49 Ibid, at 9.

50 Martha A. Fineman, 'Equality, Autonomy and the Vulnerable Subject in Law and Politics' in Martha Albertson Fineman and Anna Greer (eds.) *Vulnerability: Reflections on a New Ethical Foundation for Law and Politics* (Farnham: Ashgate Publishing 2013) 13, 22.

51 Fineman, 'The Vulnerable Subject' (n 48), at 8–15.

52 Ibid, at 10.

53 Ibid, at 11.

54 Ibid, at 12.

55 Nina A. Kohn, 'Vulnerability Theory and the Role of Government' (2014) 26(1) Yale Journal of Law and Feminism 1, at 9.

minority groups. Finally, acknowledging that vulnerability is universal encourages a holistic, rather than piecemeal, response to its reduction.

Adopting such an approach in the context of intersex variations necessitates a shift away from considering intersex as exceptional or grotesque. Rather, it requires us to refine what it is about the moment of intervention that has universal applicability. It is widely acknowledged that there is a paucity of longitudinal studies proving the efficacy or otherwise of medical and surgical intervention on people with intersex variations.[56] Indeed Lee et al. expressly acknowledge this and call for research to be conducted in this area.[57] Given this lack of authoritative information on its impact, Cheryl Chase argues that each individual procedure was effectively an experiment.[58]

Although the terms 'research' and 'experimentation' are often used interchangeably, Mason and Laurie opine that they are not in fact the same thing.[59] Research implies a predetermined protocol with a clearly defined end point, whereas experimentation involves a more speculative, ad hoc approach to an individual subject. This is an important distinction, as the researcher cannot deviate from the predetermined protocol, whereas when conducting an experiment it can be altered and modified to take into account the individual response of the subject.[60] Additionally, the aims of research and experimentation are usually different. Research is defined as 'the attempt to derive generalisable new knowledge by addressing clearly defined questions with systematic and rigorous methods' and thus its aim is not directly related to the research subject.[61] By contrast, experimentation is focused on the diminishing health of the patient and therefore responds to any changes in the individual patient.

There are a variety of approaches to the treatment of intersex variations.[62] Yet, while some advocate introduction of a formal treatment protocol,[63] others decry such a step as 'too prescriptive'.[64] Nonetheless, there is some guidance regarding suggested interventions for particular intersex variations, which

56 American Academy of Pediatrics, 'Evaluation of the Newborn with Developmental Anomalies of the External Genitalia' (n 11); Dreger, *Hermaphrodites and the Medical Invention of Sex* (n 8); Fausto-Sterling, *Sexing the Body* (n 9).

57 Lee et al., 'Consensus Statement on Management of Intersex Disorders' (n 1).

58 Cheryl Chase, *ISNA's Amicus Brief on Intersex Genital Surgery* www.isna.org/node/97 (last accessed 14 December 2020) at point 12.

59 J. Kenyon Mason and Graeme T. Laurie, *Mason & McCall Smith's Law and Ethics* (7th edn, Oxford University Press 2006) 651.

60 B. M. Dickens, 'What is a Medical Experiment?' (1975) 113 Canadian Medical Association Journal 635.

61 Department of Health, *Research Governance Framework for Health and Social Care* (London, UK: Department of Health 2005) at 3.

62 Ní Mhuirthile, *Realising Gender Recognition* (n 45) at 6–8.

63 Lee et l., 'Consensus Statement on Management of Intersex Disorders' (n 1).

64 N. R. Maharaj, A. Dhai, R. Wiersma and J. Moodley, 'Intersex Conditions in Children and Adolescents: Surgical, Ethical, and Legal Considerations' (2005) 18 Journal of Pediatric and Adolescent Gynaecology 399, at 401.

suggests that treatment can be considered research. However, as each intersex child is treated individually and the treatment evolves as the child grows, develops and responds to previous interventions, it could be argued that the treatment should be considered experimentation. Thus, whether treatment would be considered research or experimentation depends on the particular circumstances of each individual case.

International ethical guidelines on research and experimentation were developed in the aftermath of the Second World War[65] and subsequently endorsed by the medical professions in the Declaration of Helsinki (1964). These principles have been restated by national authorities.[66] At a regional level, in 2005, an Additional Protocol to the Council of Europe's Convention on Human Rights and Biomedicine (1997) was opened for signature.[67] All these guidelines share an appreciation for the need for human research subjects while simultaneously accepting that, in order to produce scientifically accurate research, the right to self-determination of the individual research subject will necessarily be sacrificed. It is for this reason that the importance of the informed consent of the research subject is emphasised.[68] They all include specifications regarding the inclusion of children and mentally disordered research subjects. Generally speaking, in such circumstances the informed consent of a legally authorised representative is required in accordance with the applicable domestic law.[69] Furthermore, children and other medical incompetents can only become research subjects where such research is necessary to promote the health of the population represented and the research cannot be conducted on legally competent persons.

For those conducting research/experimentation, the protection afforded by the common law test will not be forthcoming.[70] By definition, if the procedure is research or an experiment, it is not endorsed by a reasonable body of medical opinion. Yet, if the deviation for normal practice is deemed to be logical in all circumstances of the case, it may not offend legal principles. As stated in the Declaration of Helsinki:

> In the treatment of a patient, where proven interventions do not exist or have been ineffective, the physician, after seeking expert advice, with informed consent from the patient or a legally authorized representative,

65 George J. Annas and Michael A. Grodin (eds.) *The Nazi Doctors and the Nuremberg Code: Human Rights in Human Experimentation* (Oxford University Press 1992).

66 www.mrc.ac.uk/Ourresearch/Ethicsresearchguidance/MRC002578.

67 Available online at http://conventions.coe.int/treaty/EN/Treaties/Html/195.htm.

68 Declaration of Helsinki, paras 19–25, Additional Protocol Articles 13–17.

69 Ibid, para 24, Additional Protocol 15–17.

70 *Dunne v National Maternity Hospital* [1989] IR 91 and *Bolam v Friern Hospital Management Committee* [1957] 1 WLR 582.

> may use an unproven intervention if in the physician's judgement it offers hope of saving life, re-establishing health or alleviating suffering.[71]

Thus the importance of informed consent is clear. However, even in situations where informed consent is not possible, experimental treatment may be legal if it is deemed to be in the best interests of the patient.

Simms v An NHS Trust concerned two teenagers suffered from advanced stages of variant Creutzfeldt-Jakob disease (vCJD), a degenerative, incurable and terminal brain condition.[72] Both sets of parents sought a declaration that it would be lawful to undertake a highly experimental course of treatment, the risks and benefits of which were unknown, but which had shown some marginal varying success in mice, rats and dogs in Japan. It was accepted by all parties that the minors would not recover from the disease and that this treatment was a 'last chance'. The Court applied the best interests test and ruled that the experiment was justified, as there was no witness who was willing to rule out the possibility that some benefit might accrue to the children in question. However, the permission to conduct the experiment was qualified by the fact that the disease was invariably progressive and fatal, there was no alternative treatment and, so long as the experiment did not increase the suffering of the children, then it would not be unlawful to try. Finally, because there was evidence that did not entirely rule out some chance of benefit, Dame Butler-Sloss held that the Bolam test had been complied with. From this case, it becomes evident that a fine balance must be maintained between the child's rights and the interests of progress.

The situation with interventions on intersex children is different to that in *Simms*. Applying Butler-Sloss's qualifications: there are alternative treatment options to performing surgery in infancy, the available evidence indicates that being treated in this manner does increase the physical suffering of the intersex child, and finally a substantial number of medical professionals would contend that performing surgery does not benefit the child.[73] As interventions on bodies with intersex variations meet the criteria for the qualifications to the best interests test in the context of undergoing an experimental and/or research procedure, proxy consent cannot be given to these procedures. In this way, the right of children with intersex variations to develop without restriction or impediment, and to participate in decisions about interventions, is vindicated.

Conclusion

Recent leaps forward in LGBT rights in Ireland have left those with intersex variations behind. In permitting movement between legally recognised

71 Declaration of Helsinki (n 68), para 37.

72 *Simms v An NHS Trust* [2002] EWHC 2734.

73 See *supra* (n 24).

genders, the Gender Recognition Act 2015 has further embedded the primacy of the binary gender paradigm underpinning the law. Thus, it fails to protect those with intersex variations from unnecessary interventions. In this way, law becomes complicit in rendering healthy bodies vulnerable. Adopting the vulnerability lens enables law to refocus from the obvious doctrinal dogma around negligence and to consider instead the question of interventions on intersex bodies from the perspective of experimentation. Applying directly the doctrinal law on consent to experimentation carves out a space where children with an intersex variation can be enabled to determine for themselves what, if any, interventions they should undergo.

Bibliography

Primary sources

Constitution

Constitution of Ireland, 1937.

Cases

Australia

In the Marriage of C and D (falsely called C) (1979) 35 FLR 340.
New South Wales v *LePore* [2003] HCA 4, 212 CLR 511.
PAO, BJH, SBM, IDF and PMA v *Trustees of the Roman Catholic Church for the Archdiocese of Sydney* [2011] NSWSC 1216.
Prince Alfred College Incorporated v *ADC* [2016] HCA 37.
Woolcock Street Investments v *CDG* (2004) 216 CLR 515.

Canada

Bazley v *Currey* (1999) 144 DLR (4th) 45.
EB v *Order of the Oblates of Mary Immaculate in the Province of British Columbia* [2005] 3 SCR 45.
Jacobi v *Griffiths* (1999) 174 DLR (4th) 71.
John Doe v *Bennett* [2004] 1 SCR 436.

European Court of Human Rights

Akkoç v. *Turkey* Application nos. 22947/93 and 22948/93 Judgment (Merits and Just Satisfaction) 10 October 2000.
Aksoy v. *Turkey* Application no. 21987/93 Judgment (Merits and Just Satisfaction) 18 December 1996.
Al-Khawaja & Tahery v *United Kingdom* (2012) 54 EHRR 23.
Angelova and Iliev v *Bulgaria* Application No. 55523/00 Judgment (Merits and Just Satisfaction) 26 July 2007.
Aydın v. *Turkey* Application no. 23178/94 Judgment (Merits and Just Satisfaction) (Grand Chamber) 25 September 1997.
Centre for Legal Resources on behalf of Valentin Câmpeanu v *Romania* 47848/08 Judgment (Merits and Just Satisfaction) (Grand Chamber) 17 July 2014.

Chapman v *the United Kingdom* Application no. 27238/95 Judgment (Merits and Just Satisfaction) 18 January 2001.

Confederation française de l'encadrement v *France* Complaint No 9/2000.

Connors v. *the United Kingdom* Application nos. 39665/98 40086/98 Judgment (Merits and Just Satisfaction) 15 July 2002.

D.H. and others v *the Czech Republic* Application no. 57325/00 Judgment (Merits and Just Satisfaction) (Grand Chamber) 13 November 2007.

Dahlab v *Switzerland* Application no. 42393/98 Judgment (Merits and Just Satisfaction) 15 February 2001.

Denmark et al. v *Greece* Application no. 3321/67 Commission Report of 5 November 1969, Yearbook 12.

Dikme v Turkey, Application no. 20869/92 Judgment (Merits and Just Satisfaction) 11 July 2000.

Edwards v *United Kingdom* Application nos. 39647/98 40461/98 Judgment (Merits and Just Satisfaction) (Grand Chamber) 27 October 2004.

Eremia v *The Republic of Moldova* Application no. 3564/11 Judgment (Merits and Just Satisfaction) 28 May 2013.

European Roma Rights Centre (ERRC) v *Ireland* Complaint no. 100/2013 Decision on the Merits 16 May 2016.

European Roma Rights Centre v *France* Complaint no. 15/2003.

F.G. v *Sweden* Application No. 43611/11 Judgment (Merits and Just Satisfaction) (Grand Chamber) 23 March 2016.

Frimu & Ors v Romania Application no. 45312/07 7 February 2012.

Goodwin v *United Kingdom* Application no. 28957/95 [2002] 35 EHRR 447.

Hutten-Czapska v *Poland* Application no. 35014/97 Judgment (Merits and Just Satisfaction) (Grand Chamber) 19 June 2006.

I.A.A. v *the United Kingdom* Application no. 25960/13 Judgment (Admissibility) 8 March 2016.

İlhan v. *Turkey* Application no. 22277/93 Judgment (Merits and Just Satisfaction) 27 June 2000.

KAB v *Sweden* Application no. 886/11 Judgment (Merits and Just Satisfaction) 5 September 2013.

Keenan v United Kingdom Application no. 27229/95 Judgment (Merits and Just Satisfaction) 3 April 2001.

Ketreb v *France* Application no. 38447/09 19 July 2012.

Khoniakina v *Georgia* [2012] ECHR 1050.

Kiyutin v *Russia* Application no. 2700/10 Judgment (Merits and Just Satisfaction) 10 March 2011.

Kostovski v *The Netherlands* (1990) 12 21 EHRR 343

Koufaki v *Greece* Application no. 57665/12 7 May 2013.

Mamatas & Ors v Greece [2016] ECHR 694.

Mayeka and Mutunga v Belgium, Application no. 13178/03, Judgment (Merits and Just Satisfaction) 12 October 2006.

McCann v *UK* [2008] ECHR 385.

McCann v *United Kingdom* Application no. 19009/04 Judgment (Merits and Just Satisfaction) 13 May 2008.

Mehmet and Suna Yigit v Turkey [2007] ECHR 47.

Moldovan v *Romania* (2005) 44 EHRR 302.

MSS v *Belgium and Greece* Application no. 30696/09, Judgment (Merits and Just Satisfaction) (Grand Chamber) 21 January 2011.

Murray v *the United Kingdom* Application no. 14310/88 Judgment (Merits and Just Satisfaction) (Grand Chamber) 28 October 1994.

MYH and Others v *Sweden* Application no. 50859/10 Judgment (Merits and Just Satisfaction) 27 June 2013.

Opuz v *Turkey* Application no. 33401/02 Judgment (Merits and Just Satisfaction) 09 June 2009.

P Plaisier BV v *Netherlands* Application no. 46184/16 7 December 2017.

Salman v *Turkey* Application no. 21986/93 Judgment (Merits and Just Satisfaction) (Grand Chamber) 27 June 2000.

Santos Januario v *Portugal* [2013] ECHR 321.

Savickas v *Lithuania* [2013] ECHR 328.

Selmouni v *France* Application no. 25803/94 Judgment (Merits and Just Satisfaction) (Grand Chamber) 28 July 1999.

Siliadin v *France* Application no. 73316/01 Judgment (Merits and Just Satisfaction) 26 July 2005.

Soares de Melo v *Portugal* Application no. 72850/14 (ECtHR 16 May 2016)

Stanev v *Bulgaria* Application no. 36760/06 Judgment (Merits and Just Satisfaction) (Grand Chamber) 17 January 2012.

T v *United Kingdom* Application no. 24724/94 Judgment (Merits and Just Satisfaction) (Grand Chamber) 16 December 1999.

Tarakhel v *Switzerland* Application no. 29217/12 (Grand Chamber) 4 November 2014.

TW v *Malta* Application no. 25644/94 Judgment (Grand Chamber) 29 April 1999.

Uner v *The Netherlands* Application no. 46410/99, Judgment (Merits and Just Satisfaction) (Grand Chamber) 18 October 2006.

V.C. v *Slovakia* Application no. 18968/07 Judgment (Merits and Just Satisfaction) 8 November 2011.

Van Mechelen & Others v *The Netherlands* (1997) 25 EHRR 647.

Y v *Slovenia* (2016) 62 EHRR 3.

European Union

Case C-562/13 *Centre public d'action sociale d'Ottignies-Louvain-La-Neuve* v *Moussa Abdida* EU:C:2014:2453.

Case C-578/16 *CK and Others* v *Republika Slovenija* EU:C:2017:127.

Joined Cases C-411/10 and C-493/10 *NS* v *Secretary of State for the Home Department and ME and Others v Refugee Applications Commissioner and Minister for Justice, Equality and Law Reform* EU:C:2011:865, [2011] ECR I-13905.

C-13/94 *P* v *S and Cornwall County Council* ECR I-2143.

C-443/15 *Parris* v *TCD*, 24 November 2016.

Case C-61/11 *PPU Hassen El Dridi* EU:C:2011:268, [2011] ECR I-3015.

Case C-216/18 *PPU Minister for Justice and Equality* v *LM* EU:C:2018:586.

Case C-399/11 *Stefano Melloni* v *Ministerio Fiscal* EU:C:2013:107.

Ireland

Application of Gallagher [1991] 1 IR 31

Cronin v *Minister for Education* Unrep, High Court 6 July 2004.

Delahunty v *South Eastern Health Board* [2003] 4 IR 361

Donnelly v *Ireland* [1998] 1 IR 321.

Donnelly v *Ireland* [1998] 1 IR 321.

DPP v *McManus* [2011] IECCA 32 (12 April 2011).
Dunne v *National Maternity Hospital* [1989] IR 91.
Foy v *An tArd Chlá;raitheoir & Ors (No 1)* [2002] IEHC 166.
Foy v *An tArd Chlaraitheoir (No 2)* [2007] IEHC 470.
G v *An Bord Uchtála* [1980] IR 32.
Health Board v *BC* [1994] ELR 27.
Hickey v *McGowan* [2017] IESC 6.
JMcD v *PL and BM* [2010] 2 IR 199.
L v *L* [1992] 2 IR 77.
Maguire v *Ardagh* [2002] 1 IR 385.
Maguire v *Central Mental Hospital* [1996] 3 IR 1.
Mapp v *Gilhooley* [1991] 2 IR 253.
MR and DR v An tArd-Chláraitheoir [2014] IESC 60.
O'Donnell v *South Dublin County Council* [2007] IEHC 204.
O'Donnell v *South Dublin County Council* [2015] IESC 28.
O'Keeffe v *Hickey* [2009] 2 IR 302.
O'D v *DPP* [2009] IEHC 559 [2009]; [2015] IECA 273 [2015].
People (DPP) v DO [2006] 2 ILRM 61.
People (DPP) v Kelly [2006] 3 IR 115.
People v James T [1988] Frewen 141.
PP v Judges of the Dublin Circuit Court [2019] IESC 11.
Re Ellis [1990] 2 IR 291.
Re Kevin O'Kelly (1974) 108 ILTR 97.
Reilly v *Devereaux* [2009] IESC 22.
Ryan v *AG* [1965] IR 294.
Sinnott v *Minister for Education* [2001] 2 IR 545.
State (Healy) v *Donoghue* [1976] IR 325.
State (Nicolaou) v *An Bord Uchtála* [1966] IR 567.
TD v *Minister for Education* [2001] 4 IR 259.
White v *Ireland* [1995] 2 IR 268.
Zappone and Gilligan v *Revenue Commissioners* [2006] IEHC 404.

Latvia

Case no. 2009–43–01.

Portugal

Judgment 187/2013 State Budget Law for 2013.
Judgment 353/2012 State Budget Law for 2012.

United Kingdom

Armes v *Nottinghamshire County Council* [2017] UKSC 60.
Bolitho v *Hackney Health Authority* [1998] AC 232.
Canadian Pacific Railway Co v *Lockhart* [1942] AC 591.
Corbett v *Corbett (Otherwise Ashley)* [1970] 2 All ER 3.

Dubai Aluminium Co Ltd v *Salaam* [2002] UKHL 48.
Duncan v *Findlater*, 6 Cl. & Fin. 894 (1839).
Fairchild v *Glenhaven Funeral Services Ltd* [2003] 1 AC 32; [2002] 3 All ER 305.
Hyde v *Hyde* (1866) LR 1 P&D 130.
ICI v *Shatwell* [1965] AC 656.
Lister v *Hesley Hall Ltd* [2002] 1 AC 215.
Maga v *The Trustees of the Birmingham Archdiocese of the Roman Catholic Church* [2010] EWCA Civ 256; [2010] 1 WLR 1441.
Mohamud v *Wm Morrison Supermarkets plc* [2016] UKSC 11; [2016] 2 WLR 821.
R (Carmichael and Rourke) v *Secretary of State for Work and Pensions* [2016] UKSC 58.
R (Christie Elan-Cane) v *Secretary of State for the Home Department* [2018] EWHC 1530.
R (on the application of SG and others (previously JS and others)) v *Secretary of State for Work and Pensions* [2015] UKSC 16.
R v *Barker* [2010] EWCA Crim 4.
R v *Lubemba* [2015] 1 WLR 1579 (CA (Crim Div)).
R v *Willis* [2012] 1 Cr App R 2 (CA (Crim Div)).
Re J (Child's Religious Upbringing and Circumcision) [2000] 1 FCR 30.
Re TT and YY [2019] EWHC 1823 (Fam).
Simms v An NHS Trust [2002] EWHC 2734.
Steinfeld and Keidan v *Secretary of State for International Development* [2018] UKSC 32.
Various Claimants v *Catholic Child Welfare Society and others* [2012] UKSC 56, [2013] 2 AC 1 [34].
Various Claimants v *The Catholic Child Welfare Society* [2012] UKSC 56.

UN Committee on Economic, Social and Cultural Rights

IDG v *Spain* E/C.12/55/D/2/2014 decision dated 19 June 2015.
Marcia Cecelia Trujillo Calero v *Ecuador* E/C.12/63/D/10/2015 decision dated 26 March 2018.
Mohammed Ben Djazia and Naouel Bellili E/C.12/61/D/5/2015 decision dated 20 June 2017.

United States of America

M.C. v *Medical University of South Carolina*, filed 14 May 2013 in County of Richland Common Pleas http://interactadvocates.org/wp-content/uploads/2016/03/050714_Crawford_Complaint_Release_FINAL_FINAL.pdf.

Legislation

Canada

Revised Statutes of British Columbia 1960.

Council of Europe

European Convention for the Prevention of Torture and Inhuman or Degrading Treatment or Punishment ETS no. 126 (1987).
European Convention on Human Rights and Fundamental Freedoms (1950).

England and Wales

Civil Partnerships, Marriages and Deaths (Registration etc) Act 2019.

European Union

Charter of Fundamental Rights of the European Union (2000).
Directive 2000/78/EC of 27 November 2000 establishing a general framework for equal treatment in employment and occupation.
Directive 2003/9/EC laying down minimum standards for the reception of asylum seekers [2003] OJ L31/18.
Directive 2004/83/EC on minimum standards for the qualification and status of third country nationals or stateless persons as refugees or as persons who otherwise need international protection and the content of the protection granted [2004] OJ L 304/12.
Directive 2005/85/EC on minimum standards on procedures in Member States for granting and withdrawing refugee status [2005] OJ L 326/13.
Directive 2008/115/EC on common standards and procedures in Member States for returning illegally staying third-country nationals [2008] OJ L 348/98.
Directive 2011/95/EU on standards for the qualification of third-country nationals or stateless persons as beneficiaries of international protection, for a uniform status for refugees or for persons eligible for subsidiary protection, and for the content of the protection granted [2011] OJ L 337/9.
Directive 2012/29/EU establishing minimum standards on the rights, support and protection of victims of crime [2012] OJ L 325/57.
Directive 2012/29/EU establishing minimum standards on the rights, support and protection of victims of crime, and replacing Council Framework Decision 2001/220/JHA.
Directive 2013/32/EU on common procedures for granting and withdrawing international protection (recast) [2013] OJ L 180/60.
Directive 2013/33/EU laying down standards for the reception of applicants for international protection (recast) [2013] OJ L 180/96.
Opinion 2/13 *Accession to the European Convention on Human Rights* EU:C:2014:2454.
Opinion 2/94 *Accession by the Community to the European Convention for the Protection of Human Rights and Fundamental Freedoms* EU:C:1996:229, [2006] ECR I-2827.

International

International Covenant on Civil and Political Rights 1966.
International Covenant on Economic Social and Cultural Rights 1966.
UN Committee on Economic, Social and Cultural Rights, Committee Statement to the World Conference, UN Doc E/1993/22.
UN General Assembly, Draft International Covenants on Human Rights, UN Doc A2929 1955.
UN General Assembly Resolution 1985/17.
Vienna Declaration, 1993 Second World Conference on Human Rights.

Ireland

Children Act 2001.
Children and Family Relationships Act 2015.

Civil Partnership and Certain Rights and Obligation of Cohabitants Act 2010.
Criminal Evidence Act 1992.
Criminal Justice (Evidence) Act 1924.
Criminal Justice (Female Genital Mutilation) Act 2012.
Criminal Justice (Victims of Crime) Act 2017.
Criminal Law Amendment Act 1885.
Criminal Law (Rape) Act 1981.
Criminal Law (Rape) (Amendment) Act 1990.
Criminal Law (Sexual Offences) Act 1993.
Criminal Procedure Rules 2015.
Department of Finance Circular 12/88, the Prohibition of Incitement to Hatred Act 1989.
Employment Equality Act 1998.
Equal Status Act 2000.
Equality Act 2004.
Family Law (Divorce) Act 1996.
Gender Recognition Act 2015.
General Scheme of the Assisted Human Reproduction Bill 2017.
Guardianship of Infants Act 1964.
Health Insurance Act 1994.
International Protection Act 2015.
Marriage Act 2015.
Offences against the Person Act 1861.
Pensions Act 1990.
Rules of the Superior Courts 198.
Sex Offenders Act 2001.
Social Welfare and Pensions Act 2010.
Social Welfare (Miscellaneous Provisions) Act 2004.
Social Welfare, Pensions and Civil Registration Act 2018.
Thirty–First Amendment of the Constitution (Economic, Social and Cultural Rights) Bill 2012.
Thirty-Fourth Amendment of the Constitution (Economic, Social and Cultural Rights) Bill 2014.
Twenty-First Amendment of the Constitution (No. 3) Bill 1999.
Unfair Dismissals (Amendment) Act 1993.

Northern Ireland

Northern Ireland (Executive Formation etc) Act 2019.

Scotland

Housing (Scotland) Act 2001.

United Kingdom

Children Act 1975.
Civil Partnership Act 2004.
Youth Justice and Criminal Evidence Act 1999.

United States of America

Protection of Children Act.

Secondary sources

Books

Annas, G. J. and Grodin, M. A. (eds.), *The Nazi Doctors and the Nuremberg Code: Human Rights in Human Experimentation* (Oxford, UK: Oxford University Press 1992).

Atiyah, P., *Vicarious Liability in the Law of Torts* (Butterworths 1967).

Badgett, M. V. L., Durso, L. E. and Schneebaum, A. *New Patterns of Poverty in the Lesbian, Gay, and Bisexual Community* (Williams Institute 2013).

Bakhtin, M., *Rabelais and His World* (Bloomington: Indiana University Press 1984).

Bell, E., *Criminal Justice and Neoliberalism* (Palgrave Macmillan 2011).

Besselink, L. A., *Composite European Constitution* (Europa Law Publishing 2007).

Brown, W., *States of Injury: Power and Freedom in Late Modernity* (Princeton University Press 1995).

Bumiller, K., *In an Abusive State: How Neoliberalism Appropriated the Feminist Movement Against Sexual Violence* (Duke University Press 2009).

Burrows, D., *Children's Views and Evidence* (Bloomsbury 2018).

Buzawa, E. and Buzawa, C., *Domestic Violence: The Criminal Justice Response* (3rd edn, Sage 2003).

Capitaine, B. and Vanthuyne K. (eds.), *Power through Testimony: Reframing Residential Schools in the Age of Reconciliation* (UBC Press, 2017).

Coke, Sir E., *The First Part of the Institutes of the Law of England* (Robert H. Smith, 1853).

Conrad, R. (ed.), *Against Equality: Queer Critiques of Gay Marriage* (Against Equality Press 2010).

Conway, G., *The Limits of Legal Reasoning and the European Court of Justice* (Cambridge University Press, 2012).

Cruz, J. B., *What's Left of the Law of Integration? Decay and Resistance in European Union Law* (Oxford University Press 2018).

Cunneen, C. and Hoyle, C., *Debating Restorative Justice* (Hart Publishing, 2010).

Davis, G., *Contesting Intersex: The Dubious Diagnosis* (New York University Press, 2015).

Dembour, M. B., *When Humans Become Migrants* (Oxford University Press 2015).

Denzin, N. K., *The Research Act: A Theoretical Introduction to Sociological Methods* (3rd edn, Prentice Hall International 1989).

Doak, J., *Victims' Rights, Human Rights and Criminal Justice: Reconceiving the Role of Third Parties* (Hart Publishing 2008).

Dobash, R. and Dobash, R., *Violence Against Wives: A Case Against the Patriarchy* (New York: Free Press 1979).

Dreger, A. D., *Hermaphrodites and the Medical Invention of Sex* (Harvard University Press 1998).

Duggan, L., *The Twilight of Equality: Neoliberalism, Cultural Politics, and the Attack on Democracy* (Beacon Press 2003).

Durso, L. E. and Gates, G. J., *Serving Our Youth: Findings from a National Survey of Service Providers Working with Lesbian, Gay, Bisexual and Transgender Youth Who Are Homeless or At Risk of Becoming Homeless* (Williams Institute 2012).

Ellison, L., *The Adversarial Process and the Vulnerable Witness* (Oxford University Press 2001).

Fennell, C., *The Law of Evidence in Ireland* (3rd edn, Bloomsbury Professional 2009).

Ferriter, D., Occasions of Sin, Sex and Society in Modern Ireland (Profile Books 2009).

Fineman, M. A., *The Autonomy Myth* (The New Press 2004).

Fineman, M. A. and Fineman, J. (eds.), *Vulnerability and the Legal Organisation of Work* (Routledge 2017).

Fineman, M. A., Mattsson, T. and Andersson, U. (eds.), *Privatization, Vulnerability, and Social Responsibility* (Routledge 2016).

Foucault, M., *The History of Sexuality*, vol. 1, *An Introduction* (Random House 1978).

Ganiel, G., *Transforming Post-Catholic Ireland* (Oxford University Press 2016).

Garland, D., *The Culture of Control: Crime and Social Order in Contemporary Society* (Oxford University Press 2002).

Godwin Phelps, T., *Shattered Voices: Language, Violence, and the Work of Truth Commissions* (University of Pennsylvania Press 2004).

Goode, H., McGee, H. and O'Boyle, C., *Time to Listen: Confronting Child Sexual Abuse by Catholic Clergy in Ireland* (Dublin: Liffey Press 2003).

Goodin, R., *Protecting the Vulnerable: A Re-Analysis of Our Social Responsibilities* (University of Chicago Press 1986).

Halley, J., Kotiswaran, P., Rebouché, R. and Shamir, H., *Governance Feminism: An Introduction* (University of Minnesota Press 2018).

Hammarberg, T., *Human Rights in Europe: No Grounds for Complacency* (Council of Europe Publishing 2011).

Heffernan, L., *Evidence in Criminal Trials* (Bloomsbury Professional 2014).

Hemreijck, A., *Changing Welfare States* (Oxford University Press 2013).

Henderson, J. and Wakeham, P. (eds.), *Reconciling Canada: Critical Perspectives on the Culture of Redress* (University of Toronto Press 2013).

Jacobs, J. and Geerson, J., *The Time Divide: Work, Family and Gender Inequality* (Harvard University Press 2004).

Karakazis, K., *Fixing Sex: Intersex, Medical Authority and Lived Experience* (London: Duke University Press 2008).

Kessler, S., *Lessons from the Intersexed* (Rutgers University Press, 1998).

Kilcommins. S., Leahy, S. and Moore Walsh, K., *The Victim in the Irish Criminal Process* (Manchester University Press, 2018).

Kittay, E., *Love's Labor: Essays on Women, Equality and Dependency* (Routledge 2013).

Kosciw, J. G., Greytak, E. A., Zongrone, A. D., Clark, C. M., and Truong, N. L., *The 2017 National School Climate Survey: The Experiences of Lesbian, Gay, Bisexual and Transgender Youth in our Nation's Schools* (GLSEN, 2018).

Lupton, D., *Risk* (Routledge 1999).

MacGréil, M., *Prejudice in Ireland Revisited* (St Patrick's College 1996).

Mackenzie, C. and Stoljar, N., *Relational Autonomy: Feminist Perspectives on Autonomy, Agency, and the Social Self* (Oxford University Press 2000).

Mackenzie, C., Rogers, W. and Dodds, S., *Vulnerability: New Essays in Ethics and Feminist Philosophy* (Oxford University Press 2014).

Madden-Dempsey, M., *Prosecuting Domestic Violence: A Philosophical Analysis* (Oxford University Press 2009).

Marshall, T. H., *Citizenship and Social Class and Other Essays* (Cambridge University Press 1950).

Mason, J. K. and Laurie, G. T., *Mason & McCall Smith's Law and Ethics* (7th edn, Oxford University Press 2006).

McGrath, D., *Evidence* (2nd edn, Thomson Roundhall 2014).

Mitsilegas, V., *EU Criminal Law after Lisbon* (Hart 2016).

Nedelsky, J., *Law's Relations: A Relational Theory of Self, Autonomy and Law* (Oxford University Press 2011).

Norrie, A., *Law and the Beautiful Soul* (Glass House 2005).

Nussbaum, M., *Creating Capabilities: The Human Development Approach* (Harvard University Press 2013).

O'Hanlon, G., *The Quiet Revolution of Pope Francis: A Synodal Catholic Church in Ireland?* (Dublin: Messenger Publications 2018).

Okin, S., *Justice, Gender and the Family* (University of Chicago Press 1989).

Pavlich, G., *Governing Paradoxes of Restorative Justice* (Glasshouse Press 2005).

Peers, S., *EU Justice and Home Affairs Law*, vol. 1, *EU Immigration and Asylum Law* (Oxford University Press 2016).

Pescatore, P, *Le Droit de l'intégration* (A. W. Sijthoff 1972).

Preves, S. E., *Intersex and Identity: The Contested Self.* (New Brunswick, NJ: Rutgers University Press 2003).

Putnam, R. D., *Bowling Alone: The Collapse and Revival of American Community* (Simon and Schuster 2000).

Putnam, R. D., *Democracy in Flux: The Evolution of Social Capital in Contemporary Society* (Oxford University Press 2002).

Reynaud, A. M., *Emotions, Remembering and Feeling Better: Dealing with the Indian Residential Schools Settlement Agreement in Canada* (transcript 2017).

Rothblatt, M. A., *The Apartheid of Sex: A Manifesto on the Freedom of Gender* (Crown Publishing 1995).

Rubin, H. and Rubin, I., *Qualitative Data: The Art of Hearing Data* (Thousand Oaks: Sage Publications 2012).

Salmond, J. W. and Heuston, R., *Salmond and Heuston on the Law of Torts* (19th edn, Sweet and Maxwell 1987).

Sen, A, *Development as Freedom* (Oxford University Press 2001).

Sharpe, A. N., *Transgender Jurisprudence. Dysphoric Bodies of Law* (Cavendish Publishing 2002)

Smith, J. M., *Ireland's Magdalen Laundries and the Nation's Architecture of Containment* (University of Notre Dame Press 2007).

Smyth, C. M., *Social and Economic Rights in Ireland* (Clarus Press 2017).

Steiner, H., Alston, P. and Goodman, R., *International Human Rights in Context: Law Politics and Morals* (3rd edn, Oxford University Press 2008).

Streeck, W., *How Will Capitalism End?* (Verso 2017).

Umbreit, M. S., and Armour, M. P., *Restorative Justice Dialogue: An Essential Guide for Research and Practice* (Springer Publishing 2011).

Vaughan-Whitehead, D., *Work Inequalities in the Crisis: Evidence from Europe* (International Labour Organisation 2012).

Woolford, A., *The Politics of Restorative Justice. A Critical Introduction* (Fernwood Publishing 2009).

Zehr, H., *Changing Lenses: A New Focus for Crime and Justice* (Herald Press 1990).

Contribution to edited books

Andrieu, K., 'Political Liberalism after Mass Violence: John Rawls and a "Theory" of Transitional Justice', in Susanne Buckley-Zistel, Teresa Koloma Beck, Christian Braun and Fridererike Mieth (eds.), *Transitional Justice Theories* (Routledge 2014).

Aptel, C., 'International Criminal Justice and Child Protection', in Saudamini Siegrist, Mindy Jane Roseman and Theo Sowa (eds.), *Children and Transitional Justice: Truth-Telling, Accountability and Reconciliation* (UNICEF 2010).

Bourdieu, P., 'Forms of Capital', in J. Richardson (ed.), *Handbook of Theory and Research for the Sociology of Education* (Greenwood 1993).

Chung, R. and Hunt, M. R., 'Justice and Health Inequalities in Humanitarian Crises: Structured Health Vulnerabilities and Natural Disasters', in Patti Lenard and Christine Straehle (eds.), *Health Inequalities and Global Justice* (Edinburgh University Press 2012).

Cloud, M., 'More than Utopia', in Martha Fineman and Anna Grear (eds.), *Vulnerability: Reflections on a New Ethical Foundation for Law and Politics* (Ashgate 2013).

Conway, G. S. and Mouriquand P. D. E., 'Congenital Adrenal Hyperplasia', in Adam H. Balen, Sarah M Creighton, Melanie C. Davies, Jane MacDougall and Richard Stanhope (eds.), *Paediatric and Adolescent Gynaecology: A Multidisciplinary Approach* (Cambridge University Press, 2004).

de Búrca, G., 'The Evolution of EU Human Rights Law', in Paul Craig and Gráinne de Búrca (eds.), *The Evolution of EU Law* (2nd edn, Oxford University Press 2011).

de Greiff, P., 'Justice and Reparations', in Pablo de Greiff (ed.), *The Handbook of Reparations* (Oxford University Press 2006) 451.

Dodds, S., 'Dependence Care and Vulnerability,' in C. Mackenzie, W. Rogers, and S. Dodds (eds.), *Vulnerability: New Essays in Ethics and Feminist Philosophy* (Oxford University Press 2014).

Ettelbrick, P. 'Since When Is Marriage a Path to Liberation?', in William Rubenstein (ed.), *Lesbians, Gay Men and the Law* (New Press 1993).

Everson, M., 'The Legacy of the Market Citizen', in Jo Shaw and Gillian More (eds.), *New Legal Dynamics of European Union* (Clarendon Press 1995).

Fausto-Sterling, A., *Sexing the Body: Gender Politics and the Construction of Sexuality* (New New York: Basic Books 2000).

Fineman, M. A., 'Equality, Autonomy, and the Vulnerable Subject in Law and Politics', in Martha Fineman and Anna Grear (eds.), *Vulnerability: Reflections on a New Ethical Foundation for Law and Politics* (Ashgate 2013).

Fineman, M. and Grear, A., 'Introduction', in Martha Fineman and Anna Grear (eds.), *Vulnerability: Reflections on a New Ethical Foundation for Law and Politics* (Ashgate 2013).

Ganiel, G., 'Negating the Francis Effect? The Effect of the Abuse Crisis in Ireland', in Giuseppe Giordan (ed.), *Research in the Social Scientific Study of Religion* (Leiden: Brill 2019).

Harwell, E. E. and Le Billon, P., 'Natural Connections: Linking Transitional Justice and Development Through a Focus on Natural Resources', in Pablo de Grieff and Roger Duthie (eds.), *Transitional Justice and Development: Making Connections* (ICTJ 2009).

Hughes, J. 'The New Victims: Perpetrators Before the Canadian Truth and Reconciliation Commission', in B. Capitaine and K. Vanthuyne (eds.), *Power through Testimony: Reframing Residential Schools in the Age of Reconciliation* (UBC Press, 2017).

Keeley, H., Ó Súilleabháin, F. and Leane, M., 'Sexual and Gender Minority Populations and Suicidal Behaviours', in Danuta Wasserman (eds.), *Oxford Textbook of Suicidology and Suicide Prevention* (Oxford University Press 2021).

Lira, E., 'The Reparations Policy for Human Rights Violations in Chile', in Pablo de Grieff, *The Handbook of Reparations* (Oxford University Press 2006).

Mackenzie, C., 'The Importance of Relational Autonomy and Capabilities for an Ethics of Vulnerability', in Catriona Mackenzie, Wendy Rogers and Susan Dodds (eds.), *Vulnerability: New Essays in Ethics and Feminist Philosophy* (Oxford University Press 2014).

Mackenzie, C., Rogers, W. and Dodds, S., 'Introduction: What is Vulnerability, and Why Does it Matter for Moral Theory?', in Catriona Mackenzie, Wendy Rogers and Susan Dodds (eds.), *Vulnerability: New Essays in Ethics and Feminist Philosophy* (Oxford University Press 2014).

Maruna, S. and Koch, T., 'The Impact of Imprisonment on the Desistence Process', in J. Travis and C. Visher (eds.), *Prisoner Reentry and Crime in* America (Cambridge University Press 2005).

McCold, P., 'What Is the Role of Community in Restorative Justice Theory and Practice?' in Harry Zehr and Barry Toews (eds.), Critical Issues in Restorative Justice (New York: Criminal Justice Press 2004).

McCold, P. and Wachtel, B., 'Community is not a Place: A New Look at Community Justice Initiatives', in Gerry Johnstone (ed.), *A Restorative Justice Reader* (Willan Publishing, 2003).

Naffine, N., 'Sexing the Subject (of Law)', in Margaret Thornton (ed.), *Public and Private: Feminist Legal Debates* (Oxford University Press 1995).

Ní Mhuirthile, T., 'Building Bodies: A Legal History of Intersex in Ireland', in Jennifer Redmond, Sonia Tiernan, Sandra McAvoy and Mary McAuliffe, *Sexual Politics in Modern Ireland* (Irish Academic Press, 2015).

Ní Mhuirthile, T, 'Foy v An tArd Chláraitheoir', in Máiréad Enright, Julie McCandless and Aoife O'Donoghue (eds.), *Northern/Irish Feminist Judgments: Judges Troubles and the Gendered Politics of Identity* (Oxford: Hart Publishing 2017).

Ní Mhuirthile, T., 'Gender Identity, Intersex and Law in Ireland', in Lynsey Black and Peter Dunne (eds.), *Law and Gender in Modern Ireland: Critique and Reform* (Hart Publishing 2019), 191.

Ní Mhuirthile, T., 'Legal Recognition of Preferred Gender Identity in Ireland: An Analysis of Proposed Legislation', in M. Leane and E. Kiely (eds.), *Sexualities and Irish Society: A Reader* (Orpen Press 2014).

Peers, S., 'Justice and Home Affairs Law since the Treaty of Lisbon: A Fairy-Tale Ending?' in Diego Acosta Arcarazo and Cian Murphy (eds.), *EU Security and Justice Law* (Hart 2014).

Petrich, D. and Morrison, B., 'The Alternatives to Violence Project: Using Positive Criminology as a Framework for Understanding Rehabilitation and Reintegration' in T. Gavrielides (ed.), *Offenders no More: An Interdisciplinary Restorative Justice Dialogue* (NOVA Science Publishers 2015).

Ryan, F., 'Mapping a Transformed Landscape: Sexual Orientation and the Law in Ireland', in Lynsey Black and Peter Dunne (eds.), *Law and Gender in Modern Ireland: Critique and Reform* (Hart Publishing 2019).

Sandoval, C., 'Reflections on the Transformative Potential of Transitional Justice and the Nature of Social Change in Times of Transition', in Roger Duthie and Paul Seils (eds.), *Justice Mosaics: How Context Shapes Transitional Justice in Fractured Societies* (International Centre for Transitional Justice 2017).

Smyth, C. M., 'Social and Economic Rights and the Struggle for Equivalent Protection in International Law', in Lora Windenthal and Jean Quatet (eds.), The Routledge History of Human Rights (Routledge 2019).

Smyth, C. M., 'Social and Economic Rights in a Post Neo-Liberal Society', in Claire-Michelle Smyth and Richard Lang (eds.), *The Future of Human Rights in the UK* (Cambridge Scholars Publishing 2017).

Smyth, M., 'Putting the Past in its Place: Issues of Victimhood and Reconciliation in Northern Ireland's Peace Process', in Nigel Biggar (ed.), *Burying the Past: Making Peace and Doing Justice after Civil Conflict* (Georgetown University Press 2001).

Tombs, D., 'Lived Religion and the Intolerance of the Cross', in R. R. Ganzevoort and S. Sremac (eds.), *Lived Religion and the Politics of (In)tolerance* (Cham, Switzerland: Palgrave Macmillan 2017).

Walker, M. U., 'Moral Vulnerability and the Task of Reparations', in Catriona Mackenzie, Wendy Rogers and Susan Dodds (eds.), *Vulnerability: New Essays in Ethics and Feminist Philosophy* (Oxford University Press 2014).

Weeks, J., 'Necessary Fictions: Sexual Identities and the Politics of Diversity', in J. Weeks, J. Holland and M. Haites (eds.), *Sexualities and Society: A Reader* (Polity Press 2003).

Whittle, S., 'Gender Fucking or Fucking Gender: Current Cultural Contributions to Theories of Gender Bending', in R. Ekins and D. King (eds.), *Blending Genders: Social Aspects of Cross-Dressing and Sex-Changing* (Routledge 1996).

Wiebelhaus-Brahm, E., 'After Shocks: Exploring the Relationships between Transitional Justice and Resilience in Post-Conflict Societies', in Roger Duthie and Paul Seils (eds.), *Justice Mosaics: How Context Shapes Transitional Justice in Fractured Societies* (International Centre for Transitional Justice 2017).

Williams, A, 'Human Rights in the EU' in Anthony Arnull and Damian Chalmers (eds.), *The Oxford Handbook of European Union Law* (Oxford University Press 2015).

Zehr, H., 'Retributive Justice, Restorative Justice', in Gerry Johnstone (ed.), *A Restorative Justice Reader* (Willan Publishing 2003).

Journal articles

American Academy of Pediatrics, 'Evaluation of the Newborn with Developmental Anomalies of the External Genitalia' (2000) 106 Pediatrics 138.

Anderson, P., 'Autonomy, Vulnerability and Gender' (2003) 4(2) Feminist Theory 149.

Ashworth, A., 'Responsibilities, Rights and Restorative Justice' (2002) 43 British Journal of Criminology 578.

Baldaccini, A., 'The Return and Removal of Irregular Migrants under EU Law: An Analysis of the Returns Directive' (2009) 11 European Journal of Migration and Law 1.

Bender, L., 'Changing the Values in Tort Law' (1989–1990) 25 Tulsa Law Journal 759.

Beuermann, C., 'Conferred Authority Strict Liability and Institutional Child Sexual Abuse', (2015) 37 Sydney Law Review 113.

Blackless, M., Charuvastra, A., Derryck, A., Fausto-Sterling, A., Lauzanne, K. and Lee, E., 'How Sexually Diamorphic Are We? Review and Synthesis' (2000) 12 American Journal of Human Biology 151.

Bohmert, M. N., Duwe, G. and Kroovand Hipple, N., 'Evaluating Restorative Justice Circles of Support and Accountability: Can Social Support Overcome Structural Barriers' (2018) 62(3) International Journal of Offender Therapy and Comparative Criminology 739.

Brodie, D., 'Enterprise Liability: Justifying Vicarious Liability' (2007) 27 Oxford Journal of Legal Studies 493.

Brown, K., '"Vulnerability": Handle with Care' (2011) 5(3) Ethics and Social Welfare 313.

Bryan, A. and Mayock, P., 'Supporting LGBT Lives? Complicating the Suicide Consensus in LGBT Mental Health Research' (2017) 20(1–2) Sexualities 65.

Buel, S., '50 Obstacles to Leaving aka Why Victims Stay' (1999) 28 Colorado Lawyer 1.

Burton, M., Evans, R. and Sanders, A., 'Implementing Special Measures for Vulnerable and Intimidated Witnesses: The Problem of Identification' (2006) Criminal Law Review 229.

Cabanyes Truffinoa, J., 'Resilience: An Approach to the Concept' (2010) 3(4) Revista de Psiquiatría y Salud Mental 145.

Carney, P., 'The Role of the Victim in the Irish Criminal Process' (2007) Judicial Studies Institute Journal 7.

Chalmers, D. and Barroso, L., 'What Van Gend en Loos Stands for' (2014) 12 International Journal of Constitutional Law 105.

Chung, C., 'Victims' Participation at the International Criminal Court: Are Concessions of the Court Clouding the Promise?' (2008) 6(3) Northwestern Journal of International Human Rights 459.

Clamp, K. and Paterson, C., 'Rebalancing Criminal Justice Potentials and Pitfalls for Neighbourhood Justice Panels' (2011) 9 British Journal of Community Justice 21.

Clark, T. C. et al., 'The Health and Well-Being of Transgender High School Students: Results from the New Zealand Adolescent Health Survey' (2014) 55(1) Journal of Adolescent Health 93.

Coker, D., 'Crime Control and Feminist Law Reform in Domestic Violence Law' (2001) British Columbia Law Review 80.

Cole, A., 'All of Us are Vulnerable, but Some Are More Vulnerable than Others: The Politics Ambiguity of Vulnerability Studies, an Ambivalent Critique' (2016) 17(2) Critical Horizons 260.

Colker, R., 'Marriage' (1991) 3 Yale Law Journal of Law and Feminism 321.

Conron, K. J., Scott, G., Stowell, G. S. and Landers S. J., 'Transgender Health in Massachusetts: Results from a Household Probability Sample of Adults' (2012) 102(1) American Journal of Public Health 118.

Cooper, F. R., 'Always Already Suspect: Revising Vulnerability Theory' (2015) 93 North Carolina Law Review 1399.

Coppel, J, and O'Neill, A., 'The European Court of Justice: Taking Rights Seriously?' (1992) 29 Common Market Law Review 669.

Cretney, A. and Davis, G., 'Prosecuting Domestic Assault: Victims Failing Courts, or Courts Failing Victims?' (1997) 36(2) The Howard Journal of Crime and Justice 146.

Cullen, F., 'Social Support as an Organising Concept for Criminology: Presidential Address to the Academy of Criminal Justice Sciences' (1994) 11 Justice Quarterly 527.

Cullen, H., 'The Collective Complaints System of the European Social Charter: Interpretative Methods of the European Committee on Social Rights' (2009) 9(1) Human Rights Law Review 61.

de Albuquerque, C., 'Chronicle of an Announced Birth: The Coming into Life of the Optional Protocol to the International Covenant on Economic Social and Cultural Rights – The Missing Piece of the International Bill of Human Rights' (2010) 32 Human Rights Quarterly 144.

de Búrca, G., 'After the EU Charter of Fundamental Rights: The Court of Justice as a Human Rights Actor?' (2013) 20 Maastricht Journal of European and Comparative Law 168.

de Greiff, P., 'Theorizing Transitional Justice' (2012) 51 Nomos 31.

Dennis, M. J. and Stewart, D. P., 'Justiciability of Economic, Social and Cultural Rights: Should there be an International Complaints Mechanism to Adjudicate the Rights to Food, Water, Housing and Health?' (2004) 98 American Journal of International Law 462.

Diamond, M. and Sigmundson, H. K., 'Management of Intersexuality: Guidelines for Dealing with Persons with Ambiguous Genitalia' (1997) 151(10) Archives of Pediatric and Adolescent Medicine 1046.

Dickens, B. M., 'What is a Medical Experiment?' (1975) 113 Canadian Medical Association Journal 635.

Doan, P. L., 'Queers in the American City: Transgendered Perceptions of Urban Space' (2007) 14(1) 57–74 Gender, Place and Culture 58.

Doan, P. L., 'The Tyranny of Gendered Spaces – Reflections from Beyond the Gender Dichotomy' (2010) 17(5) Gender, Place and Culture 634.

Ehrenreich, N. and Barr, M., 'Intersex Surgeries, Female Genital Cutting, and the Selective Condemnation of "Cultural Practices"' (2005) 40(1) Harvard Civil Rights – Civil Liberties Law Review 71.

Eichner, M., 'Dependency and the Liberal Polity: On Martha Fineman's "The Autonomy Myth"' (2005) 93 Californian Law Review 1285.

Ellison, L., 'Prosecuting Domestic Violence Without Victim Participation' (2002) 65(6) Modern Law Review 834.

Factor, R. J. and Rothblum, E., 'A Study of Transgender Adults and their Non-Transgender Siblings on Demographic Characteristics, Social Support and Experiences of Violence' (2008) 3(3) Journal of LGBT Health Research 11.

Feldman, K. W. and Smith, D. W., 'Fetal Phallic Growth and Penile Standards for Newborn Male Infants' (1975) 86(3) Journal of Pediatrics 395.

Fineman, M. A., 'Cracking the Foundational Myths: Independence, Autonomy, and Self-Sufficiency' (2000) 8 American University Journal of Gender Social Policy and Law 13.

Fineman, M. A., 'Gender and the New Legal Realism' (2005) University of Wisconsin Law Review 405.

Fineman, M. A., 'Elderly as Vulnerable: Rethinking the Nature of Individual and Societal Responsibility' (2012) 20(2) Elder Law Journal 71.

Fineman, MA., 'Equality and Difference: The Restrained State', (2015) 66(3) Alabama Law Review 608.

Fineman, M. A., 'Feminism, Masculinities and Multiple Identities' (2013) 13 Nevada Law Journal 619.

Fineman, M. A., 'Vulnerability and Inevitable Inequality' (2017) 4(3) Oslo Law Review 133.

Fineman, M. A., 'Vulnerability, Resilience, and LGBT Youth' (2014) 23(2) Temple Political & Civil Rights Law Review 307.

Fineman, M. A., 'The Vulnerable Subject: Anchoring Equality in the Human Condition' (2008) 20(1) Yale Journal of Law and Feminism 1.

Fineman, M. A., 'The Vulnerable Subject and the Responsive State' (2010) 60 Emory Law Journal 251.

Gallen, J., 'Jesus Wept: The Roman Catholic Church, Child Sexual Abuse and Transitional Justice' (2016) 10 International Journal of Transitional Justice 332.

Giliker, P., 'Rough Justice in an Unjust World' (2002) 65 Modern Law Review 269.

Giliker, P., 'Vicarious Liability or Liability for the Acts of Others in Tort: A Comparative Perspective' (2011) 2 Journal of European Tort Law 31.

Gleeson, K., 'Why the Continuous Failures in Justice for Australian Victims and Survivors of Catholic Clerical Child Sexual Abuse?' (2016) 28(2) Current Issues in Criminal Justice 239.

Gleeson, K. and Zanghellini, A., 'Graceful Remedies: Understanding Grace in the Catholic Church's Treatment of Clerical Child Sexual Abuse' (2015) 41 Australian Feminist Law Journal.

Gready, P. and Robins, S., 'From Transitional to Transformative Justice: A New Agenda for Practice' (2014) 8 International Journal of Transitional Justice 339.

Gridley, S. J. et al., 'Youth and Caregiver Perspectives on Barriers to Gender-Affirming Health Care for Transgender Youth' (2016) 59(3) Journal of Adolescent Health 254.

Gunning, I. R. 'Arrogant Perception, World-Travelling and Multicultural Feminism: The Case of Female Genital Surgeries' (1992) 23 Columbia Human Rights Law Review 189.

Halberstam, D., '"It's the Autonomy, Stupid!' A Modest Defence of Opinion 2/13 on EU Accession to the ECHR, and the Way Forward' (2015) 16 Guernsey Law Journal 105.

Hall, M., 'After Waterhouse: Vicarious Liability and the Tort of Institutional Abuse' (2000) 22 Journal of Social Welfare and Family Law 159.

Harvey, D., 'The "New" Imperialism: Accumulation by Dispossession' (2004) 40 Socialist Register 63.

Heffernan, L., 'The Participation of Victims in the Trial Process' (2017) Northern Ireland Law Quarterly 491.

Heikkilä, M., Katsui, H. and Mustaniemi-Laakso, M., 'Disability and Vulnerability: A Human Rights Reading of the Responsive State' (2020) 24(8) International Journal of Human Rights 1180.

Henderson, E., 'Best Evidence or Best Interests? What Does the Case Law Say About the Function of Cross-Examination' (2016) 20(3) International Journal of Evidence and Proof 183.

Hendricks, M., 'Is It a Boy or a Girl?' (1993) (November) Johns Hopkins Magazine 10.

Hill, J. L., 'Exploitation' (1993) 79 Cornell Law Review 631.

Hoyle, C. and Sanders, A., 'Police Response to Domestic Violence: From Victim Choice to Victim Empowerment' (2000) 40 British Journal of Criminology 14.

Hughto, J. M. W., Reisner, S. L. and Pachankis, J. E., 'Transgender Stigma and Health: A Critical Review of Stigma Determinants, Mechanisms, and Interventions' (2015) 147 Social Science & Medicine 224.

Ibáñez, A. M. and Moya, A., 'Vulnerability of Victims of Civil Conflicts: Empirical Evidence for the Displaced Population in Colombia' (2010) 38(4) World Development 647.

Imamović, Š. and Muir, E., 'The Dublin III System: More Derogations to the Duty to Transfer Individual Asylum Seekers?' (2017) 2 European Papers 719.

Ismail, I. and Creighton, S., 'Surgery for Intersex' (2005) 5 Reviews in Gynaecological Practice 57.

Jackson, C., 'Evidence – Part IV of the Criminal Evidence Act 1992: Competence and Compellability of Spouses and Former Spouses to Give Evidence' (1993) 15 Dublin University Law Journal 202.

James, M., 'A Carnival of Truth? Knowledge, Ignorance and the Canadian Truth and Reconciliation Commission' (2012) 6 International Journal of Transitional Justice 195.

James, M., 'Changing the Subject: The TRC and the Displacement of Substantive Reconciliation in Canadian Media Representations' (2017) 51(2) Journal of Canadian Studies 366.

James, M., 'On Carnival and Context: A Response to Bridget Storrie' (2015) 9 International Journal of Transitional Justice 486.

James, M., 'Uncomfortable Comparisons: The Canadian Truth and Reconciliation Commission in International Context' (2010) 5(2) The Ethics Forum/Les ateliers de l'éthnique 26.

Keane, A., 'Cross-Examination of Vulnerable Witnesses: Towards a Blueprint for Re-Professionalisation' (2012) 16 International Journal of Evidence and Proof 175.

Kim, M. E., 'Challenging the Pursuit of Criminalisation in an Era of Mass Incarceration: The Limitations of Social Work Responses to Domestic Violence in the USA' (2012) 43(7) British Journal of Social Work 1276.

Kinder, R., 'Vicarious Liability: For Whom Should the Employer Be Liable?' (1995) 15 Legal Studies 47.

Kohn, N. A., 'Vulnerability Theory and the Role of Government' (2014) 26(1) Yale Journal of Law and Feminism 1.

Leckie, S., 'Another Step Towards Indivisibility: Identifying Key Features of Violations of Economic, Social and Cultural Rights' (1998) 20 Human Rights Quarterly 81.

Lee, P. A., Houk, C. P., Hughes, I. A. and Ahmed, S. F., 'Consensus Statement on Management of Intersex Disorders' (2006) 118(2) Pediatrics e 488.

Lid, I. M., 'Vulnerability and Disability: A Citizenship Perspective' (2015) 30(10) Disability and Society 1554.

Maas,. S M. and Hage, J. J., 'Functional and Aesthetic Labia Minora Reduction' (2000) 105(4) Plastic and Reconstructive Surgery 1453.

Madden-Dempsey, M., 'Toward a Feminist State: What Does Prosecution of Domestic Violence Mean?' (2007) 70(6) Modern Law Review 908.

Maharaj, N. R., Dhai, A., Wiersma, R. and Moodley, J., 'Intersex Conditions in Children and Adolescents: Surgical, Ethical, and Legal Considerations' (205) 18 Journal of Pediatric and Adolescent Gynaecology 399.

Mahon, C., 'Progress at the Front: The Draft Optional Protocol to the International Covenant on Economic Social and Cultural Rights' (2008) 8 Human Rights Law Review 617.

Marchia, J. and Sommer, J. M., '(Re)defining Heteronormativity' (2019) 22 Sexualities 267.

McAlinden, A. M., 'An Inconvenient Truth: Barriers to Truth Recovery in the Aftermath of Institutional Child Abuse in Ireland' (2013) Legal Studies 189.

Mclvor, C., 'The Use and Abuse of the Doctrine of Vicarious Liability' (2006) 35 Common Law World Review 268.

McStravick, D., 'Adult Reparation Panels and Offender-Centric Meso-Communities: An Answer to the Conundrum' (2018) 1(1) International Journal of Restorative Justice 96.

Meredith, V. M., 'Victim Identity and Respect for Human Dignity: A Terminological Analysis' (2009) 91 (874) International Review of the Red Cross 259.

Meyers-Steifer, C. H. and Charest, N. J. 'Diagnosis and Management of Patients with Ambiguous Genitalia' (1992) 16(5) Seminars in Perinatology 332.

Miller, A., 'Sexuality, Violence Against Women and Human Rights: Women Make Demands and Ladies get Protection' (2004) Health and Human Rights 17.

Moffett, L., 'Reparations for "Guilty Victims": Navigating Complex Identities of Victim-Perpetrators in Reparation Mechanisms' (2016) 10(1) International Journal of Transitional Justice 146.

Moffett, L., 'Victim Personal Statements in Managing Victims' Voices in Sentencing in Northern Ireland: Taking a More Procedural Justice Approach' (2017) 68 Northern Ireland Legal Quarterly 4.

Morgan, P., 'Vicarious Liability for Group Companies: The Final Frontier of Vicarious Liability?' (2015) 31(4) Professional Negligence 276.

Moses, J., 'Social Citizenship and Social Rights in an Age of Extremes: T. H. Marshall's Social Philosophy in the *Longue Durée*' (2019) 16 Modern Intellectual History 155.

Munro, V., 'Shifting Sands? Consent, Context and Vulnerability in Contemporary Sexual Offences Policy in England and Wales' (2017) Social & Legal Studies 417.

Munro, V. and Scoular. J., 'Abusing Vulnerability? Contemporary Law and Policy Responses to Sex Work in the UK' (2012) 20(3) Feminist Legal Studies 189.

Nagy, R. L., 'The Scope and Bounds of Transitional Justice and the Canadian Truth and Reconciliation Commission' (2013) 7 International Journal of Transitional Justice 64.

Neyers, J., 'A Theory of Vicarious Liability' (2005–2006) 43 Alberta Law Review 287.

Nichols, A., 'No-Drop Prosecution in Domestic Violence Cases' (2014) 29(11) Journal of Interpersonal Violence 2114.

Nussbaum, M., 'Capabilities and Human Rights' (1997) 66(2) Fordham Law Review 273.

O'Carroll, J. P., 'Cultural Lag and Democratic Deficit in Ireland: Or, "Da's Outside de Terms of d'Agreement"' (2002) 37(1) Community Development Journal 11.

O'Cinneide, C., 'The Social Security (Scotland) Act 2018 – A Rights Based Approach to Social Security?' 23(1) Edinburgh Law Review 1.

O'Malley, P., 'Neoliberalism, Crime and Criminal Justice' (2016) 16(10) Sydney Law School Research 1.

O'Neill, K. L., 'Writing Guatemala's Genocide: Truth and Reconciliation Commission Reports and Christianity' (2005) 7(3) Journal of Genocide Research.

O'Rourke, C. and Swaine, A., 'Gender, Violence and Reparations in Northern Ireland: A Story Yet to Be Told' (2017) 21(9) International Journal of Human Rights 1302.

Oberfeld, S. E. et al., 'Clitoral Size in Full-Term Infants' (1989) 6(4) American Journal of Perinatology 453.

Olsen, F., 'The Family and the Market: A Study of Ideology and Legal Reform' (1983) 96(7) Harvard Law Review 1497.

Olson, S. M. and Dzur, A. W., 'Revisiting Informal Justice and Democratic Professionalism' (2004) 38 Law and Society Review 139.

Oyama, I. A., Steinberg, A. C., Holzberg, A. S. and Maccarone, J. L., 'Reduction Clitoroplasty: A Technique for Debulking the Enlarged Clitoris' (2004) 17 Journal of Pediatric and Adolescent Gynecology 393.

Packer, H., 'Two Models of the Criminal Process' (1964) 113(1) University of Pennsylvania Law Review 1.

Peroni, L. and Timmer, A., 'Vulnerable Groups: The Promise of an Emerging Concept in European Human Rights Convention Law' (2013) 11(4) International Journal of Constitutional Law 1056.

Porter, A., 'Prosecuting Domestic Abuse in England and Wales: Crown Prosecution Service "Working Practice" and New Public Managerialism' (2019) 28(4) Social & Legal Studies 493.

Regan, E., 'Church, Culture and Crediblity: A Perspective from Ireland' (2012) 94(1050) New Blackfriars 166.

Reis, E., 'Divergence or Disorder: The Politics of Naming Intersex' (2007) 50(4) Perspectives in Biology and Medicine 535.

Robins, S., 'Towards Victim-Centred Transitional Justice: Understanding the Needs of Families of the Disappeared in Postconflict Nepal' (2011) 5(1) International Journal of Transitional Justice 75.

Roen, K., 'Rethinking Queer Failure: Trans Youth Embodiments of Distress' (2019) 22(1–2) Sexualities 48.

Rooke, A., 'Trans Youth, Science and Art: Creating (Trans) Gendered Space' (2010) 17(5) Gender, Place and Culture 655.

Rooney, E. and Ní Aoláin, F., 'Transitional Justice from the Margins: Intersections of Identities, Power and Human Rights' (2018) 12(1) International Journal of Transitional Justice 1.

Rossner, M. and Bruce, J., 'Community Participation in Restorative Justice. Rituals, Reintegration and Quasi-Professionals' (2016) 11(1) Victims and Offenders 107.

Ryan, D., 'From Opportunity to Occasion: Vicarious Liability in the High Court of Australia' (2017) 76(1) Cambridge Law Journal 14.

Sen, A., 'Elements of a Theory of Human Rights' (2004) 32(4) Philosophy & Public Affairs 315.

Shabot, S. C., 'The Grotesque Body: Fleshing Out the Subject' (2007) 15 Thamyris/Inter secting: Place, Sex and Race 57.

Shumer, D. E., Nokoff, N. J. and Spack, N. P., 'Advances in the Care of Transgender Children and Adolescents' (2016) 63(1) Advances in Pediatrics 79.

Sköld, J., 'The Truth About Abuse? A Comparative Approach to Inquiry Narratives on Historical Institutional Child Abuse' (2016) 45(4) History of Education 492.

Stanton, K., 'Canada's Truth and Reconciliation Commission: Settling the Past?' (2011) 2(3) International Indigenous Policy Journal 11.

Stapleton, J., 'The Golden Thread at the Heart of Tort Law: Protection of the Vulnerable' (2003) 24 Australian Bar Review 135.

Stotzer, R. L., 'Violence Against Transgender People, a Review of United States Data' (2009) 14(3) Aggression and Violent Behaviour 170.

Stychin, C., 'The Vulnerable Subject of Negligence Law' (2012) 8(3) International Journal of Law in Context 337.

Tong, S. Y. C., Donaldson, K. and Hutson, J. M. 'When is Hypospadias not Hypospadias?' (1996) 164 (5 February) Medical Journal of Australia 153.

Tran, B. X. et al., 'Understanding Global HIV Stigma and Discrimination: Are Contextual Factors Sufficiently Studied?' (2019) 16(11, June) International Journal of Environmental Research and Public Health 1899.

Uprimny Yepes, R., 'Transformative Reparations of Massive Gross Human Rights Violations: Between Corrective and Distributive Justice' (2009) 27(4) Netherlands Quarterly of Human Rights 625.

Vandenhole, W., 'Completing the UN Complaint Mechanisms for Human Rights Violations Step by Step: Towards a Complaints Procedure Complementing the International Covenant on Economic Social and Cultural Rights' (2003) 21 Netherlands Quarterly of Human Rights 423.

Vicini, G., 'The Dublin Regulation Between Strasbourg and Luxembourg: reshaping non-refoulement in the name of trust' (2015) 8 European Journal of Legal Studies 50.

Waldorf, L., 'Anticipating the Past: Transitional Justice and Socio-Economic Wrongs' (2012) 21(2) Social & Legal Studies 171.

Wall, I. R., 'On Pain and the Sense of Human Rights' (2008) 29 Australian Feminist Law Journal 53.

Wangmann, J., 'Liability for Institutional Child Sexual Assault: Where does Lepore leave Australia?' (2004) 28 Melbourne University Law Review 169

Ward, J., 'Vulnerable Witnesses and Cross-Examination: A Path to Reform' (2017) 7(1) Irish Journal of Legal Studies 36.

Watts, B., 'Rights, Needs and Stigma: A Comparison of Homelessness Policy in Ireland and Scotland' (2013) 7 European Journal of Homelessness 41.

Weiler, J. H. H. and Lockhart, N., '"Taking Rights Seriously" Seriously: The European Court and its Fundamental Rights Jurisprudence – Part I' (1995) 32 Common Market Law Review 51.

Weiler, J. H. H. and Lockhart, N., '"Taking Rights Seriously" Seriously: The European Court and its Fundamental Rights Jurisprudence – Part II' (1995) 32 Common Market Law Review 579.

Wendell Holmes, O., 'Agency' (1890–1891) 4 Harvard Law Review 345, (1891–1892) 5 Harvard Law Review 1.

Williams, G., 'Vicarious Liability: Tort of the Master or of the Servant?' (1956) 72 Law Quarterly Review 522.

Williams, W., 'The Equality Crisis: Some Reflections on Courts, Culture and Feminism' (1982) 7 Women's Rights Law Reports 175.

Yoshino, K., 'Covering' (2002) 111 Yale Law Journal 769.

Official publications

Canada

Truth and Reconciliation Commission of Canada: Calls to Action (Truth and Reconciliation Commission of Canada – 2015).

Council of Europe

2nd General Report of the European Committee for the Prevention of Torture (1992) https://rm.coe.int/1680696a3f (last visited 15 January 2020).

Council of Europe, *Explanatory Report on the Collective Complaints Protocol* [1995] COETSER 3 (9 November 1995).

European Committee of Social Rights, *Conclusions XXI-2 (2017) United Kingdom*, January 2018.

European Union

European Union Agency for Fundamental Rights, *LGBT Survey* (FRA 2012).

Ireland

Central Statistics Office, *Census Report* (2016) www.cso.ie/en/releasesandpublications/ep/p-cp4hf/cp4hf/fmls/ (last accessed 14 December 2020).

Department of Children and Youth Affairs, *The LGBTI+ National Youth Strategy* (DCYA 2018–2020).

Department of Employment Affairs and Social Protection, *Review of the Gender Recognition Act 2015* (June 2018) www.welfare.ie/en/downloads/GRA%20Review%20Report.pdf (last accessed on 14 December 2020).

Judy Walsh and Fergus Ryan, *The Rights of De Facto Couples* (Irish Human Rights Commission 2006).

Law Reform Commission, *Report on Child Sexual Abuse* (LRC 30–1990).

Law Reform Commission, *Sexual Offences Against the Mentally Handicapped* (LRC 33–1990).

Minister for Social Protection's response, *Gender Recognition Act 2015: Report to the Oireachtas under Section 7 of the Act* (November 2019) www.welfare.ie/en/downloads/GenderRecognitionAct2015MinistersReportUnderSection7.pdf.

Press release, 'Minister for Social Protection Publishes Revised General Scheme for Gender Recognition Bill 2014' (Dublin: Department of Social Protection, 18 June 2014) www.welfare.ie/en/pressoffice/Pages/pr180614.aspx (last accessed 14 December 2020).

Review of the Gender Recognition Act 2015 (June 2018) www.welfare.ie/en/downloads/GRA%20Review%20Report.pdf.

Speech of An Taoiseach, Leo Varadkar, on the occasion of the visit of Pope Francis (25 August 2018) www.taoiseach.gov.ie/eng/News/Taoiseach's_Speeches/Speech_of_An_Taoiseach_Leo_Varadkar_on_the_occasion_of_the_Visit_of_Pope_Francis.html (last accessed 14 December 2020).

Northern Ireland

Haass–O'Sullivan Proposed Agreement 31 December 2013 www.northernireland.gov.uk/publications/haass-report-proposed-agreement (last accessed 14 December 2020).

House of Commons Northern Ireland Affairs Committee, *Consultative Group of the Past, Final Report 2009* https://publications.parliament.uk/pa/cm200910/cmselect/cmniaf/171/171.pdf (last accessed 14 December 2020).

Stormont House Agreement (2014) www.dfa.ie/media/dfa/alldfawebsitemedia/ourrolesandpolicies/northernireland/Stormont-House-Agreement.pdf (last accessed 14 December 2020).

Scotland

Scottish Government, *Fairer Scotland Duty – Interim Guidance for Public Bodies* (March 2018) www.gov.scot/Publications/2018/03/6918 (last accessed 14 December 2020).

United Kingdom

www.cps.gov.uk/sites/default/files/documents/publications/cps-vawg-report-2017.pdf (last accessed 14 December 2020).

Burton, M., Evans, R. and Sanders, A., *Are Special Measures for Vulnerable and Intimidated Witnesses Working? Evidence from the Criminal Justice Agencies* Report No 01/06 (Home Office 2006).

Crown Prosecution Service, 'Violence Against Women and Girls Crime Report, 2010–2011' (CPS 2011).

Crown Prosecution Service, 'Violence Against Women and Girls Crime Report, 2015–16' (CPS 2016).

Crown Prosecution Service, 'Violence Against Women and Girls Crime Report, 2016–17' (CPS 2017).

Crown Prosecution Service, 'Violence Against Women and Girls Report, 2017–18' (CPS 2018) www.cps.gov.uk/sites/default/files/documents/publications/cps-vawg-report-2018.pdf (last accessed 14 December 2020).

Department of Health, *Research Governance Framework for Health and Social Care* (Department of Health 2005).

HM Government, 'Together We Can End Violence Against Women and Girls: A Strategy' (Home Office 2009).

Ministry of Justice, *National Report to the UN Universal Periodic Review*, February 2017.

United Nations

Committee on Economic, Social and Cultural Rights, *Concluding Observations: UK*, July 2016, UN doc: E/C.12/GBR/CO/6.

Committee on Economic, Social and Cultural Rights, 'Letter by the Chairperson of the CESCR to States Parties to the ICESCR', 12 May 2012.

Committee on Economic Social and Cultural Rights, *List of Issues in Relation to the Third Periodic Report of Ireland* E/C.12/IRL/Q/3, 17 December 2014.

Committee on Economic Social and Cultural Rights, *List of Issues in Relation to the Third Periodic Report of Ireland, Addendum, Replies of Ireland to List of Issues* E/C.12/IRL/Q/3/Add.1, 8 April 2015.

Committee on Economic, Social and Cultural Rights, *Public Debt, Austerity Measures and the ICESCR: Statement by the CESCR*, 24 June 2016, UN doc: E/C.12/2016/1.

Committee on the Elimination of Discrimination Against Women, *Concluding Observations on the Combined Sixth and Seventh Periodic Reports of Ireland* (Geneva: United Nations, 2017) UN doc: CEDAW/C/IRL/CO/6–7.

Committee on the Rights of Persons with Disabilities, *Inquiry Concerning the United Kingdom of Great Britain and Northern Ireland* 2016, UN doc: CRPD/C/15/R.2/Rev.1

Committee on the Rights of the Child, *Concluding Observations: UK*, July 2016, UN doc: CRC/C/GBR/CO/5.

Committee on the Rights of the Child, *Concluding Observations on the Combined Third and Fourth Periodic Reports of Ireland* (Geneva: United Nations, 2016) UN doc.: CRC/C/IRL/CO/3–4.

Committee on the Rights of the Child, *Concluding Observations of the Third Periodic Report of Ireland*, UN doc: E/C.12/IRL/CO/3 (19 June 2015)

Development Programme, *Human Development Report 2014 Sustaining Human Progress: Reducing Vulnerabilities and Building Resilience* (UNDP 2014).

Human Rights Office of the High Commissioner, *Basic Principles, and Guidelines on the Right to a Remedy and Reparation for Victims of Gross Violations of International Human Rights Law and Serious Violations of International Humanitarian Law*, A/RES/60/147.

Special Rapporteur on Extreme Poverty and Human Rights, 'Statement on Visit to the UK', 16 November 2018 www.ohchr.org/EN/NewsEvents/Pages/DisplayNews.aspx?NewsID=23881&LangID=E (last accessed 14 December 2020).

Special Rapporteurs on Housing, on Rights of Persons with Disabilities, on Extreme Poverty, and on the Right to Food, 'Joint Letter to the UK Government', UN doc: AL GBR 1/2016, April 2016.

World Medical Association

World Medical Association, 'Declaration of Helsinki – Ethical Principles for Medical Research Involving Human Subjects' (1965) www.wma.net/policies-post/wma-declaration-of-helsinki-ethical-principles-for-medical-research-involving-human-subjects/ (last accessed 14 December 2020).

Working papers

Ní Mhuirthile, T., 'Realising Gender Recognition: Rendering the Vulnerable Visible or Further Vulnerabilising the Invisible?' *UCD Working Papers in Law, Criminology and Socio-Legal Studies*, Research Paper no. 41/2010 http://ssrn.com/abstract=1680899 (last accessed 14 December 2020).

Conference papers

Barron, M. N., Background paper to the thematic session 'Non-Discrimination of Lesbian, Gay, Bisexual, Transgender and Intersex (LGBTI) Children and Young People', Conference on the Council of Europe Strategy for the Rights of the Child (2016–2021), Sofia, Bulgaria, 5–6 April 2016.

Biggs, C. and Delahunt, M., '*Prosecutorial Challenges – Vulnerable Victims and Witnesses*', 17th National Annual Prosecutors' Conference, Dublin, 12 November 2016, 8–10, www.dppireland.ie (last accessed 14 December 2020).

Brazil, P. 'Applications for Asylum by Lesbian, Gay, Bisexual, Transgender and Intersex (LGBTI) Persons', paper presented to the RIPN, 25 January 2011 www.legalaidboard.ie/en/about-the-board/press-publications/newsletters/applications-for-asylum-by-lesbian-gay-bisexual-transgender-and-intersex-lgbti-persons-.html.

Claassen, R., 'Restorative Justice – Fundamental Principles', paper presented at the National Commission for the Protection of Child Rights (NCPCR), revised May 1996 at the UN Alliance of NGO's Working Party on Restorative Justice http://peace.fresno.edu/docs/rjprinc.html.

Fineman, M. A., speaking at 'A Workshop on Vulnerability and Social Justice', Leeds University, 17 June 2016.

Websites and blogs

BBC News, 'Business: The Economy The Pink Pound' http://news.bbc.co.uk/2/hi/business/142998.stm (last accessed 14 December 2020).

British Institute of Human Rights et al., *Joint Civil Society Report to the UN Universal Periodic Review of the UK (3rd Cycle)*, 2016 www.bihr.org.uk/Handlers/Download.ashx?IDMF=899c9202-602e-4244-b776-52ddaf6e79d3 (last accessed 14 December 2020).

Campaign for Better Transport, *Buses in Crisis: A Report on Bus Funding Across England and Wales 2010–2018*, June 2018 https://bettertransport.org.uk/buses-in-crisis-2018 (last accessed 14 December 2020).

Constitutional Convention, 'Terms of Reference' www.constitution.ie/Convention.aspx#terms-of-reference (last accessed 24 November 2016).

Crown Prosecution Service, 'Domestic Abuse Guidelines for Prosecutors www.cps.gov.uk/legal-guidance/domestic-abuse-guidelines-prosecutors (last accessed 14 December 2020).

Focus Ireland, 'About Homeless' www.focusireland.ie/resource-hub/about-homelessness/ (last accessed 14 December 2020).

Gender Equality in Ireland, 'Gender Pay Gap' www.genderequality.ie/en/GE/Pages/GenderPayGap (last accessed 14 December 2020).

Gender Equality Index 2017, European Institute for Gender Equality available at https://eige.europa.eu/gender-equality-index/2015/domain/time/IE (last accessed 14 December 2020).

House of Commons Library, *Welfare Savings 2010–11 to 2020–2021*, July 2016 https://commonslibrary.parliament.uk/research-briefings/cbp-7667/ (last accessed 14 December 2020).

House of Commons Public Accounts Committee, *Benefit Sanctions*, February 2017 https://publications.parliament.uk/pa/cm201617/cmselect/cmpubacc/775/775.pdf (last accessed 14 December 2020).

House of Commons Work and Pensions Committee, *Benefit Sanctions*, October 2018 https://publications.parliament.uk/pa/cm201719/cmselect/cmworpen/955/955.pdf (last accessed 14 December 2020).

ICAP, 'Redress Scheme for Magdalene Survivors', 28 June 2013 www.icap.org.uk/redress-scheme-for-magdalene-survivors/ (last accessed 1 September 2016.

Institute for Fiscal Studies, *Living Standards, Poverty and Inequality in the UK: 2017–18 to 2021–2022*, November 2017 www.ifs.org.uk/publications/10028 (last accessed 14 December 2020).

Just Fair, 'Visit by the UN Special Rapporteur on Extreme Poverty and Human Rights, Philip Alston, to the UK from 5 to 16 November 2018: Written Submission' http://

justfair.org.uk/wp-content/uploads/2018/09/Just_Fair_15_Alston_Submission-FINAL.pdf (last accessed 20 December 2020).

Kelly, M., 'ICCL Welcomes Commencement of Gender Recognition Act 2015 – Irish Council of Civil Liberties Press Release 4 September 2015' www.iccl.ie/?s=gender+recognition (last accessed 14 December 2020).

Lloyds Bank Foundation and New Policy Institute, *A Quiet Crisis: Local Government Spending on Disadvantage in England*, September 2018 www.npi.org.uk/files/7715/3669/7306/A_quiet_crisis_final.pdf (last accessed 14 December 2020).

Oakley, M., *Looked After Children* (Social Market Foundation 2018) www.smf.co.uk/publications/looked-after-children/ (last accessed 14 December 2020).

National Audit Office, *Benefit Sanctions*, November 2016 www.nao.org.uk/report/benefit-sanctions/ (last accessed 14 December 2020).

National Audit Office, *Financial Sustainability of Local Authorities*, March 2018 www.nao.org.uk/report/financial-sustainability-of-local-authorities-2018/ (last accessed 14 December 2020).

National Audit Office, *Rolling out Universal Credit*, June 2018 www.nao.org.uk/report/rolling-out-universal-credit/ (last accessed 14 December 2020).

Office for Budget Responsibility, *Welfare Trends Report*, October 2016 http://obr.uk/wtr/welfare-trends-report-october-2016/ (last accessed 14 December 2020).

Office for National Statistics, *Family Spending in the UK: Financial Year Ending March 2016*, February 2017 www.ons.gov.uk/peoplepopulationandcommunity/personalandhouseholdfinances/expenditure/bulletins/familyspendingintheuk/financialyearendingmarch2016 (last accessed 14 December 2020).

Office for National Statistics, *UK Government Debt and Deficit: March 2018*, July 2018 www.ons.gov.uk/economy/governmentpublicsectorandtaxes/publicspending/bulletins/ukgovernmentdebtanddeficitforeurostatmaast/march2018. (last accessed 14 December 2020).

Phillips, D. and Simpson, P., *Changes in Councils' Adult Social Care and Overall Service Spending in England, 2009–10 to 2017–2018*, Institute for Fiscal Studies, June 2018 www.ifs.org.uk/publications/13066 (last accessed 14 December 2020).

Progressive Policy Think Tank, *Capital Gains: Broadening Company Ownership in the UK Economy*, December 2017 www.ippr.org/research/publications/CEJ-capital-gains (last accessed 14 December 2020).

Resolution Foundation, *Britain's Increasingly Unevenly Shared Property Wealth is Driving up Inequality After a Decade-Long Fall*, June 2017www.resolutionfoundation.org/media/press-releases/britains-increasingly-unevenly-shared-property-wealth-is-driving-up-inequality-after-a-decade-long-fall/%20I (last accessed 3 March 2020).

Resolution Foundation, *The Living Standards Outlook*, February 2018, 65 www.resolutionfoundation.org/publications/the-living-standards-outlook-2018/ (last accessed 14 December 2020).

Ryan, F., 'Ireland's Marriage Referendum: A Constitutional Perspective' *DPCE Online (Diritto Pubblico Comparato Ed Europeo)* 2015–2 http://mural.maynoothuniversity.ie/8934/ (last accessed 14 December 2020).

Smith, N. A., Phillips, D. and Simpson, P., *Council-Level Figures on Spending Cuts and Business Rates Income*, Institute for Fiscal Studies, November 2016 www.ifs.org.uk/publications/8780 (last accessed 14 December 2020).

Social Justice Ireland, 'Budget 2017 Analysis and Critique', October 2017 www.socialjustice.ie/sites/default/files/attach/publication/4566/2016-10-12-budget2017responsefinalweb.pdf (last accessed 14 December 2020).

Social Justice Ireland, 'Budget 2019 Analysis and Critique', October 2019 www.socialjustice.ie/sites/default/files/attach/publication/5500/budget2019analysisfinaled.pdf?cs=true (last accessed 14 December 2020).

Social Justice Ireland Policy Briefing, 'Poverty, Deprivation and Inequality', July 2016 www.socialjustice.ie/sites/default/files/attach/publication/4471/2016-07-04-sjipolicybriefingpoverty2016final2.pdf (last accessed 14 December 2020).

Transgender Equality Network Ireland www.teni.ie.

UK Addiction Treatment Centres, *Our Campaign Reveals Cuts to Addiction Treatment Funding, as Drug Deaths Rise*, August 2018 www.ukat.co.uk/addiction-treatment/ukat-campaign-reveals-cuts-addiction-treatment-funding-drug-deaths-rise/ (last accessed 14 December 2020).

Women's Budget Group and Runnymede Trust, *Intersecting Inequalities: The Impact of Austerity on Black and Minority Ethnic Women in the UK*, October 2017 www.intersecting-inequalities.com/ (last accessed 14 December 2020)

Newspaper articles and news reports

Anonymous, 'Gun Victim Loses Appeal', *BBC News* (9 November 2001) http://news.bbc.co.uk/2/hi/uk_news/northern_ireland/1646915.stm

Anonymous, 'Ian Elliott May Sue Catholic Bishop over Child Protection Report', *BBC News* (8 March 2014) www.bbc.com/news/uk-northern-ireland-26495820

Anonymous, 'Lara Spencer Apologizes for "Insensitive" Remark on Prince George's Ballet Lessons', *Guardian* (26 August 2019) lara-spencer-prince-george-ballet-lessons-apology

Anonymous, 'Ottawa Launches Inquiry into Missing and Murdered Indigenous Women', *BBC News* (3 August 2016) www.bbc.com/news/world-us-canada-36968381

Anonymous, 'Religious Congregations Refuse to Contribute to Magdalene Redress Fund', *RTE News* (Dublin, 16 July 2013) www.rte.ie/news/2013/0716/462816-magdalenes-laundries/

Brennan, C., 'Ireland is Facing a Human Rights Case over the Awful State of Social Housing Here', *Journal.ie* (Dublin, 24 March 2015) www.thejournal.ie/social-housing-human-rights-2009407-Mar2015 (last accessed 14 December 2020).

Carswell, S., 'Varadkar Sets out His Blueprint for New Covenant', *Irish Times* (Dublin, 27 August 2018).

Carswell, S., 'Victims' Group Calls on Pope to Name Sex Abusers', *Irish Times* (Dublin, 25 August 2018).

Cusack, J. and McConnell, D., 'Lawyers Profit as Cost of Clerical Abuse Tops €1bn', *Irish Independent* (Dublin, 14 October 2012).

Hicklin, A. 'Power of the Pink Pound', *Financial Times*, 28 September 2012 www.ft.com/content/a3a5d9be-0788-11e2-92b5-00144feabdc0 (last accessed 14 December 2020).

Lally, C., 'Gardaí Suspect "Vicious" Train Station Stabbing Was Hate Crime', *Irish Times* (2 February 2020).

MacDonald, S., 'Archbishop says it would be 'disaster' if church watchdog loses trust', *Irish Independent* (Dublin, 10 March 2014).

Mas S, 'Truth and Reconciliation Final Report Points to "Growing Crisis" for Indigenous Youth', *CBC News* (14 December 2015).

McDonald, H., 'Dáil and Church Agree €1.3bn Payout to Child Abuse Victims', *Guardian* (London, 1 January 2006).

McGarry, P., 'Archbishop Says All Allegations of Clerical Abuse Must Be Reported', *Irish Times* (Dublin, 11 February 2016).

McGarry, P., 'Vatican Has Never Co-operated with Irish Inquiries into Clerical Child Sex Abuse', *Irish Times* (Dublin, 7 August 2018).

O'Loughlin, E., 'Ireland Diagnosed Record Number of HIV Infections in 2018, Health Data Suggests', *New York Times* (25 February 2019).

O'Mahony, C., 'Same-Sex Marriage Referendum: A Legal Review', *Irish Times* (22 January 2015).

Omand, G. 'Troubles Inquiry into Missed, Murdered Indigenous Women Seeks Two More Years', *CTV News* (6 March 2018) www.ctvnews.ca/politics/troubled-inquiry-into-missing-murdered-indigenous-women-seeks-two-more-years-1.3831204

Power, J., 'PrEP Programme to Be Rolled out in Health Service from Next Month', *Irish Times* (20 October 2019).

Power, J. and Carswell, S., 'Pope Asks for Forgiveness for Abuses and Exploitation During Papal Mass', *Irish Times* (Dublin, 27 August 2018).

Press Association, 'Religious Orders Have Paid Just 13% of Bill for Child Abuse Inquiry – Watchdog', *Irish Independent* (Dublin, 9 March 2017).

Siddique, H., 'Swedish Model Gets Rape Threats after Ad Shows Her Unshaved Legs', *Guardian* (6 October 2017).

Other secondary sources

'Pastoral Letter of the Holy Father Pope Benedict XVI to the Catholics of Ireland' (2010) http://w2.vatican.va/content/benedict-xvi/en/letters/2010/documents/hf_ben-xvi_let_20100319_church-ireland.html (last accessed 14 December 2020.

Borrows, J., 'Residential Schools, Reconciliation, Churches and Indigenous Peoples' (unpublished paper, no date) www.iclrs.org/content/events/123/3419.pdf (last accessed 14 December 2020.

Bramley, G., Hirsch, D., Littlewood, M. and Watkins, D., *Counting the Cost of UK Poverty* (Joseph Rowntree Foundation 2016).

Breen Smyth, M., *The Needs of Individuals and Their Families Injured as a Result of the Troubles in Northern Ireland* (WAVE 2012).

Catterall, E, in association with McEvoy, K. et al., *Apologies and Institutional Child Abuse* (Queen's University Belfast – 2018) 1 https://apologies-abuses-past.org.uk/assets/uploads/Apologies-Institutional-Abuse-Report_Sept-2018.pdf (last accessed 14 December 2020).

Chase, C., *ISNA's Amicus Brief on Intersex Genital Surgery* www.isna.org/node/97 (last accessed 14 December 2020).

Collins, B., Keating, S. and Morgan, M., *All Together Now! Pilot Project on Homophobic and Transphobic Bullying in Primary Schools Final Report* (St Patrick's College Dublin and BeLong To 2016).

Correa, C., 'Reparations in Peru: From Recommendations to Implementation' (ICTJ, June 2013).

de Grieff, P. and Duthie, R. (eds.), *Transitional Justice and Development: Making Connections* (ICTJ 2009).

Dunne, P. and Turraoin, C., *It's Time to Hear Our Voices: National Trans Youth Forum Report 2015* (TENI, 2015).

Equality and Human Rights Commission, *Measurement Framework for Equality and Human Rights* (Equality and Human Rights Commission 2017).

Equality and Human Rights Commission, *The Cumulative Impact on Living Standards of Public Spending Changes* (Equality and Human Rights Commission 2018).

Fineman, M. A., 'What it Means to Be Human: Vulnerability and the Human Condition' (2013) Emory Law School Lecture www.youtube.com/watch?v=MEgeTrzOm1o (last accessed 14 December 2020).

Haynes, A. and Schweppe, J., *Gendered Policing and Policing Gender: The Trans Community and An Garda Síochána* (Transgender Equality Network Ireland (TENI 2018).

Haynes, A. and Schweppe, J., *Life-Cycle of a Hate Crime* (Irish Council for Civil Liberties 2018).

Higgins, A. et al., *LGBT Ireland Report: National Study of the Mental Health and Wellbeing of Lesbian, Gay, Bisexual, Transgender and Intersex People in Ireland* (GLEN and BeLonG To 2016).

Higgins, A. et al., *Visible Lives: Identifying the Experiences and Needs of Older Lesbian, Gay, Bisexual and Transgender People in Ireland* (GLEN 2011).

International Federation for Human Rights, 'Nairobi Declaration on Women's and Girls' Rights to a Remedy and Reparation' www.fidh.org/IMG/pdf/NAIROBI_DECLARATIONeng.pdf (last accessed 14 December 2020).

Lindsey, C., *Women Facing War* (International Committee of the Red Cross 2015).

Magee, S., *Exploring Models for the Proposal of Special Pension Provision for Those Injured in the Northern Ireland 'Troubles'* (WAVE 2011).

Mayock, P., Bryan, A., Carr, N. and Kitching, K., *Supporting LGBT Lives: A Study of the Mental Health and Well-being of Lesbian, Gay, Bisexual and Transgender People* (GLEN and BeLonG To Youth Service 2009).

McNeil, J., Bailey, L., Ellis, S. and Regan, M., *Speaking from the Margins: Trans Mental Health and Wellbeing in Ireland* (Transgender Equality Network Ireland/TENI 2013).

Meadows, L., Albertson, K., Ellingworth, D. and Senior, P., *Evaluation of the South Yorkshire Restorative Justice Programme* (Hallam Centre for Community Justice: Sheffield Hallam University 2012).

Meadows, L. et al., *Evaluation of Sheffield's City Council Community Justice Panels Project* (Hallam Centre for Community Justice: Sheffield Hallam University, 2010).

Mee, J. and Ronayne, K., *The Partnership Rights of Same-Sex Couples* (Equality Authority 2000).

O'Sullivan, O. (ed.) *Touching the Surface: Trans Voices in Ireland* (TENI 2012).

Truth and Reconciliation Commission of Canada, *The Survivors Speak: A Report of the Truth and Reconciliation Commission of Canada* (TRC 2015).

Wilcox, A. and Hoyle, C., *The National Evaluation of the Youth Justice Board's Restorative Justice Project* (Youth Justice Board: Oxford 2004) 42 yjbpublications,justice.gov.uk/.../restorativejusticefull.pdf (last accessed 14 December 2020).

World Bank, *World Development Report 2014, Risk and Opportunity – Managing Risk for Development* (World Bank 2014).

Index

For Product Safety Concerns and Information please contact our EU representative GPSR@taylorandfrancis.com
Taylor & Francis Verlag GmbH, Kaufingerstraße 24, 80331 München, Germany

www.ingramcontent.com/pod-product-compliance
Lightning Source LLC
LaVergne TN
LVHW011129300926
849160LV00008B/570

* 9 7 8 1 0 3 2 0 7 5 3 3 4 *